CONNECTING RESEARCH AND PRACTICE FOR EDUCATIONAL IMPROVEMENT

Connecting Research and Practice for Educational Improvement presents richly illustrated cases of and arguments for how more collaborative relationships between researchers and educators can yield more relevant research that impacts practice. The chapters are useful for anyone teaching or learning about research–practice partnerships, in both school and out-of-school settings. The cases highlight the different dispositions and skills needed to cultivate ethical relationships that promote equity through partnerships and provide rich frameworks for guiding future work.

Bronwyn Bevan is Senior Research Scientist at the University of Washington, College of Education, USA.

William R. Penuel is Professor of Learning Sciences and Human Development at the University of Colorado, USA.

CONNECTING RESEARCH AND PRACTICE FOR EDUCATIONAL IMPROVEMENT

Ethical and Equitable Approaches

Edited by Bronwyn Bevan and William R. Penuel

Routledge
Taylor & Francis Group

NEW YORK AND LONDON

First published 2018
by Routledge
711 Third Avenue, New York, NY 10017

and by Routledge
2 Park Square, Milton Park, Abingdon, Oxon, OX14 4RN

Routledge is an imprint of the Taylor & Francis Group, an informa business

© 2018 Taylor & Francis

Library of Congress Cataloging-in-Publication Data
A catalog record for this book has been requested

ISBN: 978-1-138-28728-0 (hbk)
ISBN: 978-1-138-28731-0 (pbk)
ISBN: 978-1-315-26830-9 (ebk)

Typeset in Bembo
by Apex CoVantage, LLC

CONTENTS

Contributors   x

Preface   xix

PART I

Rethinking the Relationship Between Research
and Practice   1

1   Democratizing Evidence in Education   3
    Vivian Tseng, Steve Fleischman, and Esther Quintero

2   Learning, Generalizing, and Local Sense-Making
    in Research–Practice Partnerships   17
    *Bronwyn Bevan, William R. Penuel, Philip Bell,
    and Pamela J. Buffington*

PART II

RPPs That Impact Practice   31

3   Sustaining Research–Practice Partnerships: Benefits
    and Challenges of a Long-Term Research
    and Development Agenda   33
    M. Suzanne Donovan and Catherine Snow

4 Figuring it Out Together: A Research–Practice
Partnership to Improve Early Elementary
Mathematics Learning With Technology   51
Josephine Louie and Pamela J. Buffington

5 The Evolution of a Multi-Stakeholder Research–Practice
Partnership on Equity in School Discipline   66
*Yolanda Anyon, Jessica Yang, Katherine Wiley, Eldridge Greer,
Barbara J. Downing, Ricardo Martinez, and Daniel Kim*

PART III
Expanding Models of RPPs   **83**

6 Rethinking "the Community" in University–Community
Partnerships: Case Studies From CU Engage   85
*Ben Kirshner, Jennifer Pacheco, Manuela Stewart Sifuentes,
and Roudy Hildreth*

7 Messy, Sprawling, and Open: Research–Practice
Partnership Methodologies for Working in Distributed
Inter-Organizational Networks   100
*Rafi Santo, Dixie Ching, Kylie Peppler,
and Christopher Hoadley*

PART IV
Designing for Equity in RPPs   **119**

8 Five Equity-Related Tensions in Project-Based Learning:
How Research–Practice Partnerships Can Spread
and Sustain Deeper Learning   121
Angela Haydel DeBarger and Marc Chun

9 Configurations in Co-Design: Participant Structures
in Partnership Work   135
*Ashley Seidel Potvin, Rebecca G. Kaplan, Alison G.
Boardman, and Joseph L. Polman*

10 But What Does It Actually Look Like?
Representations of Teaching Practice in the Work of
Research–Practice Partnerships   150
Vera Michalchik and Jennifer Knudsen

11 Our House Could Be a Very, Very, Very Fine House:
The Tensions and Disenchantment of Collaborative
Digital Tools Within Partnerships   164
Antero Garcia and Bud Hunt

Index   *181*

CONTRIBUTORS

Yolanda Anyon, Ph.D., is Assistant Professor in the Graduate School of Social Work at the University of Denver. She is the principal investigator of the University of Denver-Denver Public Schools research–practice partnership on school discipline. Her mixed methods research is organized around three general areas of inquiry: racial disparities in youth service systems, contextual influences on the delivery of school-based preventive interventions, and social justice youth development. Across these topics, she is interested in the role of schools and community-based organizations in shaping the life outcomes of low-income students and youth of color.

Philip Bell is Professor of the Learning Sciences at the University of Washington and holds the Shauna C. Larson Chair in Learning Sciences. He pursues a cognitive and cultural program of research across diverse environments focused on how people learn in ways that are personally consequential to them. His research focuses on everyday expertise in science and health, culturally responsive science instruction, the use of emerging learning technologies in science classrooms, children's argumentation and conceptual change in science, and new approaches to inquiry instruction in science. Bell is Executive Director of the UW Institute for Science + Math Education, co-directs the Learning in Informal and Formal Environments (LIFE) research center, directs the Learning Sciences Graduate program at UW, and directs the Everyday Science & Technology Research Group. He recently served on the Board on Science Education at the National Academy of Sciences. Bell has a background in human cognition and development, science education, computer science, and electrical engineering.

Bronwyn Bevan is Senior Research Scientist at the University of Washington College of Education. She is also Principal Investigator of the Research + Practice

Collaboratory. Her research examines how learning opportunities, across formal and informal settings, can be organized to advance equity in education. Her work spans research, professional development, and policy advocacy in the out-of-school time arena. She served on the National Research Council's Committee on Out-of-School Time STEM Learning and is on the editorial board of *Science Education*.

Alison G. Boardman, Ph.D., is Associate Professor in Educational Equity and Cultural Diversity in the School of Education at the University of Colorado Boulder. A former middle and elementary school special education teacher, she works closely with teachers and school leaders to conduct research and to innovate instruction in learning environments that include emergent bilingual learners and students with disabilities. Her research focuses on shifting participant structures in classrooms and in professional development, improving reading comprehension instruction across content areas, and infusing project-based learning that supports all learners to develop literacy skills in meaningful and authentic ways

Pamela J. Buffington, Ph.D., is Co-Director of the Science and Mathematics Programs unit at Education Development Center, where she focuses on bridging research and practice with STEM researchers and practitioners in her role as Co-Principal Investigator on the NSF-funded Research + Practice Collaboratory. At EDC, Buffington is also a Co-PI on an NSF-funded grant to develop and study a blended-learning professional development program to support mathematics teachers in enhancing English learners' mathematics learning. She has served as PI on a U.S. Department of Education Institute of Education Sciences–funded mathematics formative assessment development and validation grant and as a Rural Research Alliance Facilitator and State Liaison for the Regional Educational Laboratory Northeast and Islands. She is responsible for outreach, needs sensing, synthesis, dissemination, and knowledge utilization of evidence-based research with educational leadership across the northeast region.

Dixie Ching, Ph.D., leads the Youth Pathways & Trajectories research strand of the Hive Research Lab project, a research–practice partnership with Mozilla Hive NYC Learning Network. A former cell biologist, Ching has dedicated her career to helping people see the relevance of science, technology, engineering, art, and math (STEAM) to their lives and in developing a better-informed public through STEAM literacy. She has worked on the design and implementation of educational tools and media at various organizations, including the Center for Children & Technology/Education Development Center, Inc., New York Hall of Science, Discovery Communications, WGBH/NOVA, and Beijing Television.

Marc Chun, Ph.D., is a Program Officer at the William and Flora Hewlett Foundation. He manages a portfolio on deeper learning strategy, which aims to ensure that all students are prepared for careers and civic life. He invests in research, measurement of deeper learning competencies, and understanding how innovative teaching and learning practices reach scaled impact. He has taught at Stanford University, Columbia University/Teachers College, the New School, and Vanderbilt University. He has previously worked at the Council for Aid to Education and the RAND Corporation. Marc earned his Ph.D. from Stanford University and held a postdoctoral fellowship at Columbia University/Teachers College.

Angela Haydel DeBarger is a Program Officer in Education at the William and Flora Hewlett Foundation. Previously, she served as a Program Officer for Lucas Education Research at the George Lucas Educational Foundation, where she facilitated research–practice partnerships for project-based learning (PBL). Angela has worked for SRI International as a Senior Research Scientist. While at SRI, her research focused on developing classroom assessment practices that promote student learning and engagement in science. She also developed project-based science courses and studied the efficacy of these courses. Angela received her Ph.D. in educational psychology from Stanford University.

M. Suzanne Donovan is the founding Executive Director of the SERP Institute, an organization incubated at the National Research Council and established as independent in 2003. SERP has engaged school districts and researchers in problem-solving partnerships focused on issues of mathematics, literacy, science, school organization, and classroom climate. She served as study director and editor of numerous National Research Council reports, including *How People Learn: Bridging Research and Practice* (1999), *How Students Learn: History, Mathematics, and Science in the Classroom* (2005), and *Strategic Education Research Partnership* (2003).

Barbara J. Downing, Ph.D., is a School Psychologist in the Division of Student Equity and Opportunity at Denver Public Schools. Supporting the social-emotional learning of all students is the focus of Dr. Downing's work at DPS, and she is responsible for the coordination of student discipline policy and practice. Downing is also the developer and manager of the Deployment Platform and process for the DPS Whole Child Supports Team.

Steve Fleischman serves as the Chief Executive Officer of Education Northwest, providing overall leadership for the nonprofit based in Portland, Oregon. Through more than 150 current projects, Education Northwest partners with teachers, school administrators, state department personnel and leaders, families, students, community members, and local, state, and national policymakers on applied research, evaluation, professional development, and technical assistance efforts that strengthen schools and communities. Fleischman has spent the past two decades advocating for and supporting numerous initiatives to use evidence to improve schools. He began his 30-year education career as a middle and high school social studies teacher, and since the mid-1990s, he has served in leadership positions in numerous nonprofit organizations and evidence use projects. He is a frequent author and presenter on the topic of evidence-informed policymaking and practice in education.

Antero Garcia, Ph.D., is Assistant Professor in the Graduate School of Education at Stanford University. Through work focused on increasing equitable teaching and learning opportunities for urban youth through the use of participatory media and gameplay, Garcia co-designed the Critical Design and Gaming School, a public high school currently open in South Central Los Angeles. His research has appeared in numerous journals, including the *Harvard Educational Review*, *Teachers College Record*, and *Reading & Writing Quarterly*. He has written several book chapters and authored or co-authored six books, including *Good Reception: Teens, Teachers, and Mobile Media in a Los Angeles High School* (2017), *Doing Youth Participatory Action Research: Transforming Inquiry with Researchers, Educators, and Students* (2015), and *Pose, Wobble, Flow: A Culturally Proactive Approach to Literacy Instruction* (2015). Garcia received his Ph.D. in the Urban Schooling division of the Graduate School of Education and Information Studies at the University of California, Los Angeles.

Eldridge Greer, Ph.D., is the Associate Chief of the Division of Student Equity and Opportunity at Denver Public Schools, where his focus is removing structural barriers that negatively impact educational opportunity. Greer has been nationally recognized for his work in Denver for discipline reform efforts, with a particular focus on eliminating racial disparities in discipline. His current work is focused on leading DPS in creating Whole Child supports. He is the proud parent of current and former DPS students.

Roudy Hildreth, Ph.D., is Associate Director of CU Engage and Faculty Affiliate in the Educational Foundations, Policy, and Practice program in the School of Education at the University of Colorado Boulder. With CU Engage, he supervises undergraduate learning programs, conducts evaluation research, and works with faculty on engaged pedagogy. He is co-author of *Becoming Citizens: Deepening the Craft of Youth Civic Engagement* (2009) and co-editor of *Civic Youth Work: Co-Creating Democratic Youth Spaces* (2012). Hildreth has also published numerous scholarly articles and book chapters on topics such as community-based pedagogy, democratic theory, the political philosophy of John Dewey, youth civic engagement, and qualitative research. He received his Ph.D. in Political Science in from the University of Minnesota.

Christopher Hoadley, Ph.D., is Associate Professor at New York University. Hoadley designs and studies technologies for learning and empowerment. He previously served as a Fulbright Scholar in India and Nepal, as an affiliated scholar to the National Academy of Engineering's Center for the Advancement of Scholarship in Engineering Education, and as the director of the National Science Foundation's Cyberlearning program. He chaired the American Educational Research Association's Special Interest Group in Education, Science, and Technology (now SIG: Learning Sciences) and was the first president and co-founder of the International Society for the Learning Sciences.

Bud Hunt is a teacher, writer, and instructional technologist who serves as the IT and Technical Services Manager for the Clearview Library District in northern Colorado. He believes in creating environments that support innovative teaching and learning while preserving freedom, choice, and opportunity for all learners across multiple contexts. His extensive experience in both pedagogy and technical systems helps him build bridges between the educational and technological sides of educational institutions. Hunt advises others across the country on the thoughtful implementation of technology to support teaching and learning in schools and public spaces. He is a teacher-consultant with the Colorado State University Writing Project and an affiliate of the National Writing Project, and in 2013, he was named a ConnectED Champion of Change by the White House.

Rebecca G. Kaplan is a Ph.D. candidate in Education in the Learning Sciences and Human Development department at the University of Colorado at Boulder. A former middle and high school English teacher, she currently teaches for the INVST Community Leadership program, where she supports students as they work toward a more just and sustainable world. She works with researchers and teachers to design, implement, and evaluate educator professional development, innovative curriculum, civic engagement initiatives, and participatory research. Her interests include teacher learning, anti-oppressive pedagogy, and queering literacy.

Daniel Kim is the State Organizing Director at Padres & Jóvenes Unidos. He is the lead organizer for its youth-led campaign to End the School-to-Jail Track, which since 2003 has made Padres & Jóvenes Unidos a founder and leader of the national movement to end the school-to-prison pipeline. Kim has been a movement organizer since 2001, organizing in schools and neighborhoods, on college campuses, and on the buses of Los Angeles to build the power of working-class communities of color. He has also been a faculty member of the English Department at the University of Colorado Boulder.

Ben Kirshner, Ph.D., is Professor in the Learning Sciences and Human Development program at the University of Colorado Boulder's School of Education. He is also Faculty Director of CU Engage: Center for Community-Based Learning and Research. Through his work with CU Engage, Kirshner seeks to develop and sustain university–community research partnerships that address persistent public challenges. His scholarly work examines how young people learn when working together on projects that are relevant to their everyday lives and dreams for the future, such as in community-based youth organizing, participatory action research, and new forms of digital media. His book *Youth Activism in an Era of Education Inequality* (2015) received the Social Policy Publication Award for Best Authored Book from the Society for Research on Adolescence. He received his Ph.D. in Education from Stanford University.

Jennifer Knudsen is a senior mathematics educator for SRI International's Center for Technology in Learning. Her research and products include innovative performatory approaches for learning to teach mathematical practices and curriculum integrated with technology to provide powerful mathematical experiences for students. She directs Bridging Professional Development, in which teachers learn new teaching moves for supporting students' mathematical argumentation. Knudsen previously directed curriculum and professional development efforts for a comprehensive middle school program.

Josephine Louie, Ed.D., is a Research Scientist at Education Development Center and has been the lead researcher for the research–practice partnership in Auburn, Maine. Her work focuses on research and evaluation of education policy and school improvement efforts, particularly in STEM learning. She is currently leading a cluster-randomized trial examining the impacts of a professional development program designed to promote knowledge of visual representations and language strategies in mathematics for middle school teachers serving English learners. She has served as the Co-Principal Investigator of a project designed to promote data literacy among high school students with marine science data, and she has led studies of high school algebra curricula and elementary school mathematics practices for struggling learners. She received an Ed.D. from the Harvard Graduate School of Education, a M.C.P. from the Massachusetts Institute of Technology, and an A.B. in Social Studies from Harvard University.

Ricardo Martinez is Co-Executive Director and Co-Founder of Padres & Jóvenes Unidos, a grassroots educational justice and immigrant rights organization based in Denver, built from the roots of the historic Chicano movement. Martinez's family was part of the field organizing in California that eventually became the United Farm Workers Union. He has served in leadership roles in the Service Employees International Union and the Coalición Para los Derechos de Niños Indocumentados, which was part of the campaign and lawsuit that resulted in the historic Supreme Court ruling *Plyler v. Doe* (1982). He is a recipient of the Leadership for a Changing World Award from the Ford Foundation.

Vera Michalchik is a Learning Officer at the Gordon and Betty Moore Foundation, where she applies her background in learning sciences, program evaluation, and social science research to enhance funding strategies. She served as research director in the Office of the Vice Provost for Teaching and Learning at Stanford University and, for many years, led the informal learning research practice at SRI International's Center for Technology in Learning, where she worked with colleagues on Bridging Professional Development and other projects supporting teacher learning and representational practices.

Jennifer Pacheco, currently a Ph.D. student in the Learning Sciences and Human Development Program at the University of Colorado Boulder, is interested in the intersection of education and health equity. Most recently, she worked as a family engagement coordinator in a school network, which informs her work with families and schools. She aims to use both community participatory research and design-based methods to address complex systemic challenges. Jennifer received her B.A. in Human Biology with a concentration in Urban Education from Stanford University and her M.A. in Educational Psychology from the University of Colorado Denver. She was born and raised in Pueblo, Colorado.

William R. Penuel is Professor of Learning Sciences and Human Development in the School of Education at the University of Colorado Boulder. His research focuses on the design and implementation of innovations in STEM education and on the relation of research in practice. He is a Co-Principal Investigator of the Research + Practice Collaboratory and Principal Investigator of the National Center for Research in Policy and Practice, a U.S. Department of Education–funded center focused on evidence use in education. With Dan Gallagher, he is author of *Creating Research–Practice Partnerships in Education* (2017).

Kylie Peppler, Ph.D., is Associate Professor of Learning Sciences and serves as Director of the Creativity Labs at Indiana University. Peppler is an advisor to the Connected Learning Research Network and a member of the 2016 and 2017 National Educational Technology Plan Committee, sponsored by the U.S. Department of Education. She is also the recipient of several recent awards, including the Mira Tech Educator of the Year and NSF Early CAREER, as well as grants from the Spencer Foundation, Moore Foundation, National Science Foundation, and MacArthur Foundation, among others.

Joseph L. Polman is Professor of Learning Sciences and Science Education, as well as Associate Dean for Research, in the School of Education at the University of Colorado Boulder. He designs and studies project-based learning environments for youth in schools and community programs. He focuses on learning and identity development connected to practices of science, literacy, history, and journalism, with a particular aim of fostering more engaged democratic participation. He serves on the editorial board of *Journal of the Learning Sciences* and the *American Educational Research Journal* and is President-elect of the International Society of the Learning Sciences.

Ashley Seidel Potvin is a Ph.D. candidate in Curriculum and Instruction: Research on Teaching and Teacher Education in the School of Education at the University of Colorado Boulder. A former middle and high school social studies teacher, she works with teachers and researchers to design and implement project-based learning curriculum and currently supports teachers in building positive relationships with and among their students. She has also taught in the Elementary Education program at CU Boulder. Her research interests include supporting teacher learning and professional development through participatory approaches to research, design-based implementation research, improvement science, and responsive pedagogy.

Esther Quintero, Ph.D., is a Senior Fellow at the Albert Shanker Institute. Her work focuses on conducting and synthesizing research on schools as organizations, teachers' social capital, diversity in the teaching workforce, and the sociology of the classroom. In July 2014, Quintero launched the Social Side of Education Reform initiative, highlighting how interpersonal aspects of teachers' workplaces can enable or constrain their growth and development. She is the editor of *Teaching in Context: The Social Side of Education Reform* (2017). Quintero is Co-Principal Investigator of a multi-year research project funded by the Institute of Education Sciences that will develop a novel instrument to capture rich evidence about teachers' professional activity. Other areas of work include social inequality, the sociology of gender and race, and group processes. Quintero has a B.A. from the University of Seville (Spain) and a Ph.D. in sociology from Cornell University.

Rafi Santo, Ph.D., is a learning scientist focused on the intersection of digital culture, education, and large-scale institutional change. He leads research on organizational learning and innovation networks within Hive Research Lab, a research–practice partnership with Mozilla Hive NYC Learning Network, a collective of 70 informal learning organizations including museums, libraries, and afterschool programs. His work on hacker literacies has appeared in journals including *International Journal of Learning and Media* and *Digital Culture & Education*, and he is co-author of a four-volume collection on digital making from MIT Press called *Interconnections: Understanding Systems Through Digital Design*. His work has been supported by the Spencer Foundation, the MacArthur Foundation, the Mozilla Foundation, and the Susan Crown Exchange.

Manuela Stewart Sifuentes is Director of Community Partnerships at CU Engage, where she builds and sustains relationships with community leaders and organizations carrying out collaborative projects that advance the public good. Having spent her childhood going back and forth between Guatemala and the United States, she learned to straddle both worlds and move seamlessly between two languages and cultures. Sifuentes began her career coordinating medical interpreter services for immigrants in Washington, DC, an experience that solidified her desire to work in the areas of social justice and equity, particularly with immigrant, migrant, border, and other marginalized communities on issues such as language access, sexual and reproductive health, fair housing, and educational achievement. She holds a B.A. in International Relations from the University of Colorado, as well as M.P.H. and M.P.A. degrees from the University of Michigan.

Catherine Snow is the Patricia Albjerg Graham Professor at the Harvard Graduate School of Education. She studies language and literacy development among students learning in their first and second languages, with a focus on those placed at risk of poor academic outcomes. She has published many dozens of research articles related to these topics and led the committees that produced the National Research Council report *Preventing Reading Difficulties in Young Children* (1998), as well as the RAND Reading Study Group report *Reading for Understanding* (2000).

Vivian Tseng, Ph.D., is Senior Vice President, Program, at the William T. Grant Foundation, a national funder that supports research to improve the lives of young people. In 2009, she launched the Foundation's focus on the use of research evidence in policy and practice, and in 2012, she created a national network of partnerships between school districts and researchers. Tseng was previously on the faculty in Psychology and Asian American Studies at California State University, Northridge. Her research has focused on the use of research evidence; the role of culture, immigration, and race on child development; improving youth's social settings; and promoting social change. She serves on the Board of Directors of the Forum for Youth Investment, Asian Americans and Pacific Islanders in Philanthropy, and the international journal *Evidence and Policy*. She holds a Ph.D. from New York University and a B.A. from the University of California, Los Angeles.

Kathryn E. Wiley, Ph.D., is a postdoctoral researcher in the Education Studies Department at the University of California, San Diego. She uses qualitative and quantitative methods to answer research questions related to equity and K–12 education policy, and her primary areas of expertise are school discipline and school governance policies. Wiley was a 2016 National Academy of Education/ Spencer Dissertation Fellow.

Jessica Yang, Ph.D., is Assistant Professor in the Department of Social Work at Winthrop University. Yang's research focuses on the experiences of former foster youth, including adverse childhood experiences and aging out of foster care, and child welfare policy. Additionally, Yang's research attempts to examine disproportionality and disparity among marginalized youth served across systems including child welfare, foster care, and education.

PREFACE

Advancing Equity by Embracing Equity in Research–Practice Partnerships

Most researchers concerned with advancing equity in education are deeply committed to developing knowledge that can support learners from economically and racially marginalized communities. Many of us work to challenge deficit models that position young people as lacking skills or a capacity to learn because of their backgrounds. Instead, we seek to develop and study expansive and inclusive methods of teaching that leverage young people's funds of knowledge, experiences, and interests to engage them more deeply in a wide range of epistemic practices.

Current education reform efforts are calling for the use of more research-based evidence in practice. But many of these calls are underpinned by a deficit model of practice. Such calls suggest that practice needs to learn from research, but not vice versa. They entail a unidirectional flow of knowledge from one domain (research) into another (practice). Moreover, there's an assumption that educators need only one kind of research evidence—evidence from impact studies—when, in fact, they can and do draw on a wide range of research in their work (Penuel et al., 2017). Deficit models of educators as consumers rather than producers of knowledge are disrespectful, counterproductive, and not grounded in the evidence of how many educators engage with research. They work against the adaptation of research into practice and thus undermine the relevance, and therefore rigor, of research (Gutiérrez & Penuel, 2014).

This volume posits that research for equity in education must itself adopt an equity lens with respect to knowledge production. It must be designed to recognize and leverage the knowledge and experience of educators and community members who will, it is hoped, utilize the results of the research.

Researchers and education practitioners—in both formal and informal settings, and across the spectrum of roles and activities—have much to learn from each other. Working together, we can learn how to improve practice and promote equity within complex and challenging environments.

A Need for More Equitable Relationships

The story of research and practice in education is fundamentally one of power that derives from a division of labor that has existed in education since the early 1900s (Atkin & Black, 2003; Lagemann, 1989). For decades, the voices of educational researchers, when compared to the voices of those who actually teach, have been seen as more legitimate and therefore more valued by those who set policies and professional standards. Policymakers have required educational practitioners to adopt programs with a strong evidence base from research, whether or not the research has taken into account the local contexts in which educators operate.

Researchers typically operate from a position of privilege in the research and development world: It is usually they, not teachers, who direct the use of resources (including dollars) in improvement studies that generate evidence of impact. It is usually they who possess the symbolic forms of knowledge, instantiated in advanced degrees, academic positions, and technical language. They are the ones who write and publish, establishing authorship of and recognition for knowledge derived from practice. Researchers are the ones typically asked to speak to the press or sit on panels that produce reports that tell practitioners what to do.

Recognizing this power differential is an essential part of shifting the relationship between research and practice to be more equitable and, we would argue, more ethical such that the experiences and voices of practice play a more central role in the formulation of questions, the design of research plans, and the interpretation of results. This is a more ethical stance because it includes and integrates the experiences and concerns of those individuals who are closest to the work and who are ultimately responsible for using and sustaining the results of research. There is also perhaps an ethical issue related to using public resources to generate knowledge without building in, from the start, structures and relationships that enhance the viability and sustainability of the results (Penuel & Fishman, 2012). This volume will explore what such research–practice relationships look like in the context of educational improvement efforts conducted in both formal and informal settings.

Establishing equal footing has implications: Research may need to produce more actionable results at a quicker pace so that the results have more immediate value and use in practice (see Donovan & Snow, Chapter 3 this volume). This does not mean lowering professional standards, but it may mean identifying tentative and emerging knowledge in more timely ways (Cobb, Jackson, Smith, Sorum, & Henrick, 2013). Recognizing and leveraging educators' funds of knowledge is something that will require *methodological* innovations, in terms of how researchers and practitioners work together, as well as *axiological* ones, in terms of how they value one another's work (Bang, Faber, Gurneau, Marin, & Soto, 2016). Raising the curtain on emerging findings by sharing and considering them together, researchers with educators, has the added benefit to research of potentially surfacing factors, forces, or explanations that might otherwise go unidentified because they have taken place beyond the focal length of the researcher but within the notice of the practitioner.

Research may also need to take detours as researchers learn that their questions may be too big or too small to have value to practitioners. For example, a study we undertook in California to understand major issues of implementation of STEM-Rich Maker programs in afterschool was transformed, through a research–practice partnership (RPP), into a study of professional development needs and strategies to support equity in STEM-Rich Making. This focus emerged from the practical needs of the program leaders, who were concerned that Making programs might otherwise fail to deeply engage youth from communities historically excluded from STEM and STEM education (Bevan, Ryoo, & Shea, 2017). A feature of RPPs is that the work together can change the conditions, the conversation, and at times, the focus.

As such, and as this volume will explore, two-way relationships between research and practice may in fact produce more robust and usable results and ideas that practitioners can take up to expand educational opportunity. Indeed, studies in a wide range of fields, including education, have found that close partnerships between researchers and field practitioners can accelerate the implementation of research findings, through *adaptation* rather than *adoption*, developing more practical and therefore sustainable uses (Coburn & Penuel, 2016; National Research Council, 2012; Palinkas et al., 2009).

Outcomes of Equitable Research–Practice Relationships

As has been noted, equity is not *sameness* (Nasir, Rosebery, Warren, & Lee, 2006). Researchers and practitioners bring different experiences and skill sets to shared work and may play different roles in that work. But true partnerships are long-term and mutualistic, serving the needs and advancing the causes of both researchers and practitioners (Coburn, Penuel, & Geil, 2013). Importantly, this kind of mutualism emerges from close relationships between researchers and practitioners, and successful partnerships strengthen and expand those relationships and enrich the practice of partners (see Louie & Buffington, Chapter 4 this volume). These networks are then available as resources when unforeseen, just-in-time needs arise. At those times, one party may call upon the other's expertise or expanded networks for assistance. Those moments may look like one party acting in service to the other—and they are. However, these acts of one-way service are phases, maybe important ones, in long-term relationships oriented toward shared mutualistic goals.

Another key benefit of more equitable approaches to research and practice is the theorization of expert practice, surfacing the unarticulated assumptions and beliefs about teaching and learning that underpin expert educational practice (Bevan, 2016). Theorizing is key to supporting the spread, through *principled adaptation* (Penuel & Gallagher, 2009), of key features or strategies of practice from one context to another. It can also sometimes surface tensions between theory and practice. For example, educators deeply committed to learner-centered instruction can, by uncovering the theory embedded in their practice, come to see the ways in which their specific instructional practices might be advancing or sometimes derailing the learner-centered nature of their work because of theoretical (in)consistencies.

The use of evidence as a basis for professional decision-making is yet another benefit of rethinking the relationship between research and practice. For example, RPPs commonly place data, in the form of field notes, video and audio recordings, or transcripts of interviews, at the center of reflective professional conversations regarding sense-making and critique of a given question of practice (Coburn et al., 2013). Evidence-based discussions can be mutually enlightening. For example, researchers can come to new understanding through the expert inferences of educators whose scope of understanding always exceeds the scope of a given slice of data. At the same time, practitioners can come to think more explicitly about indicators and evidence of effective teaching and learning as they are challenged to support their inferences and ideas based on what they see in the data and what they know from practice (see, e.g., Bevan, Gutwill, Petrich, & Wilkinson, 2015).

Altogether, these benefits can add up to more than the sum of their parts by building capacity and insight among educators involved in the improvement enterprise. Many partnerships organize themselves to include educators across multiple levels of the system: classroom teachers, curriculum supervisors or program directors, building or organizational leaders, and so forth (Severance, Leary, & Johnson, 2014). These conversations engage multiple perspectives around visions for equitable teaching and learning and research evidence, build interest and buy-in across levels (thus enhancing sustainability), and develop a shared a language and sometimes new forms of representation for articulating and continuing to investigate and communicate key issues of practice.

This Volume

In this volume, we share accounts from the front lines of projects where educational researchers and practitioners are working together to identify problems, design solutions, and test out new strategies. In this reimagined relationship, knowledge, interests, and experiences from each community are equally valued in shaping the work. At the center of each chapter is a shared commitment to improvement that can advance educational equity.

Across the chapters, RPPs are explored in terms of seven defining characteristics: (1) long-term or open-ended; (2) pragmatic (organized to address pressing problems of practice); (3) of mutual benefit to all parties; (4) involving processes of iteration, where questions and strategies are developed, tested, reviewed, and retested; (5) integrating mechanisms or routines that intentionally nurture the developing relationship; (6) engaging in original data analysis; and, when problems are related to equity in education, (7) creating mechanisms to surface and directly address relevant histories of racism, classism, sexism, and other forms of inequity (Bevan, 2017; Coburn et al., 2013).

Part I: Rethinking the Relationship Between Research and Practice

In Chapter 1, Tseng, Fleischman, and Quintero set the stage for this important work by exploring the potential rewards and benefits of democratizing the creation and use of evidence in education. As they note, too often research has been undertaken to *prove* rather than to *improve*. This chapter can serve as foundational reading for why the field needs to take this step forward in reshaping the relationship between research and practice.

Chapter 2, by Bevan, Penuel, Bell, and Buffington, addresses issues of how RPPs can produce research-based findings with applicability to other researchers and settings of practice, or what is typically referred to as generalizable results. They reframe generalizability for partnerships, drawing on reports from the four Labs of the NSF-funded Research + Practice Collaboratory. These reports describe three different ways that locally produced and locally relevant knowledge was used to engage national conversations and perspectives in ways that produced concrete new resources and action plans across a wide variety of settings. The paper highlights measures RPP teams can take to ensure that their work can build the evidence base and be used to improve practice.

Part II: RPPs That Impact Practice

In Part II, we share three detailed accounts of strong RPPs. These chapters describe how partnerships unfolded and reflect on key dimensions that afforded or constrained their development, such as the dispositions of good partners, issues related to funding, how research questions were negotiated, developing trust and buy-in across multiple actors in the systems, and how data were used to direct the inquiries as well as to impact practices in the districts.

Donovan and Snow describe the development and evolution of the Strategic Educational Research Partnership in Chapter 3. This longitudinal account brings to life how long-term, mutualistic relationships allow for much deeper and broader knowledge development as partnerships ride out and respond to shifting priorities, needs, and opportunities. Begun with a focus on middle grades English language arts, this partnership, over the course of a decade, came to also address mathematics, science, and equity for English language learners. Their chapter also points to the need to compromise, redirect, and reframe goals and strategies as district contexts shift, as well as the fragility of such partnerships when they are not integrated into the organizational infrastructure and funding streams.

In Chapter 4, Louie and Buffington describe how they started and supported their RPP with a rural district in Maine. Their work focused on bringing learning sciences research on learning trajectories to support the meaningful use of technology in early grades mathematics. Their careful attention to integrating their project with district priorities on one level and with teachers' questions and constraints on another level led to significant teacher-led uptake of new mathematics-rich instructional practices. The chapter also highlights the importance of building trusting relationships early in partnerships through co-defining the focus of joint work.

Anyon and colleagues provide in Chapter 5 a detailed account of their partnership, designed to address a district's historical inequities in practices of discipline and punishment. They describe how urban schools adopting restorative justice interventions led to changes in K–12 students' disciplinary experiences and outcomes. Their project brings together a powerful configuration of partners from a university, a school district, and a community organizing group that had long lobbied the school district to address racial disparities in discipline practice. Their chapter also reflects on the role of social and historical context, in this case a contemporaneous increase in media attention to police relationships with communities of color, which created a sense of urgency and personal commitment on the part of many in the partnership.

Part III: Expanding Models of RPPs

Most RPPs are between researchers and a given school district, or sometimes a set of schools within a district. There are also RPPs between researchers and informal learning institutions, such as the San Jose Children's Museum and the University of California, Santa Cruz (see Sobel & Jipson, 2016, for a compendium of museum RPPs), or networks of afterschool organizations such as the California Tinkering Afterschool Network. Part III of this volume includes descriptions of RPPs that are organized at different scales and with different types of partners than most of the others in this book and in the literature.

Kirshner, Pacheco, Sifuentes, and Hildreth, in Chapter 6, describe social justice–oriented RPPs that seek to engage community members, as opposed to educators, in partnerships that can uncover historical processes of marginalization in an effort to address more equitable arrangements. This chapter describes three different RPPs: one with undergraduate students, one with facilities maintenance staff at a university, and one with parents in a local community. Among many other contributions, this chapter calls out the tension between wanting to work

democratically, to allow the research agenda to emerge through true joint exploration, and the sometimes awkward pauses and gaps that this process creates for
participants who may be accustomed to more predetermined, or even researcher-
led, ways of working.

In Chapter 7, Santo, Ching, Peppler, and Hoadley describe an RPP developed
within a distributed inter-organizational network. They describe their strategies
for working across a network of 70 informal learning organizations in New York
City who had come together to improve learning outcomes for youth engaged
in a range of digital learning opportunities. Their chapter describes how they
negotiated the research questions through a counsel-based model, the nature of
productive research questions in distributed networks, how they attempted to
keep this large network engaged with and aware of the research activities, and
how they designed activities to support collective sense-making and knowledge
building from the data they collected. The chapter provides insights and strategies
for organizing and managing complex networked relationships.

Part IV: Designing for Equity in RPPs

This part contains four chapters that address particular dimensions of the work
of RPPs.

In Chapter 8, DeBarger and Chun describe how RPPs can be deployed to support stronger and more equitably distributed approaches to project-based learning
(PBL). Their chapter summarizes the case for PBL but notes the many questions that are raised about how PBL can be implemented in ways that ameliorate
rather than exacerbate current inequities in education. They identify five central
tensions to achieving this end and argue that RPPs can help bridge these tensions by building supportive infrastructures for teacher learning and by ensuring
appropriate localization of projects. They highlight ways that these are particularly
important strategies for scaling PBL, because for many teachers, project-based
approaches represent a significant departure from current practice and making
projects locally relevant is a key strategy for promoting broad interest and engagement of students.

Potvin, Kaplan, Boardman, and Polman, in Chapter 9, describe two different
approaches they took to organizing co-design processes with teachers integrating
PBL into high school English language arts classes. Co-design is a strategy within
RPPs for democratizing participation in the design of educational innovations. At
present, however, there are few examples of different ways to organize co-design.
This chapter illustrates the different ways that co-design can be analyzed and studied
and the consequences of these decisions. As such, it contributes to our understanding of how and when different strategies might balance goals of promoting teacher
agency with the need for designs to cohere around shared goals for learning.

Michalchik and Knudsen, in Chapter 10, explore the ways in which representations of instructional practice are critical tools for developing educators' vision,

understanding, and confidence to enact and embrace educational innovations. They explore the ways that co-developing such representations can provide powerful contexts for the development of RPPs. They also note that such representations, when co-developed, can produce *portable* results of the research, which can be used to inform the practice and improvement efforts of others.

Communication is critical to RPPs, and in Chapter 11, Garcia and Hunt describe how their partnership experimented with a range of digital tools to support collaboration and communication. In particular, their account reveals the tensions and challenges that can arise from the demands that RPPs place on participants to communicate and collaborate, often in new ways. Their chapter emphasizes the need to foreground the purposes for using technology when selecting tools. They also describe the trade-offs involved in the choice of tools for their partnership. Their chapter underscores the primacy of communication and coordination within RPPs in selecting tools to build an infrastructure that can support the dynamic and fast-moving rhythms of partnership work.

Conclusion

Research on creativity stresses the importance of colliding perspectives—from multiple disciplines, cultures, or media types—for gaining new insights and developing new ideas (Peppler & Solomou, 2011; Sawyer, 2006). This is the core argument for RPPs: Colliding and converging perspectives, organized around the seven characteristics of RPPs described earlier, will lead to relevant, usable, and feasible improvement strategies, argued to be criteria of true rigor (Gutiérrez & Penuel, 2014).

As these chapters show, RPPs can be deeply rewarding. Through establishing equitable relationships, researchers and practitioners contribute, in practical and real-time ways, to the improvement of teaching and learning. Thinking is deepened, methods are innovated, and social networks are expanded. RPPs provide a more equity-oriented approach to knowledge generation, theory development, and STEM education improvement.

We envision readers making use of this volume in different ways. Some readers, whether educational leaders or researchers, are likely to be forming partnerships, and for them, this book will yield a set of organizing principles and values for anticipating how inequities might show up in partnership formation and how those inequities can be confronted in building relationships among partners. Other readers are likely to be experienced in RPPs and find the specific case examples, as well as the chapters focused on particular dimensions of PBL, co-design, representations, and communication, useful for identifying strategies to address common challenges in partnerships. For instructors, this book can serve as a reader for graduate students in education who are preparing to become researchers or education leaders with an emphasis on equity in education. We hope that for all readers, this volume will be a springboard for advancing the field through their own efforts to expand, challenge, and revise the ideas found here in the interest of advancing equity in education.

References

Atkin, J. M., & Black, P. (2003). *Inside science education reform: A history of curricular and policy change*. New York: Teachers College Press.

Bang, M., Faber, L., Gurneau, J., Marin, A., & Soto, C. (2016). Community-based design research: Learning across generations and strategic transformations of institutional relations toward axiological innovations. *Mind, Culture, and Activity, 23*(6), 28–41.

Bevan, B. (2016). Wanted: A new cultural model for the relationship between research and practice. In D. Sobel & J. Jipson (Eds.), *Relating research and practice: Cognitive development in museum settings* (pp. 181–189). New York: Psychology Press.

Bevan, B. (2017). Research and practice: One way, two way, no way, or new way? *Curator: The Museum Journal, 60*(2), 133–141. doi:10.1111/cura.12204

Bevan, B., Gutwill, J., Petrich, M., & Wilkinson, K. (2015). Learning through STEM-rich tinkering: Findings from a jointly negotiated research project taken up in practice. *Science Education, 99*, 98–120.

Bevan, B., Ryoo, J. J., & Shea, M. V. (2017). What-if? Building creative cultures for STEM making and learning. *Afterschool Matters, 25*, 1–8.

Cobb, P., Jackson, K., Smith, T., Sorum, M., & Henrick, E. C. (2013). Design research with educational systems: Investigating and supporting improvements in the quality of mathematics teaching at scale. In B. J. Fishman, W. R. Penuel, A-R. Allen, & B. H. Cheng (Eds.), *Design-based implementation research: Theories, methods, and exemplars: National society for the study of education yearbook* (pp. 320–349). New York: Teachers College Record.

Coburn, C. E., & Penuel, W. R. (2016). Research–practice partnerships in education: Outcomes, dynamics, and open questions. *Educational Researcher, 45*(1), 48–54.

Coburn, C. E., Penuel, W. R., & Geil, K. (2013). *Research–practice partnerships at the district level: A new strategy for leveraging research for educational improvement*. Berkeley, CA and Boulder, CO: University of California and University of Colorado.

Gutiérrez, K. D., & Penuel, W. R. (2014). Relevance to practice as a criterion for rigor. *Educational Researcher, 43*(1), 19–23. doi:10.3102/0013189X13520289

Lagemann, E. C. (1989). The plural worlds of educational research. *History of Education Quarterly, 29*(2), 185–214.

Nasir, N. S., Rosebery, A. S., Warren, B., & Lee, C. D. (2006). Learning as a cultural process: Achieving equity through diversity. In R. K. Sawyer (Ed.), *The Cambridge handbook of the learning sciences* (pp. 567–580). New York: Cambridge University Press.

National Research Council. (2012). *Using science as evidence in public policy*. Washington, DC: The National Academies Press.

Palinkas, L. A., Aarons, G. A., Chorpita, B. F., Hoagwood, K., Landsverk, J., & Weisz, J. (2009). Cultural exchange and the implementation of evidence-based practices: Two case studies. *Research on Social Work Practice, 19*(5), 602–612.

Penuel, W. R., & Fishman, B. J. (2012). Large-scale intervention research we can use. *Journal of Research in Science Teaching, 49*(3), 281–304.

Penuel, W. R., & Gallagher, L. P. (2009). Comparing three approaches to preparing teachers to teach for deep understanding in Earth science: Short-term impacts on teachers and teaching practice. *The Journal of the Learning Sciences, 18*(4), 461–508.

Peppler, K. A., & Solomou, M. (2011). Building creativity: Collaborative learning and creativity in social media environments. *On the Horizon, 19*(1), 13–23.

Sawyer, R. K. (2006). *Explaining creativity: The science of human innovation.* New York: Oxford University Press.

Severance, S., Leary, H., & Johnson, R. (2014). Tensions in a multi-tiered research partnership. In J. L. Polman, E. Kyza, D. K. O'Neill, I. Tabak, A. S. Jurow, K. O'Connor, & W. R. Penuel (Eds.), *Proceedings of the 11th international conference of the learning sciences* (Vol. 2., pp. 1171–1175). Boulder, CO: ISLS.

Sobel, D. M., & Jipson, J. (2016). *Relating research and practice: Cognitive development in museum settings.* New York: Psychology Press.

PART I

Rethinking the Relationship Between Research and Practice

1

DEMOCRATIZING EVIDENCE
IN EDUCATION

*Vivian Tseng, Steve Fleischman,
and Esther Quintero*

In this chapter, we invite readers into a dialogue on how we can collectively democratize the evidence movement in education. Significant strides have been made to build and use evidence in U.S. education over the past 15 years (Tseng, 2016), but these efforts have produced mixed responses to their effectiveness and in the degree of support for them among different stakeholders. Many initiatives have been driven by top-down forces and imperatives, with too little attention provided to the perspectives, expertise, and diversity of people who are concerned with education. All too often, teachers have perceived evidence-based policies as something done *to* them rather than *with* them (Finnigan, Daly, & Che, 2013). Educators more broadly have seen research conducted *on* schools and not *with* them. Those perceptions have contributed to a distrust of data and research evidence and of policymakers' efforts to use them to drive change.

A desire to address these issues is already palpable in the education sector, but many of us are grappling with how to make our work more inclusive. Going forward, we believe that the movement for evidence in education could accomplish much more by aligning our efforts with democratic principles. We must aim for a more engaged and evidence-informed "citizenry" in which different stakeholders can meaningfully participate in the production and use of data and research evidence to inform educational improvement.

What would this mean? In a more democratic evidence movement, the power to define research agendas would be shared among a broader cross-section of researchers, practitioners, decision-makers, and communities. In our current context, research questions often arise out of researchers' discussions and debates with each other in academic journals and at scholarly conferences. Imagine instead a world in which the research questions arose from vibrant back-and-forth exchanges between researchers and educators as they jointly addressed the roadblocks to teaching and learning. Imagine, too, that parents, students, and community stakeholders had a say in determining the unanswered questions that future research should address. And what if the demand for evaluation was not driven primarily and punitively by policymakers but by educators seeking knowledge to enhance their professional work and by parents and community groups invested in improving education? Setting research goals would become less an academic exercise or a policy mandate and more a matter of deliberation, negotiation, and compromise among diverse stakeholders. The process would likely be messier and less efficient, but it would also yield more meaningful agendas.

When it came to evidence-informed decision-making, research and data would not just be a tool for policymakers; evidence would also be accessible to community organizations, parents, students, and the broader public as they seek to drive change in education. There would be a stronger focus on developing a shared understanding of what the research says and what its implications are for practice and policy. Of course, disagreements will remain about values, the proper role of government, and where to direct resources. Data and research evidence cannot resolve those debates, but they can be tools for forging consensus about the problem at hand and the likely outcomes—both intended and unintended—of moving in particular policy directions.

In this chapter, we discuss why it is important to democratize the evidence movement in education and the urgency of tackling it now. We offer our views on what a more democratic evidence system could look like in action by focusing on shared values; redefining relationships, roles, and professional identities; and putting in place new practices and structures. For the purposes of this chapter, we focus intensively on researchers and practitioners, but we see them as only two sets of stakeholders within a broader democratic movement. For work on community stakeholders, we refer readers to Kirshner, Pacheco, Sifuentes, and Hildreth (Chapter 6, this volume).

Why Democratize the Evidence Movement? Why Now?

It is commonly believed that more or better evidence and greater science literacy could settle disagreements. According to recent studies in cognitive and social psychology, however, the primary source of controversies is not a lack of information or a feeble ability to understand it, but differences in people's "goals and needs, knowledge and skills, and values and beliefs" (National Academies, 2017, p. 3). Taken in this light, how evidence is produced, debated, and communicated is as important—if not more so—than having the right evidence or having sufficient evidence.

Researchers Matthew Feinberg and Robb Willer (2013) found that tapping into people's preexisting beliefs influences their support for specific policies. In an experiment, they tested whether using images that resonate with conservative values could increase skeptical Republicans' support for climate change policies. Conservative individuals were shown images of the consequences of climate change; some saw images that tapped into conservative beliefs about purity (e.g., once-pure water contaminated), and others saw images that invoked liberal beliefs about protection from harm (e.g., a coral reef system harmed by global warming). Climate change skeptics who saw images that appealed to their conservative beliefs reported greater support of climate change policies than those who saw images that appealed to liberal beliefs. The alignment of the message with the viewer's belief system mattered.

Similarly, Dan Kahan and his colleagues (2012) set out to investigate why good evidence isn't more effective in resolving disagreements. The researchers surveyed the attitudes and beliefs of 1,000 Americans, then administered a test to evaluate their math skills, and finally presented them with various scenarios that required them to use those skills to evaluate information and make a recommendation. When the scenario was related to an issue on which participants did not have strong views, their math skills predicted their answers. That is, participants with stronger math skills were more likely than those with weak skills to make the right recommendation. However, when the scenario was related to an issue for which participants held strong views, math ability ceased to be predictive of how well they did. In fact, people with stronger math skills were *less* likely to make the correct choice when such a choice conflicted with their beliefs.

Like Feinberg and Willer (2013), Kahan and colleagues (2012) concluded that the problem was not one of needing more information or a stronger ability to judge it. Instead, the researchers attributed this phenomenon to the ways people's preexisting beliefs influence how they process information. In general, individuals want to avoid the tension that arises when they confront information that conflicts with their beliefs. It is much easier to resolve this tension by changing how you look at a specific piece of evidence rather than by changing your beliefs or how you look at the world.

It might be tempting at times to see the world as divided between those on the evidence side and those outside it, but the studies just discussed suggest that this distinction might be more situational. It depends on the issue at hand, the specific context, and people's beliefs. Rather than staking out "sides" for or against evidence, we may be better off broadening and opening up the evidence movement to account for real-world complexities and the ways people's beliefs and values influence their positions on social issues. There must be room for different stakeholders to participate in building and using evidence to improve education.

Evidence as Weapon Versus Evidence for Dialogue

The need for the evidence movement to become more democratic is urgent because of increasing concerns about the political motives behind research and its use:

> You know, you can find research to support anything. The problems we have in our society today . . . People are now using research to say that all the

problems are the teacher, and if you can correct the teacher, all our problems go away, which is ridiculous. . . . The point is research can be slanted to support many different viewpoints.

(Daly & Finnigan, 2011)

This view of research as a political weapon is not inevitable. In *Teaching in Context*, Elaine Allensworth (2017, pp. 156–157) explains how evidence can also be used to facilitate productive conversations:

> In 2009, schools in Chicago started using data on early warning indicators in the ninth grade to help students have a strong transition to high school and keep them on track to graduation. Before this, conversations in schools about issues around dropout often focused on factors other than student course performance. School staff considered dropout and course failure to be problems that were outside of their control, that stemmed from students' lives outside of the school. By focusing attention on students' grades and attendance, conversations became about how students were performing in school and what school staff and parents could do to support better attendance and performance in classes, rather than trying to fix problems outside the school, such as crime and teenage pregnancy. . . . By keeping the focus on data related to outcomes everyone cares about for the student, . . . conversations can move away from finger-pointing about who is to blame for problems at school (the student, the parent, the teacher) to making plans for improving how students are actually doing in school.

As this example suggests, research evidence can be used as a tool for productive dialogue rather than as ammunition to take down another argument. Research can help different stakeholders come to a shared understanding of the problems that they care about and to jointly determine the productive directions to take and the solutions to try out. But to have these kinds of dialogues, we need to reenvision the relationship between the research community and other stakeholders and we need a different infrastructure for connecting research, policy, and practice (Tseng & Nutley, 2014).

Some might think that this is a particularly challenging time with regard to science. There has been extensive commentary and debate about whether we are in a post-truth, post-fact, post-evidence environment (Brown, 2016; Stewart, Dubow, Hofman, & van Stolk, 2016). These challenges are all the more reason to reflect on where we have been in our evidence work and where we want to go. In this time of uncertainty and reevaluation, a window of opportunity has opened for redefining the role of education research in policy, practice, and broader public discourse. There are related efforts led by organizations around the world, including Sense About Science, Evidence for Democracy, the African Institute for Development Policy, the Alliance for Useful Evidence, and the Scholars Strategy

Network. How we come out of this period will depend a great deal on whether we use this as a time to consider alternative ways of thinking and working or whether we retrench.

Democratizing Evidence in Action

What will it take to achieve a more democratic evidence system, where diverse stakeholders have a voice in both the production and use of research evidence? A democratic political system is bolstered when there are respectful relationships, shared values, well-defined roles and identities, and a supportive infrastructure. In the sections that follow, we discuss how we might rethink these same elements to create a more democratized evidence system.

About a decade ago, the second author attended a meeting bringing together district administrators and educators with education researchers to learn about promising school improvement approaches. The meeting started well, at least from the researchers' perspectives: After all, they were able to present the latest research evidence on school improvement to practitioners. Soon, however, the meeting degenerated into recriminations against the research side and the practice side. The practitioners complained about being dragged to "yet another meeting" at which researchers presented irrelevant studies and then told practitioners what to do. In turn, the researchers expressed frustration and disdain that educators neither read nor used their research. This disagreeable dynamic went on for a day and a half.

This all-too-common story illustrates how important it is to foster productive relationships and to work toward shared values. Educators too often feel like second-class citizens, spoken down to by research "experts" in these mixed-role settings. Researchers who care about education and feel their work could benefit educators are frustrated that they are distrusted. In this environment, the parties are at an impasse, and forward movement is all but impossible.

One of the more important benefits of a democratic system is that it can help a diverse citizenry reconcile differences in a peaceful manner, enabling collective action and progress. To democratize evidence, we must bridge the different perspectives and interests held by various stakeholders in our education system. We need to recognize the interdependencies of different people—teachers, administrators, parents, students, policymakers, and researchers—and the varying roles they play within our education system.

Building Relationships

If researchers disrespect educators—for example, by assuming that they disregard research evidence in their teaching—and, in turn, if educators disparage researchers as "ivory tower" intellectuals who produce nothing of practical value, then we cannot build a system in which evidence informs change. Fortunately, there's a lot to build on in developing more constructive relationships between educators and researchers.

Across the country, we are witnessing an emerging field of research–practice partnerships (RPPs) in education (Coburn, Penuel, & Geil, 2013). As the recently formed National Network of Education Research–Practice Partnerships describes, these efforts are "long-term mutually beneficial formalized collaborations between education researchers and practitioners" that focus on "producing more relevant research, improving the use of research evidence in decision making, and engaging both researchers and practitioners to tackle problems of practice" (National Network of Education Research–Practice Partnerships, n.d.).

If the key to success in real estate is "location, location, location," then the key to effective partnerships is "relationships, relationships, relationships" (Barton, Nelsestuen, & Mazzeo, 2014, p. 2). While robust relationships among researchers, educators, and policymakers certainly exist outside of RPPs, these entities have codified some of the relational elements that foster success. Chief among them is *mutualism*, a commitment to "sustained interaction that benefits both researchers and practitioners" (Coburn et al., 2013, p. 3). Partnerships depart from the typical ways researchers and practitioners work together wherein one group or the other sets the agenda. For example, "collaborative" work often entails researchers reaching out to practitioners because they need a site to conduct their studies or practitioners contracting with a researcher to fulfill specific technical needs. While there may be some negotiation around the work, those adaptations are often made around the edges, and the project goals do not rise to the level of being co-defined. In RPPs, there is a commitment to jointly setting the research agendas and the projects that stem from them (Coburn et al., 2013).

Working Toward Shared Values

Identifying shared values can provide a foundation for productive relationships. Values that we think are necessary to promote a more democratic evidence system fall into three categories: interpersonal (values regarding social interaction), scientific (values that support rigorous research evidence), and civic (values that promote democratic engagement). In the next sections, we discuss these mutually reinforcing values and the relationships they can generate.

Interpersonal Values

Three interpersonal values stand out in building a more democratic system: respect, humility, and curiosity (see also Palinkas, Short, & Wong, 2015, for a discussion of intra- and interpersonal characteristics). Of these three values, mutual respect is perhaps the most fundamental. In a functioning evidence system, researchers and practitioners respect what the other brings to the table. Respect can engender trust, and trust is the glue that holds relationships together and makes collective action possible, even when disagreements arise.

Humility is also vital given the enormous complexity and difficulty of educational improvement. With humility, researchers and practitioners can acknowledge the limitations of what they "know," remain open to the possibility of being wrong, and be willing to learn and improve their own knowledge and work over time.

Finally, everyone in the democratic evidence system must remain curious about each other, about the work, and about whether there are better—but unexplored—ways to improve education. Educators cannot shut their classroom doors and look only to their own experiences, without consideration of external sources of evidence, to guide their actions. Researchers too must look beyond academic walls and consider how their work can be more relevant to improving education.

Scientific Values

Core scientific values such as a commitment to systematic observation and analysis, appropriate skepticism, and openness to alternative hypotheses must also be widely shared if we are to build a more democratic evidence system. A National Research Council report (2012, p. 3) observes that science "is a process of producing knowledge directed by systematic and rule-governed efforts that guard against self-deception—against believing something is true because one wants it to be true."

Nearly 15 years ago, Paula and Keith Stanovich made the hopeful observation that the values of science are well aligned with those held by educators. They wrote, "Researchers and educators are kindred spirits in their approach to knowledge, an important fact that can be used to forge a coalition to bring hard-won research knowledge to light in the classroom" (2003, p. 35). In their experience, educators

> believe that some explanations and methods are better than others. . . . They believe that there are valid, if fallible, ways of finding out which educational practices are best. Teachers believe in a world that is predictable and controllable by manipulations that they use in their professional practice, just as scientists do.
>
> *(Stanovich & Stanovich, 2003, p. 35)*

Maintaining skepticism about what we think we know and openness to alternative hypotheses are important values that science can contribute to education decision-making. We do not presume that it will be easy. As Stanovich and Stanovich (2003) acknowledged, it is challenging for educators and policymakers—and researchers themselves—to adhere to these scientific values. The authors observed:

> [Some] educators reject public, depersonalized knowledge in social science because they believe it dehumanizes people. Science, however, with

its conception of publicly verifiable knowledge, actually democratizes knowledge. It frees practitioners and researchers from slavish dependence on authority. . . . Empirical science, by generating knowledge and moving it into the public domain, is a liberating force.

Civic Values

The civic values of dialogue, negotiation, and optimism also need to be mobilized to support a more democratic evidence movement. Dialogue is necessary for the resolution of difference. It allows researchers, practitioners, and other stakeholders to come to an understanding of others' viewpoints, and that knowledge is critical for defining research agendas that matter to a broad public. Dialogue is also critical for interpreting research findings. Research evidence never speaks for itself: human beings must always make sense of what research results mean for particular problems at hand (Honig & Coburn, 2008; Tseng, 2012). Researchers bring to that dialogue an analysis of what constitutes more plausible versus less plausible conclusions that can be drawn from studies, given the methods and designs that were employed. Practitioners also need to be at the table to consider plausible explanations because they have the experiential and practical on-the-ground knowledge of what is possible.

In a diverse democracy, negotiation is always necessary. Disagreement is inevitable, but negotiation and compromise allow diverse stakeholders to forge a path forward. Transparency is also key because stakeholders must be able to appraise and comment on the evidence upon which decisions are based (O'Neil, 2016; Sense About Science, 2016). As researchers and practitioners deliberate over research priorities or the policy implications of research findings, there must be a give-and-take. How democratic societies—and a democratic evidence movement—navigate, deliberate, and negotiate those differences is critical.

Finally, democratic societies are often characterized by optimism and faith in the future based on confidence that, if given the chance and the necessary tools, people who are affected by a problem can also resolve it.

Redefining Professional Roles and Identities

Closely related to the values and relationships that are required to build a more democratic evidence system are the new professional roles and identities that must be assumed. In our vision of a more democratic future, researchers are not the exclusive producers or arbiters of empirical knowledge. Educators are not simply the willing or unwilling consumers of this knowledge. Both groups assume responsibilities in developing and using evidence. Doing so does not deny the significance of experts: Researchers have expertise in scientific methods, just as educators have expertise in teaching. But the boundaries of expertise do not need to be rigidly defined. In a democratic evidence movement, roles would be more fluid and there would be room for different forms of participation. Some teachers want to deeply engage with research, and others prefer to be consumers of the findings. But all would gain from a system in which teachers' collective voices shape research agendas and the policy priorities that stem from the findings.

Researchers will also need to reconsider their roles, and not all researchers will choose the same form of participation. Some researchers will want to work side by side with teachers to improve practice while others will prefer to stick with doing research in their offices. The more important point, as Fleischman (2014, p. 23) observed, is that "complexity, and the stubborn entrenchment of many critical social issues, requires [researchers and] evaluators to rethink their roles. Evaluators should consider behaving as co-developers, 'critical friends,' informants, and conveners, rather than experts with all the answers or equivocators with no solutions." Although there are only a few places that prepare researchers to take on these collaborative roles, resources to support role redefinition are increasing. For example, researchers at the University of Washington Institute for Science and Mathematics Education outlined core operating principles for researchers working in RPPs (Bell, Rhinehart, & Peterman, 2015):

- Act as a thoughtful and responsive sense-maker.
- Work to build interpersonal relationships with teachers and students, and be transparent in your work.
- Co-design, co-teach, and co-research in response to problems of practice.
- Understand and work within the realities, needs, and demands of classrooms and educational systems.

In a new book, Penuel and Gallagher (2017) suggested additional ways that researchers can support educators' work: surfacing tensions between the central office and schools, identifying those people who need extra help, brokering relationships to other researchers, and identifying funding opportunities.

Educators will also need to take on new roles, identities, and skills as we democratize the evidence movement. For practitioners, the core operating principles for working in RPPs might include the following:

- Remain open-minded about the value of research, and ask questions when the findings go against your instincts; help researchers identify potential blind spots by sharing your expertise and knowledge of the local context.
- Demand training on how to use research and data to improve your practice, your school, and the teaching profession.
- Communicate your needs to researchers, allowing time and space for the back-and-forth engagement.
- Learn about the constraints under which researchers operate and work with them to build better infrastructures and incentive systems.

Intermediaries will need to reimagine their roles as well. Well-meaning consultants often end up working on the wrong problem, misunderstanding the client organization's culture, or ignoring the possibility that constant change can make today's solutions obsolete tomorrow. In *Humble Inquiry* (2013), Edgar Schein outlined a new approach. He argued that consultants and coaches must jettison the old idea of professional distance and work with their clients in a more personal way, emphasizing openness, curiosity, and humility. Schein showed how to create an atmosphere of trust and caring so that clients can share what is on their minds. Consultants and clients can then jointly discover what needs to be done. Working together from the outset also speeds things up; it obviates the need for elaborate diagnostic tests and avoids solutions that might look good on paper but don't fit an organization's on-the-ground reality.

Building a New Infrastructure Focused on Learning

Producing and using evidence simply to sift through what works and what doesn't is a recipe for disappointment (Tseng, 2016). The evidence democracy we espouse here would shift our research priorities and structures from a focus on "proving" to "improving." It would harness various types of evidence from a rich array of sources, and it would be supported by an infrastructure geared toward learning and continuous improvement.

A learning system will need to facilitate ongoing, seamless engagement between researchers, practitioners, and policymakers around research, data, expertise, and experience (Tseng, 2015). Additionally, it will need to foster engagement within agencies across research and program departments, across actors at varying levels, and in the broader ecosystem, which includes parents and community members. Smart incentive systems, cross-functional agency teams, intermediary organizations, and RPPs can all be elements of that infrastructure.

This new evidence democracy would also require its own version of civics education. As suggested earlier, both researchers and educators will need new kinds of learning opportunities, either in their professional training or in-service, so that they can perform their new roles well. Some practices that have emerged through RPPs may become standard operating procedures of this infrastructure and shape other kinds of researcher-educator relationships. For example, the University of Chicago Consortium on School Research has, since its inception, followed a "no-surprises" policy with its partner, the Chicago Public Schools, such that "the school system is always made aware of the contents of Consortium reports prior to public release" (Consortium on Chicago School Research, 2007, p. 9). This allows the agency to prepare a thoughtful response rather than scramble in the middle of a media frenzy. Many of these partnership practices are codified through formal charters, operating principles, and memoranda of understanding, which should facilitate their application by others.[1] As technology advances, digital tools and social media platforms are also providing new ways of codifying and facilitating partnership practices (see Garcia and Hunt, Chapter 11, this volume).

Finally, we need to build new structures while tearing down those that impede an evidence democracy. Both RPPs and labor-management collaborations (LMCs) are undergoing robust development (Rubinstein & McCarthy, 2016; Tseng, Easton, & Supplee, 2017). Whereas RPPs bring researchers and local or state education agencies together, LMCs take place between school districts, unions, and sometimes businesses and community organizations. Both forms of partnerships seek to redefine relationships that are conventionally in tension or distanced from one another. RPPs put practitioners and researchers on equal footing in defining research agendas, and LMCs contest the notion that labor-management relations must be adversarial. Both are long-term ventures bringing together diverse stakeholders with unique as well as shared interests to jointly identify priorities and goals, as well as ways to accomplish them. The RPP movement has already organized 23 partnerships through the National Network of Education Research–Practice Partnerships. Other organizations, such as the Research + Practice Collaboratory, the Carnegie Foundation for the Advancement of Teaching, and the Strategic Education Research Partnership, also promote and connect RPPs.

The federal government has played a central role in developing this infrastructure. The Institute of Education Sciences of the U.S. Department of Education has demonstrated leadership in creating and repurposing structures to encourage a more democratic evidence system. Its Regional Educational Laboratory program has supported more than 70 partnerships across the nation. The Institute's National Center for Education Research has created two national knowledge utilization centers and initiated grant programs that promote RPPs. The National Science Foundation has also supported design research partnerships focused on STEM learning. Looking ahead, further structural enhancements to federal research and evaluation agencies and offices would give other education stakeholders an increased voice in setting research priorities by requiring their participation on advisory boards for research and technical assistance projects and structuring an effective process for joint deliberations.

Conclusion

Efforts to improve the production and use of research evidence in education have made great strides in the past two decades, but the potential for research to inform educational improvement is still largely untapped. Top-down structures that have incentivized proving over improving—and that have focused on narrow definitions of what works rather than broader conceptions of what matters to diverse stakeholders—have fueled misconceptions and recriminations in the research, policy, and practice communities. It is difficult to imagine a productive way forward if we do not build more productive relationships, work toward shared values, rethink our professional identities and roles, and build an infrastructure that leverages the best research has to support learning.

In a more democratic evidence system, practitioners, parents, students, community stakeholders, and researchers would jointly influence the ways research is carried out, and they would participate in deliberations over the findings and their implications for educational improvement. From the definition of policy problems and research agendas through to the implementation of initiatives, diverse stakeholders would be at the table, and they would still be there to assess what's working, what isn't, and what needs to be improved. If we can engage with this diverse array of expertise and perspectives in education, the evidence movement's best days may well be ahead of us.

Looking to the future, we hope that readers will join us in bringing about a more democratized evidence movement to improve education for all students.

Acknowledgments

The authors of this chapter share deep commitments to democratic principles and the use of evidence to improve education. The views expressed here are our own. However, the organizations we work for have a deep and abiding interest in improving the lives of all students, with particular attention to those who have been underserved or marginalized in our society.

The first author thanks Tracey Brown at Sense About Science for the keen insights that spurred her to think and write about the relationship between democracy and evidence.

Note

1 See the William T. Grant Foundation Research–Practice Partnerships website: rpp.wtgrant foundation.org

References

Allensworth, E. (2017). How the organization of schools and local communities shape educational improvement. In E. Quintero (Ed.), *Teaching in context* (pp. 147–162). Cambridge, MA: Harvard Education Press.

Barton, R., Nelsestuen, K., & Mazzeo, C. (January, 2014). *Lessons learned: Addressing the challenges of building and maintaining effective research partnerships*. Portland, OR: Education Northwest. Retrieved from http://educationnorthwest.org/sites/default/files/ resources/lessons-learned-research-partnerships-v4i1.pdf

Bell, P., Rhinehart, A., & Peterman, T. (December 17, 2015). *Negotiating researcher roles within a research–practice partnership*. Research + Practice Collaboratory. Retrieved from http://researchandpractice.org/negotiating-researcher-roles/

Brown, T. (2016). Evidence, expertise, and facts in a "post truth" society. *BMJ, 355,* i6467. Retrieved from https://drive.google.com/file/d/0B3lzJori8reea0xzbmY2T3FhVFJm OTFfQkdZb0I4MHdCM1Ew/view

Coburn, C. E., Penuel, W. R., & Geil, K. E. (2013). *Research–practice partnerships: A strategy for leveraging research for educational improvement in school districts*. New York: William T. Grant Foundation. Retrieved from http://wtgrantfoundation.org/library/uploads/2015/10/ Research-Practice-Partnerships-at-the-District-Level.pdf

Consortium on Chicago School Research at the University of Chicago. (January 17, 2007). *Steering committee manual: Revised mission, new purpose and core values*. Chicago,

IL: University of Chicago. Retrieved from http://rpp.wtgrantfoundation.org/library/uploads/2015/11/CCSR-Steering-Committee-Manual.pdf

Daly, A., & Finnigan, K. (2011). *Defining, acquiring, and using research evidence: Early findings from underperforming districts and schools.* Paper presented at the Use of Research Evidence meeting, Los Angeles, CA.

Education for Democracy Project. (1987). *Education for democracy: A statement of principles: Guidelines for strengthening the teaching of democratic values.* Washington, DC: Education for Democracy Project, American Federation of Teachers.

Feinberg, M., & Willer, R. (2013). The moral roots of environmental attitudes. *Psychological Science, 24*(1), 56–62.

Feinberg, M., & Willer, R. (2015). From gulf to bridge: When do moral arguments facilitate political influence? *Personality and Social Psychology Bulletin, 41*(12), 1665–1681.

Finnigan, K. S., Daly, A. J., & Che, J. (2013). Systemwide reform in districts under pressure: The role of social networks in defining, acquiring, and diffusing research evidence. *Journal of Educational Administration, 51*(4), 476–497.

Fleischman, S. (2014). Managing complexity: How evaluators can help achieve better outcomes in policy and practice. *Zeitschrift für Evaluation, 13*(1), 7–25.

Honig, M., & Coburn, C. (2008). Evidence-based decision making in school district central offices: Toward a policy and research agenda. *Educational Policy, 22*(4), 578–608.

Kahan, D. M., Peters, E., Wittlin, M., Slovic, P., Ouellette, L. L., Braman, D., & Mandel, G. (2012). The polarizing impact of science literacy and numeracy on perceived climate change risks. *Nature Climate Change, 2*(10), 732–735.

National Academies of Sciences, Engineering, and Medicine. (2017). *Communicating science effectively: A research agenda.* Washington, DC: The National Academies Press.

National Network of Education Research–Practice Partnerships. (n.d.). *The national network of education research–practice partnerships.* Retrieved from http://nnerpp.rice.edu/

National Research Council. (2012). *Using science as evidence in public policy.* Committee on the Use of Social Science Knowledge in Public Policy, K. Prewitt, T. A. Schwandt, & M. L. Straf (Eds.), Washington, DC: Division of Behavioral and Social Sciences and Education, The National Academies Press.

O'Neil, C. (2016). *Weapons of math destruction: How big data increases inequality and threatens democracy.* New York: Crown Publishing Group.

Palinkas, L. A., Short, C., & Wong, M. (2015). *Research–practice policy partnerships for implementation of evidence-based practices in child welfare and child mental health.* New York: William T. Grant Foundation.

Penuel, W. R., & Gallagher, D. J. (2017). *Creating research–practice partnerships in education.* Cambridge, MA: Harvard Education Press.

Rubinstein, S., & McCarthy, J. (2016). Union-management partnerships, teacher collaboration, and student performance. *Industrial and Labor Relations Review, 69*(5), 1114–1132.

Schein, E. H. (2013). *Humble inquiry: The gentle art of asking instead of telling.* San Francisco, CA: Berrett-Koehler Publishers.

Sense About Science. (2016). *Transparency of evidence: An assessment of government policy proposals May 2015 to May 2016.* London: Sense About Science. Retrieved from http://senseaboutscience.org/wp-content/uploads/2016/11/SaS-Transparency-of-Evidence-2016-Nov.pdf.

Stanovich, P. J., & Stanovich, K. E. (2003). *Using research and reason in education: How teachers can use scientifically based research to make curricular and instructional decisions.* Jessup, MD: The National Institute for Literacy. Retrieved from https://lincs.ed.gov/publications/pdf/Stanovich_Color.pdf

Stewart, K., Dubow, T., Hofman, J., & van Stolk, C. (2016). *Social change and public engagement with policy and evidence.* Santa Monica, CA: RAND Corporation. Retrieved from www.rand.org/pubs/research_reports/RR1750.html.

Tseng, V. (2012). The uses of research in policy and practice. *SRCD Social Policy Report, 26*(2), 1–24.

Tseng, V. (April 30, 2015). Let's advance education as a learning system. *Psychology Today.* Retrieved from www.psychologytoday.com/blog/psyched/201504/let-s-advance-education-learning-system

Tseng, V. (March 23, 2016). *Evidence at the crossroads Pt. 11: The next generation of evidence-based policy.* New York: William T. Grant Foundation. Retrieved from http://wtgrantfoundation.org/evidence-crossroads-pt-11-next-generation-evidence-based-policy

Tseng, V., Easton, J. Q., & Supplee, L. H. (2017). Research–practice partnerships: Building two-way streets of engagement. *SRCD Social Policy Report, 30*(4), 1–17.

Tseng, V., & Nutley, S. (2014). Building the infrastructure to improve the use and usefulness of research evidence in education. In K. S. Finnigan & A. J. Daly (Eds.), *Using research evidence in education: From the schoolhouse door to Capitol Hill* (pp. 163–175). Heidelberg: Springer.

Wentworth, L., Carranza, R., & Stipek, D. (2016). A university and district partnership closes the research-to-classroom gap. *Phi Delta Kappan, 97*(8), 66–69.

2

LEARNING, GENERALIZING, AND LOCAL SENSE-MAKING IN RESEARCH–PRACTICE PARTNERSHIPS

Bronwyn Bevan, William R. Penuel, Philip Bell, and Pamela J. Buffington

A central concern voiced about research–practice partnerships (RPPs) is whether or not research findings that are, by design, the result of highly local, adaptive, responsive, and contingent inquiries can be generalized. That is, can RPP ideas, findings, and tools inform work outside the partnership in ways that can help others accomplish their own local educational improvement goals?

This concern is based on the canonical—but demonstrably tenuous—principle that education research can and should produce findings in one setting that can be replicated in other settings. Indeed the use of effectiveness studies that rely on random assignment, proven so effective in much (but not all) medical research, is held up by most policymakers and funders as the highest form of education research (e.g., see IES & NSF, 2013). Through effectiveness trials, researchers are expected to demonstrate that an innovation can be effective anywhere, under routine conditions of practice. This view of the primacy of randomized controlled trials (RCTs) reflects what Tseng, Fleischman, and Quintero (Chapter 1, this volume) refer to as a preoccupation by education policymakers with *proving* rather than *improving*. Moreover, it has been shown to have limited results, in terms of extensibility and viability, in education contexts. For example, Yeager and Walton (2011) found that the positive results of education improvements, justified by RCTs, drop off drastically within 12 months after the intervention studies end. Moreover, research has found that even small, focused interventions with proven effectiveness have to be adapted when implemented in new contexts (Penuel & Farrell, 2017).

This position may sound heretical to some because of the promise that some interventions (e.g., to reduce stereotype threat) have shown in a series of RCTs. In theory, a large number of systems can apply findings tested in a much smaller number of settings; and the need (and cost) to develop new strategies is obviated.

The wholesale adoption of tested and standardized approaches also decreases costs associated with monitoring and assessment.

At the core of this canonical vision of research, with the RCT positioned as the gold standard, is the idea of generalizability as *replication*. But as with genetics before we better understood the phenomenon of epigenetics, this vision discounts the role of environment—whether physical, social, cultural, or temporal—in shaping whether or not an organism or mechanism will thrive when introduced into a new setting. Plenty of evidence suggests that, in education, turbulent environments make replication a challenging and elusive aim (Glazer & Peurach, 2013). Faith in the potential and efficiency of replication also fails to take into account the unintended and often cascading consequences that can result from even seemingly benign disturbances in an ecosystem, which can ultimately and fatally change the conditions in which an organism (in our case, a program in an educational system) has been shown to thrive (Oyama, 2000; Thelen & Smith, 1994)

Adaptation Versus Adoption: Knowledge Production as a Social and Cultural Process

As decades of research have shown, learning is a deeply social and cultural process (NRC, 2000; Rogoff, 2003). Research has also demonstrated that learning and development are shaped by interactions occurring in a nested set of systems that extend in space and time beyond the here and now of the student sitting in a classroom. These have been described by Bronfenbrenner and colleagues (Bronfenbrenner, 2005) as including historical (chronosystem), cultural (macrosystem), sociopolitical (exosystem), environmental[1] (mesosystem), and proximal (microsystem) spheres of activity. For example, the cultural values (macrosystem) of a given historical era (chronosystem) will shape policies and possibilities (exosystem) that afford and constrain access to a range of opportunities or settings (mesosystem) in which young people engage, for example, in mathematics learning or language development activities and interactions (microsystem). The current trend to fund STEM learning ecosystems involves enhancing what Bronfenbrenner and colleagues might consider the mesosystems for supporting STEM learning. Even then, as we all know from personal experience, learning is deeply personal: not all students in that classroom or afterschool program will experience it in the same way. We know that not all people (sometimes not even our partners, parents, or children, much less our neighbors or schoolmates) share our particular passions (or aversions) for engaging with particular ideas or processes. One student's favorite teacher and class is another student's least favorite. Learning is not universal, but contingent, personal, and cultural.

Fully recognizing the cultural, nested, and contingent nature of learning does not require throwing in the towel with respect to conducting research that can spread, inform, and improve teaching and learning. In fact, one might say that *not* fully recognizing the cultural, nested, and contingent nature of learning might be the equivalent of throwing in the towel in that it has at times led to the production of studies and reforms that have caused significant disruptions in the routines of teachers and students and at the same time not led to lasting improvements. On the other hand, embedding RCTs within RPPs, as studies that fully take into account the nested systems and social dimensions of teaching and learning, can produce highly productive lines of inquiry, as Donovan and Snow (Chapter 3, this volume) describe in their long-term RPP with the Boston Public Schools.

If we redefine generalizability not as something that makes a study's results replicable (in principle because of the quality of the research design), but as an accomplishment in practice that is evident when others appropriate and adapt ideas, tools, and findings produced in one setting to a new setting, then generalizability could come in many forms. Michalchik and Knudsen (Chapter 10, this volume) demonstrate how the co-creation of *representations* of instructional innovations (such as videos, role plays, lesson studies, or practice briefs) can, in addition to serving as tools for building teacher vision and capacity, help to disseminate and support uptake of research-based ideas in new settings. Another strategy for generalizing is to identify a *package* of specific arrangements that support desired outcomes, which can then be abstracted, recontextualized, and adapted into a new setting, taking into account local history and contextual characteristics (Bell, Hoadley, & Linn, 2004; DBRC, 2003; Salomon, 1993). Central to this process is careful and ongoing theorization of practice that allows for the abstraction, or *principled adaptation*—and not whole-cloth adoption—of findings and solutions from one context to another (Penuel & Gallagher, 2009).

In long-term RPPs, partnerships can and do learn from each other, much as we learn from the study of cases in any domain (Flyvbjerg, 2001). Paradoxically, by being deeply grounded in a particular context, partnership research surfaces specific and pivotal processes and dynamics of educational systems, develops concrete strategies, and raises salient questions that can help others rethink and reframe approaches to persistent problems of practice. This approach to research fundamentally recognizes and positions knowledge production and its use as a social and cultural process that cannot exist independent of context and local meaning-making. Moreover, iteratively developing or adapting new interventions through design research that is not experimental in nature can be—in the long run—quite cost-effective because partnerships can do the work needed to integrate innovations into the infrastructure of the educational systems in which they operate.

Generalizing From RPPs: Co-Production, Synthesis, and Dissemination

From 2012 to 2017, the Research + Practice Collaboratory supported the development of three RPPs aimed at addressing inequities in STEM education. The third author has a long-term partnership with the Seattle and Renton school districts in Washington which, during the timeframe reported here, focused on a teacher-led curriculum adaptation process to support the implementation of the Next Generation Science Standards (NGSS) in ways that could leverage the cultural resources of all students. The fourth author (see Louie & Buffington, Chapter 4, this volume) partnered with the high-poverty Auburn Maine school district to investigate how iPads could be integrated into early grades mathematics instruction. The first author led a distributed RPP network (see Santo, Ching, Peppler, & Hoadley's description of networked RPPs in Chapter 7, this volume) to advance equity-oriented maker programs in urban and rural Californian after-school programs serving economically and racially marginalized youth. Working across these three educational improvement partnerships, the second author and his colleagues gathered sets of professional resources developed as part of these and other partnerships into an RPP Toolkit and organized a series of webinars and workshops to help teams nationally develop and maintain thriving partnerships to advance more equitable outcomes for young people.

Across the activities of the four Labs of the NSF-funded Research + Practice Collaboratory, three design principles guided our efforts to develop generalizable knowledge for adaptation into new settings: (1) the need to bring together researchers, administrators, and educators grappling with similar issues and challenges in their local settings as a strategy for supporting sustained sense-making related to locally developed questions, co-designed resources, and emerging evidence of improvements; (2) the need for a range of different resources integrating knowledge from both research and practice—including research briefs, research–and–practice briefs, and practice briefs, each differing in the relative weighting of the conceptual to the pragmatic—to increase the accessibility of ideas, tools, and findings to others; and (3) the need to partner with a set of national professional associations to both disseminate resources and findings and to collaboratively explore how these resources and strategies could support STEM education improvement of members of these networks. In the next section, we provide examples and results of these efforts.

Engaging Mixed Groups of Educators and Researchers to Inform Local Sense-Making and Co-Design

In the Collaboratory's theory of action, we described a part of our work as involving *cultural exchange* between individuals representing a broad range of perspectives across research and practice (cf. Palinkas, 2010). The goal of this work was to define pressing problems of practice, of importance to multiple stakeholders and communities, and to create convenings in which we, along with others, could share emerging questions and findings from our local RPPs to help in processes of analysis and meaning-making. Through this collaborative process with others, we produced frameworks, reports, professional learning resources, and recommendations that both provided direction for the ongoing work and connected local findings to national issues.

For example, in July 2015, we held a meeting in Seattle of 30 educators, district and state administrators, informal educators, and researchers to identify and develop professional learning resources to support teachers' use of classroom formative assessment to support the implementation of equitable three-dimensional science instruction, as exemplified in the NGSS. This meeting helped refine specific resource and capacity-building needs and tensions educators faced in implementing research-based approaches and fitting the practice into their ongoing teaching. The meeting engaged the participants in co-authoring a dozen practice briefs on 3D formative assessment, later added to a collection of professional learning resources called STEM Teaching Tools (discussed in the next section). This initial work and the positive, broad uptake of the practice briefs, in turn, led to the subsequent creation of additional tools that had been identified as needed, as well as an online course for teachers focused on formative assessment of 3D NGSS instruction.

We also fostered cultural exchanges to address salient policy issues. For example, in November 2016, we brought together policy leaders, educators, and researchers to discuss ways that RPPs could help states and districts with developing and implementing plans for the Every Student Succeeds Act (ESSA). ESSA includes several "evidence provisions," meaning demands for adopting programs with strong evidence of efficacy, and the group we convened contributed ideas that were later adapted into state briefs and a guide for RPPs for supporting ESSA implementation. We also held a series of webinars in early 2017 that brought together partnerships that are engaged in efforts to define a set of nonacademic indicators of school success as part of ESSA to discuss their work. This series, jointly organized with the National Education Policy Center at CU Boulder, focused on indicators that can foreground equity, such as "opportunity to learn" indicators and school safety as perceived by LGBTQ students. The Collaboratory has been exploring how to sustain this work through other groups concerned with research evidence use in education, such as Results 4 America.

Cultural exchange also directly informed the progress of our RPPs. In February 2014, in San Francisco, we held a meeting of 40 educators, researchers, and policymakers on challenges to making cross-setting connections for youth engaged in STEM learning. A dozen presentations addressed the need, current program strategies, and evaluation and assessment schemes. Results were integrated into a paper, published in an afterschool practitioner-oriented journal, conceptualizing and outlining challenges and strategies (Penuel, Clark, & Bevan, 2016). As our own California RPP narrowed its focus on professional development needs for out-of-school educators, we held a follow-up meeting with some 20 colleagues from across the country—afterschool leaders, learning scientists, and frontline staff participating in the local California RPP—to explore together, and ultimately make recommendations about, the professional development needs for educators in out-of-school programs serving historically economically and racially marginalized youth. The results of this meeting, circulated in a report, in turn informed the analytical framework the RPP used in presenting its results to the field (Bevan, Ryoo, & Shea, 2017).

Representing Knowledge With Different Balances of Abstraction and Pragmatism

The Collaboratory experimented with several different tools for synthesizing knowledge, from research and practice, relevant to the daily work of educators in our RPPs. Many of these tools were created as particular needs surfaced within the RPPs; for example, to help frame discussions in meetings organized to address a given challenge or decision. At other times, our partners would make specific requests for synthesis documents on particular topics. In addition to local use and uptake with the RPPs and within our work with professional association partners (see the next section), individuals or teams engaged in STEM education efforts elsewhere across the country have at times contributed drafts of briefs for the Collaboratory team to produce and publish, which speaks to the perceived utility of the initiative.

In producing these tools, we explored giving different relative weight to research findings versus implications for practice. STEM Research Briefs and STEM Practice Briefs were one-page (double-sided) documents. Research Briefs summarized, in practitioner-friendly language, the upshot of a single published research study. The majority of the text described the study's findings, with a section on its implications for practice. Practice Briefs were organized topically by problems of practice and provided research-based suggestions for actions to be taken in the classroom or within an improvement effort at the school or district level. Research-and-Practice Briefs sought to do both—synthesizing research findings and addressing pragmatic concerns—and were four to five pages in length.

Research Briefs could be seen as representing a transmission model wherein the findings of research are translated for use and implementation in practice. At the Collaboratory, we designed them primarily as a jumping-off point for professional conversations about practice. For example, reading about a study that investigated how to foster conversation in museums could stimulate discussions about what kinds of conversations were happening or could happen in an afterschool program and how. The Research Brief served as a tool for connecting practitioners' personal experiences to the broader research base. In an early evaluation study, we discovered that about half of those who read Research Briefs did so for "conceptual" reasons (Weiss, 1979); that is, to inform their thinking and practice but not any specific decision. The other half used them for symbolic or political reasons; that is, to support a proposal or argument.

Research-and-Practice Briefs were summaries of mathematics learning and teaching research on topics of interest to the collaborating partners. They also were used as tools to stimulate dialogue that combined practitioner experiences and strategies with research on evidence-based practices. In these discussions administrators, math coaches, classroom teachers, education researchers, and higher education faculty reflected together on how their collective knowledge from research and practice informed the improvement efforts in the participating technology-rich classrooms and schools. The collaboration and exchange provided researchers with opportunities to incorporate practitioner knowledge into the research efforts and for the educators to incorporate evidence-based practices into their instruction. Initially, we read about and discussed the use of technological tools with young learners (Lewis Presser & Busey, 2014), early mathematics learning trajectories (Clements & Sarama, 2004), and Math Congress (Fosnot & Dolk, 2001). Through these discussions, we built shared understandings and formed a culture of inquiry. As the work proceeded and strategies were being applied, partners asked for more information on research that could further inform their improvement efforts and the co-investigation taking place in classrooms. For example, during iterative cycles of co-investigation, interest grew about rich tasks (Stein, Smith, Henningsen, & Silver, 2000; National Council of Teachers of Mathematics, 2014), open questions and parallel tasks (Small, 2012), and issues around productive struggle (Warshauer, 2015). We wrote Research-and-Practice Briefs associated with these emerging topics that were utilized by both participating educators and higher education faculty.

Practice Briefs were generally co-developed by researchers and practitioners who together identified problems or opportunities of practice that could benefit from insights from relevant knowledge and tools from research and practice. The collection of Practice Briefs, which are published as STEM Teaching Tools (stemteachingtools.org), has been designed to provide pragmatic insight and guidance about actions that educators can take in their classrooms as they implement NGSS in equity-oriented ways. For example, in the Things to Consider section—where Practice Briefs highlight key concepts and research findings relevant to issues of practice—a brief on argumentation in the classroom describes how argumentation operates in professional scientific practices and provides strategies for supporting it in the classroom. Other sections include Reflection Questions, to support professional learning discussions and personal reflections, and Why It Matters to You, which lays out what different actors in the system (teachers, administrators, curriculum supervisors) can do to support the integration of the research-based findings into their improvement efforts. The briefs all include a focus on equity, and many briefs are focused on equity topics. The resources have been promoted through our professional association network (see the next section) and through a guerrilla marketing strategy on social media.

The STEM Teaching Tools effort has developed into a broad initiative. The site now organizes the collection into implementation themes (e.g., assessment, informal education, instruction), hosts playlists of sequenced tools that support different professional learning experiences (e.g., for introducing NGSS to school principals), and publishes open educational resources—professional development

(PD) resources—for use by PD providers. In a broad sense, STEM Teaching Tools has become a trusted, timely, and relevant resource to support equity-focused implementation of NGSS and the National Research Council's *Framework for K–12 Science Education* vision.

Engaging the Broader Field Through Strategic Partnerships With Professional Associations

Before the Collaboratory was funded, we invited seven professional organizations to partner with us as a part of a professional associations network; these included the National Science Teachers Association (NSTA), the Afterschool Alliance, the National Council of Teachers of Mathematics (NCTM), National Association for Research in Science Teaching (NARST), Center for the Advancement of STEM Education, the Math and Science Partnership Network (MSPnet), and the Council of State Science Supervisors (CSSS). We envisioned learning from these associations what kinds of resources would be of value to their constituencies, as well using their existing newsletters, websites, conferences, webinar series, and other communication mechanisms as a means for disseminating the products of our work. Fundamentally, our goal was to avoid trying to create new communities for our work and instead to join existing professional conversations where we could add value (Penuel, Bell, Bevan, & Buffington, 2016). Indeed, in year 3 of the grant, a study led by the second author, as part of his work with the IES-funded National Center for Research in Policy and Practice, confirmed that the top source of research for educational leaders is professional associations and networks (Penuel & Farrell, 2017).

Additionally, we hired multiple staff with external communications expertise, including a full- or part-time person located at each Lab, to serve as a communications team. This group not only oversaw the development and updating of the website but additionally developed and monitored an active social media strategy that included deep connections with the professional associations network.

These relationships developed in different ways. In some cases (e.g., MSPnet), initially robust personal interactions settled into more of a one-way relationship where the associations generously offered to announce the availability of resources we created through their regular newsletters and websites. In other cases (e.g., NSTA, NARST, NCTM), we were invited to lead or organize symposia and workshops on RPPs at the association's standing annual conferences. In still other cases (e.g., the Center for Advancement of Informal Science Education, CSSS, Afterschool Alliance), in addition to announcing the availability of reports, briefs, and other resources, we developed more ongoing and organic relationships and were invited to organize and lead live webinars where we presented the work of the Collaboratory along with the work of other colleagues engaged in the same subjects. For example, we organized a webinar for the Afterschool Alliance on the meaning of the NGSS for state leaders of the Mott-funded afterschool networks.

Presenters included afterschool educators from a state network, a state department of education, and a science museum. In another case, the second and fourth authors of this chapter organized a webinar in which key leadership in NCTM and mathematics specialists from state education agencies learned about our early mathematics and technology RPP equity-oriented improvement efforts.

The Case of CSSS: Responsiveness and Its Relationship to Impact

Most of our partner professional associations were membership-driven nonprofit organizations with a national or global reach. In one case, our partnership involved state education leaders. This partnership with CSSS—the professional association for state leaders in science education in all 50 states, the District of Columbia, and U.S. territories—shows the potential payoff of sustained involvement with a professional association of state government employees. The case study highlights how it can lead to a more lasting partnership between researchers and practitioners and how a multistate organization can help co-design more broadly useful resources for a broad diversity of educational contexts.

As with our other partnerships, our initial involvement was as individuals bringing expertise to a question the association was grappling with. In this case, the third author was invited to present a CSSS-sponsored meeting because of his role on the committee that drafted the *Framework for K–12 Science Education* (National Research Council, 2012)—the policy document that guided development of the NGSS and other science standards. CSSS then reached out to two of the Collaboratory Co-PIs (Penuel and Bell) to serve as advisors to its efforts to a new initiative called Building Capacity for State Science Education (BCSSE). That initiative funded state teams of five or six leaders from districts, advocacy groups, and community-based organizations to attend a series of meetings focused on developing plans for implementing the vision of the *Framework*.

Through ongoing engagement with CSSS, we identified a number of tools and practices from our Lab work that were useful to CSSS members and leaders. Bell's STEM Teaching Tools initiative (described earlier) led plenary and workshop sessions at CSSS conferences to identify, workshop, and share STEM Teaching Tools that were targeted to issues of concern to members. The second author was invited to help inform the planning of a new organization for the annual CSSS conference focused on committees that would do active work there and between meetings. He helped the CSSS organizer, Matt Krehbiel of Kansas, identify researchers who could embed within these committees to provide research support. One of the more successful committee efforts was the Professional Learning Committee, which developed a set of research-based standards (www.csss-science.org/SPLS.shtml) for how to organize PD focused on preparing teachers to implement the vision of teaching in the *Framework*. These collaborative efforts built trust among CSSS members in the Collaboratory researchers, and for their part, Bell and Penuel felt welcomed into a community that valued their involvement and expertise.

As BCSSE funding ended, CSSS and the Collaboratory began discussing the possibility of seeking funding together to continue the work of preparing states for NGSS implementation with a strong equity lens. This became the three-year NSF-funded Advancing Coherence and Equity in State Science Education (ACESSE) project. Due to budget constraints, the project focused on teams in 13 states who worked to co-design resources and strategies to guide and support implementation that all states could use. The Collaboratory sponsored a workshop in November 2017 to introduce ACESSE resources to teams from all 50 states, DC, and the territories.

ACESSE brought researchers together with state leaders and teams into a networked improvement community (NIC), in which a network of educational organizations forms to address a specific, persistent problem of practice and collaborates to design and test solutions (Bryk, Gomez, Grunow, & LeMahieu, 2015). In a NIC, the roles of researcher and educator are intentionally blurred. In this particular NIC, the researchers bring relevant expertise in understanding implementation needs and designing resources, and the educators contribute by co-designing strategies and testing them as well as collecting and interpreting the resulting data. The project decided to initially focus on resourcing capacity building around cognitive and cultural formative assessment—which has strong potential for having a systemic impact in support of coherence and equity.

To help the network understand problems of coherence and equity, the project is undertaking a systematic investigation of what is happening in each state. This includes a survey of teachers to assess the distance between their visions for science teaching and that of the *Framework*. That survey is also identifying where teachers would like to grow as professionals, in order to help the network focus its efforts on areas where there is energy and broad educator support for improvement. State teams are also holding focus groups, using a protocol developed collaboratively by the network, to attain better insight into different stakeholders' views of science education.

To promote equity, each state team is formed purposefully to include people from different sectors in education—people judged to be key influencers of system components and the overall direction of science education in their states. Across states, team members include not only researchers from higher education and leaders from state departments of education but also leaders from districts, education nonprofits, educator associations, and more. The purposeful effort to build teams that include community representatives is an attempt to include new voices in systems reform.

The partnership is also collaboratively designing a set of resources that state teams can use to help build a common understanding of the vision of the *Framework*, focusing specifically on the challenge of adapting and designing formative, classroom-based assessments. These open education resources for professional learning are being shared through the STEM Teaching Tools initiative. In consultation with the researchers, the states' teams are helping adapt and test these resources based on their local implementation plans and problems identified from surveys and focus groups. These resources focus specifically on strategies for promoting equity through cultural formative assessment by sharing practices for eliciting students' interests, experiences, and identities so as to link them to instruction in the classroom (Reeve & Bell, 2009). This idea is called out as a focus for formative assessment within the consensus volume *Developing Assessments of the Next Generation Science Standards* (National Research Council, 2014). The resources are also focused on cognitive formative assessment by building capacity to attend to the diversity of science-related ideas and sense-making practices of learners. To assess progress arising from use of these tools, the research team is developing a system of practical measures—measures that can be used to signal improvement goals and assess what strategies are helping states accomplish their aims (Yeager, Bryk, Muhich, Hausman, & Morales, 2013)—for states to implement. The ACESSE project is making progress on developing equity-centered professional learning sequences of resources for use with teachers broadly.

Conclusion

Researchers concerned with equity in education rightly are concerned with generating evidence and enriching the knowledge base for how best to address inequalities of opportunity linked to race, class, gender, and sexual orientation. But promoting equity in practice also deeply entails engaging local values and naming historical and persistent injustices. Developing knowledge and useful representations of knowledge in partnership with actors in the education ecosystem—whether individual teachers such as those in Maine, networks such as we described in CSSS, or professional associations and entities such as NSTA or the Afterschool Alliance—can help to ensure that research designs and outcomes fully take into account the practical contexts, resources, and needs in which findings can help improve equitable outcomes for young people.

A challenge is a lack of sufficient funding for partnerships to carry out this work. At present, although a number of private foundations and public agencies fund research within partnerships, dollar amounts are small relative to funding for research that follows the scale-up paradigm of research, in which researchers attempt to develop interventions that will work in a variety of settings. As compared to the "impact infrastructure," which exists to support scholars in developing skills for conducting efficacy trials and then carrying out such trials, the "improvement infrastructure" is relatively weak (Peurach, 2016). To build a field where RPPs are more common, we need an infrastructure that includes regular meeting spaces for partnerships, predoctoral and postdoctoral professional preparation programs for researchers, and educational leadership programs that focus on how to develop and maintain robust partnerships with researchers to support improvement efforts. Needed, too, is funding to support staff time for people to serve as brokers between researchers and practitioners and resources to build data archives that can serve as the basis for original analyses in partnerships.

The lack of infrastructure speaks to an additional challenge for partnerships focused on equity: legitimacy. Partnership advocates struggle for legitimacy of their approach, often facing opposition from those who believe it is possible to *just do what works*, as if this is a simple matter of following the prescriptions of evidence-based programs. In our view, this confidence in the power of doing *what works* is not based on research evidence—it does not reflect the evidence about how, in practice, research-based interventions must be adapted to fit the local context or the evidence about how practitioners actually access and use research. Some amount of confidence or trust in the partnership approach is needed—among policymakers, funders, educators, and researchers—so that people will view it as a legitimate complement to other approaches to conducting research. We suggest that the examples provided in this volume, as well as those generated by the Research + Practice Collaboratory and others engaged in this work, make a strong case for the capacity building, improvement outcomes, and sustainability of results made possible through RPPs.

Acknowledgments

This material is based on work supported by the National Science Foundation (NSF) under grants DUE-1238253 and DRL-1626365. Any opinions, findings, and conclusions or recommendations expressed in this material are those of the authors and do not necessarily reflect the views of the NSF.

Note

1   Also called "inter-organizational" by scholars such as Engeström and Kerosuo (2007).

References

Bell, P., Hoadley, C. M., & Linn, M. C. (2004). Design-based research in education. In M. C. Linn, E. A. Davis, & P. Bell (Eds.), *Internet environments for science education* (pp. 73–88). Mahwah, NJ: Erlbaum.

Bevan, B., Ryoo, J. J., & Shea, M. V. (2017). What-if? Building creative cultures for STEM making and learning. *Afterschool Matters, 25*, 1–8.

Bronfenbrenner, U. (Ed.) (2005). *Making human beings human: Bioecological perspectives on human development.* Thousand Oaks, CA: Sage.

Bryk, A. S., Gomez, L. M., Grunow, A., & LeMahieu, P. (2015). *Learning to improve: How America's schools can get better at getting better.* Cambridge, MA: Harvard University Press.

Clements, D. H., & Sarama, J. (2004). Learning trajectories in mathematics education. *Mathematical Thinking and Learning, 6*(2), 81–89.

Design-Based Research Collective (DBRC). (2003). Design-based research: An emerging paradigm for educational inquiry. *Educational Researcher, 32*(1), 5–8.

Engeström, Y., & Kerosuo, H. (2007). From workplace learning to inter-organizational learning and back: The contribution of activity theory. *Journal of Workplace Learning, 19*(6), 336–342. doi:10.1108/13665620710777084

Fosnot, C. T., & Dolk, M. (2001). *Young mathematicians at work: Constructing number sense, addition, and subtraction.* Portsmouth, NH: Heinemann.

Flyvbjerg, B. (2001). *Making social science matter: Why social inquiry fails and how it can succeed again.* Cambridge: Cambridge University Press.

Glazer, J. L., & Peurach, D. J. (2013). School improvement networks as a strategy for large-scale education reform: The role of educational environments. *Educational Policy, 27*(4), 676–710.

Institute of Education Sciences & National Science Foundation. (2013). *Common guidelines for education research and development.* Washington, DC. Retrieved from https://ies.ed.gov/pdf/CommonGuidelines.pdf

Lewis Presser, A., & Busey, A. (2014). *Using technology to promote mathematics learning in the early grades* (Research + Practice Brief). Education Development Center. Retrieved from http://interactivestem.org/wp-content/uploads/2016/07/Mobile-Technology-and-Math-Learning-in-the-Early-Grades.pdf

National Council of Teachers of Mathematics (NCTM). (2014). *Principles to actions: Ensuring mathematical success for all.* Reston, VA: NCTM.

National Research Council. (2000). *How people learn: Brain, mind, experience, and school.* Washington, DC: National Academy Press.

National Research Council. (2012). *A framework for K–12 science education: Practices, crosscutting concepts, and core ideas.* Washington, DC: National Research Council.

National Research Council. (2014). *Developing assessments for the Next Generation Science Standards.* Washington, DC: National Academies Press.

Oyama, S. (2000). *Evolution's eye: A systems view of the biology-culture divide.* Durham, NC: Duke University Press.

Palinkas, L. A. (2010). Commentary: Cultural adaptation, collaboration, and exchange. *Research on Social Work Practice, 20*(5), 544–546.

Penuel, W. R., Bell, P., Bevan, B., Buffington, P., & Falk, J. (2016). Enhancing use of learning sciences research in planning for and supporting educational change: Leveraging and building social networks. *Journal of Educational Change, 17*(2), 251–278. doi:10.1007/s10833-015-9266-0

Penuel, W. R., Clark, T. R., & Bevan, B. (2016). Designing for equitable learning across settings. *Afterschool Matters, 24*, 13–20.

Penuel, W. R., & Farrell, C. (2017). Research–practice partnerships and ESSA: A learning agenda for the coming decade. In E. Quintero (Ed.), *Teaching in context: The social side of reform* (pp. 181–200). Cambridge, MA: Harvard Education Press.

Penuel, W. R., & Gallagher, L. P. (2009). Comparing the efficacy of three approaches to preparing teachers to teach for deep understanding in Earth science: Short-term impacts on teachers and teaching practice. *The Journal of the Learning Sciences, 18*(4), 461–508.

Peurach, D. J. (2016). Innovating at the nexus of impact and improvement: Leading educational improvement networks. *Educational Researcher, 45*(7), 421–429.

Reeve, S., & Bell, P. (2009). Children's self-documentation and understanding of the concepts 'healthy' and 'unhealthy'. *International Journal of Science Education, 31*(14), 1953–1974.

Rogoff, B. (2003). *The cultural nature of human development.* New York: Oxford University Press.

Salomon, G. (1993). On the nature of pedagogic computer tools: The case of the writing partner. In S. P. Lajoie & S. J. Derry (Eds.), *Computers as cognitive tools* (pp. 179–196). Hillsdale, NJ: LEA.

Small, M. (2012). *Good questions: Great ways to differentiate math instruction* (2nd ed.). New York: Teachers College Press.

Stein, M. K., Smith, M. S., Henningsen, M. A., & Silver, E. A. (2000). *Implementing standards-based mathematics instruction: A casebook for professional development*. New York: Teachers College Press.

Thelen, E., & Smith, L. (1994). *A dynamic systems approach to the development of cognition and action*. Cambridge, MA: MIT Press.

Warshauer, H. K. (2015). Strategies to support productive struggle. (2015). *Mathematics Teaching in the Middle School, 20*(March), 390–393.

Weiss, C. H. (1979). The many meanings of research utilization. *Public Administration Review, 39*, 426–431.

Yeager, D., Bryk, A. S., Muhich, J., Hausman, H., & Morales, L. (2013). *Practical measurement*. Palo Alto, CA: Carnegie Foundation for the Advancement of Teaching.

Yeager, D. S., & Walton, G. M. (2011). Social-psychological interventions in education: They're not magic. *Review of Educational Research, 81*(2), 267–301. doi:10.3102/0034 654311405999

PART II
RPPs That Impact Practice

3

SUSTAINING RESEARCH–PRACTICE PARTNERSHIPS

Benefits and Challenges of a Long-Term Research and Development Agenda

M. Suzanne Donovan and Catherine Snow

In this chapter, we describe in detail a long-lasting and highly productive program of work launched in 2005 by the Strategic Education Research Partnership (SERP) and the Boston Public Schools (BPS). The focus of the partnership was middle grades literacy—the problem the BPS superintendent considered his highest priority. In chronicling the progression of the middle school literacy work over more than a decade, we highlight the ways in which the partnership model contributed both to a coherent set of programs and tools that have been taken up by practitioners in districts around the country and to the generation of new research knowledge and instruments. This chapter illuminates the ways in which the complex contexts of practice often shifted the nature of the work and triggered significant adaptations to the SERP partnership model. The history exemplifies the potential power of research–practice partnerships (RPPs), as well as their potential fragility when not supported by sustained institutional and financial relationships.

Background

SERP emerged as a late product of a lengthy series of conversations about the disappointing effectiveness of research in supporting improvements in educational practice (Ravitch, 1985; Kaestle, 1993; Lagemann, 2002). In 2003, a National Research Council (NRC) committee made the case for a fundamentally different relationship between research and practice—one in which the problems of practice become the focus of research and development, with researchers and practitioners collaborating in the effort to address those problems (Donovan, Wigdor, & Snow, 2003). Drawing on evidence from medicine, agriculture, highway safety, and other sectors, the report argued for partnerships with three defining characteristics: long-term duration, responsiveness to the needs and priorities of practitioners, and attention to the requirements for knowledge generation and accumulation.

While there are many agreements between researchers and practitioners to engage in single projects, long-term partnership arrangements have two unique affordances. First, an enduring partnership makes it possible to follow the contours of a problem over time, as progress on one dimension reveals new or initially unforeseen challenges. Second, it provides the sustained exposure required to build trust. Partnership work requires a commitment of time and effort from people with busy schedules: time for all members of the partnership to develop a common framing of the problem and its potential solutions and time to monitor and steer the work. It requires an investment by researchers in understanding the district context, as well as action from district participants to facilitate progress, remove barriers, and integrate the work into their decision-making. These investments of time and commitments to action are unlikely in the absence of relational trust, and relational trust is built on sustained connections and shared identity as members of a group (Bryk & Schneider, 2002).

While the field site partnerships were intended to support local problem framing and solution development, concentrating the investment in specific sites was considered to have broad benefits:

- Other districts would have access to solutions to common problems of practice that would be specifically designed for usability at scale.
- Funding agencies and organizations committed to using research knowledge to improve practice would be better able to accomplish their goals in stable sites where the infrastructure for collaborative work had been built.
- The field of education research would have the opportunity for capacity building among scholars interested in research on problems of practice.

The ambitious vision of the NRC committee inspired the creation of SERP as an independent, nonprofit organization in 2003. The partnership with BPS is one of several RPPs initiated by SERP with the goal of establishing long-term field sites.

The SERP partnership model is a type of RPP that has been referred to as design-based implementation research (DBIR; Fishman, Penuel, Allen, & Cheng, 2013). DBIR partnerships have a shared commitment to collaborative, problem-solving research and development. They use research knowledge to inform design (often done with practitioners) and conduct research to determine the impact of those designs on practice. They also aim to support their district partners' independent capacity to improve educational outcomes. DBIR partnerships stand in contrast to other RPP models such as research alliances, which conduct place-based research but focus on conducting analyses to uncover phenomena that promote or constrain positive outcomes for students (e.g., Roderick, Easton, & Sebring, 2009). Alliances produce reports and papers that draw out implications for education policymakers. The design of solutions, however, is generally not within their mission.

Problem-solving partnerships are particularly complex arrangements because designing solutions that are responsive to the needs of practice requires researchers, designers, and practitioners to work across institutional boundaries with agility. Initial plans that have been carefully negotiated are frequently called into question as new insights about the nature of the problem emerge. Contextual factors surface that had not previously been considered or understood, requiring new lines of work and new sources of funding. Also, churn in district and school leadership can slow or stall progress. Clarifying the defining features of design-based RPPs can be helpful in contrasting them to other types of RPPs, but the tidy list of characteristics may conceal the necessarily adaptive, and often messy, nature of the emerging enterprise.

By looking under the hood of a problem-solving RPP that is unusual in its duration and productivity, we make visible the complexity and messiness of the enterprise. We highlight points at which our work diverged from our original plans and in which adaptations challenged the partnership model itself.

Focusing on the District's Problem of Practice

In 2003, the fledgling SERP organization was challenged by the BPS superintendent to help improve literacy growth among middle school students. BPS test results showed gains in the primary grades, suggesting that the reforms introduced in early grades reading instruction were having an impact. At the other end, BPS was investing in redesigning its high schools into smaller, more learning-centered communities. Teachers and administrators, however, argued that too many of the high school students would not benefit optimally from the new structures because of poor reading skills. Indeed, district data confirmed that growth in literacy skills was largely stagnant during the middle school years (grades 6–8). This was the challenge presented to the SERP team.

The local research team set out to understand how the practitioners at the school level understood the issue raised by the superintendent. What was it exactly that they thought middle school students could not do? What did they see as the biggest obstacles to reading success? To gain some sense of the local definitions of the challenge, the team observed in middle school English language arts (ELA), science, math, and history classrooms, interviewed teachers, and examined test scores.

Most teachers were in agreement that students could decode text reasonably well, but their views of the problems varied somewhat. Among the explanations were problems with reading stamina, with making inferences, and with motivation and attention. The most widely noted issue, though, was vocabulary; teachers reported that students were unfamiliar with the meanings of words that occurred frequently in textbooks but that were not discipline-specific. While words like *photosynthesis* and *Congress* are bolded and defined for students, words like *system* and *institution*—words used to define terms in the glossaries—are often not taught. Operating on the principle that reforms should solve problems identified by the practitioners and supported by evidence, we set out to develop a program to support the teaching of all-purpose academic vocabulary words.

Discussions in partnership meetings raised concerns in addition to academic vocabulary. The superintendent argued that the data available to the district gave too little information on the nature and the extent of students' struggles in reading comprehension. Members of the team with expertise in assessment confirmed that an easily administered assessment that would provide a profile of students' reading skills was not available on the market and began the development of an assessment that met BPS' specifications. Eventually, the partners from the Education Testing Service (ETS) carried the work forward and created the Reading Inventory and Scholastic Evaluation (RISE), a computer-administered diagnostic screening test for reading and comprehension problems. The partnership model was precisely what was needed to solve the assessment problem. ETS had both foundational work and interest in creating a middle grades assessment but was not sure how to design something to serve the needs and interests of school districts. BPS gave the direction that ETS had been missing.

By 2005, the outline of an academic vocabulary program, Word Generation, was in place. The initial design principles were drawn from the research literature and were iteratively reshaped by the researchers and practitioners on the partnership team (Donovan, Snow, & Daro, 2013). For example, research has suggested the value of introducing new words in a range of semantic contexts (e.g., the word *variable* as it is used in math, in science, and as an adjective in nondisciplinary language). Practitioners on the team insisted that the activities in math, science, and history appear to teachers in those content areas as relevant to their subject. Otherwise, they argued, teachers would reject the activities, believing they were more appropriate for the ELA classroom.

The topics and the specifics of Word Generation activities were greatly influenced by teachers. One school with a particularly supportive principal and literacy coach volunteered to be the nexus of the partnership activities. Teachers provided feedback on units as they were written, shifting design features early and often. For example, the initial plan was to teach 10 words per week, but teachers who piloted the materials said that was too many. We ultimately reduced the number to five. We constructed at- and above-grade-level math problems related to each week's topic and words, aware of research suggesting that appropriate challenge increases engagement. Teachers, though, expressed a preference for problems that constituted review and test preparation over more challenging problems that were not tightly aligned to the content currently being taught. The math activities were revised to address their concerns. It is worth noting that this is precisely the kind of error researchers working outside an RPP context are likely to make. The initial math problems were conceptually more interesting; however, they simply did not meet the needs of practitioners, and meeting the needs of teachers is what matters for uptake of new materials.

Testing the Program on a Small Scale

A beta version of Word Generation piloted in the first partnership school impressed the principal, leading to broader interest among other principals in BPS, which was reinforced by the central office. We conducted a quasi-experimental study of the program, implementing it in six schools and—with district support—identifying three schools that would serve as comparison cases. The findings confirmed Word Generation's effectiveness in teaching academic vocabulary. As curriculum development expanded to provide content for grades 6, 7, and 8, the larger group of teachers and students involved in the study provided feedback about topics and activities.

It was during the extension of Word Generation to these new schools that we were able to identify the logistical arrangements needed to ensure good implementation and to learn from practitioners about locally developed innovations: making posters of the week's words for display in the hallways and in nearby shop windows, using the words in principals' PA announcements, using mobile racks or crates to move Word Generation materials across classrooms, and using visual images of the words. These supports for effective implementation would not have been identified were it not for the partnership with teachers.

The quasi-experimental study produced three important findings: First, it confirmed that students were learning the taught vocabulary and retaining that word knowledge over a subsequent academic year (Snow, Lawrence, & White, 2009). Second, language minority (LM) learners—those whose parents spoke a language other than English at home—showed greater improvements than English-only students and retained their advantages as robustly (Lawrence, Capotosto, Branum-Martin, White, & Snow, 2012). Third, and most relevant to the RPP model, leadership at the school level was key to successful introduction and implementation of the program. The schools with the largest effects were those where the principal and the literacy coach embraced the program enthusiastically and where the teachers voiced their trust in their local leadership. In contrast, in a school where the principal had garnered minimal levels of trust as an instructional leader and where the coach was being used primarily for clerical duties, data showed minimal implementation and little student growth.

Following the Contours of the Problem

Two additional lines of inquiry emerged as a result of the first phase of work. The first followed from the Word Generation results. The link between program results and the level of trust in school leadership was not an unfamiliar phenomenon. Work by others had documented the relationship before (Abelman, Elmore,

Even, Kenyon, & Marshall, 1999; Edmondson, 2002; Newmann, King, & Youngs, 2000; Goddard, Goddard, & Tschannen-Moran, 2007). Indeed, as an active member of the SERP-BPS partnership team, Richard Elmore had argued that schools without adequate internal coherence would be unable to make good use of this (or any) program. By this he meant schools without leadership focused on instructional improvement, individual and collective efficacy beliefs among teachers regarding the ability of instructional practice to support student learning, and the organizational structures to support collaboration. Prior work, however, had focused on measuring and describing rather than improving internal coherence. With the district's enthusiasm and Elmore's leadership, the partnership began a new line of work. A survey instrument was developed to determine the internal coherence level of a school, and an effort was launched to develop and test an approach to working with school-level leaders and teachers to increase coherence (ic.serpmedia.org; Forman, Stosich, & Bocala, 2017). The district itself funded the internal coherence team's engagement with principals in its middle schools.

A second new line of work was initiated as a result of the RISE assessment scores. Though teachers had expressed the belief that their students had mastered basic reading skills but struggled with more challenging texts, RISE results told another story. Between one fourth and one third of students in grades 6–8 in the schools with which we were working still struggled with foundational reading skills.

Prior to the RISE administration, district leaders had assumed that the majority of struggling readers had trouble with fluency and comprehension, not with basic word reading. The district had therefore purchased a well-known reading intervention at considerable cost to support reading fluency and comprehension (but not decoding and morphology). A member of the research team who had evaluated the program elsewhere agreed to study its use in BPS to see what could be learned about its effects.

Given that the district licenses for the program covered only a portion of the eligible population, the researcher proposed conducting a lottery. Eligibility for the lottery was to be determined by the reading level for which the intervention was designed. The researcher's logic, however, was not at all logical from the school principals' perspectives. Schools were using the program with their neediest students, many of whom were performing at a reading level well below that targeted by the program. They were not willing to engage in a study that would require them to use the program only with students at the appropriate reading level because they had no other program to serve the lowest group of struggling readers. Their only alternative would have been to place those students in the general education classroom—an option that would have widened the gap between the needs of those students and the instruction they were receiving. The researchers saw the principals' actions as ineffective for the lowest readers and costly for readers who might have benefited from the program. The fact that both were true underscored the need for an alternative solution.

The SERP-BPS partnership team had a core group of researchers, practitioners, and other partners that met monthly. One of its members was the executive director of the Boston Plan for Excellence (BPE), who happened to have a foundation grant to address the needs of struggling BPS readers in grade 9. She had administered the RISE to identify the population in need of support, but the high school teachers with whom BPE was working were frustrated in their efforts to identify materials that were appropriate for their students. While the targeted reading skills for these students were at a third- or fourth-grade level, teachers saw these students as vulnerable to disengaging from school entirely if the content with which those reading skills were taught was seen as juvenile. The goal of the partnership team was therefore to develop a program with content that would allow adolescents to feel proud to be engaged with it. Because the needs of struggling ninth-grade readers were so similar to their middle grades counterparts, BPE proposed funding the early development activity. The work was led by a researcher on the partnership team from Wheelock College.

The first draft of what is now the Strategic Adolescent Reading Intervention (STARI) was piloted in a subset of the schools using Word Generation, where relationships of trust that had already been built allowed for rapid iterations of design features and data collection on a small scale. Strict random assignment in this early phase was modified to give principals access to places in the program for students the principals identified as needing immediate extra support but who might not have qualified according to the researchers' criteria, thus achieving a compromise between researcher- and practitioner-defined goals of the work. The study provided critical information that shaped the next phase of development and laid the groundwork for an efficacy study further down the road.

Word Generation and the RISE assessment demonstrated the value of a partnership model in which researchers with varied expertise work in close collaboration with practitioners. The unique value of a *long-term* partnership is best demonstrated by the Internal Coherence and STARI projects. Uncovering the need for these initiatives required years of prior work and evidence-gathering. It also required time in routine partnership meetings, during which the evidence was digested and where potential responses to it were discussed and negotiated. Finally, the ability to move these two new lines of work forward in partner schools rested on the relationships of mutual trust built in the earlier years of collaboration with school administrators and teachers.

Moving Beyond the Field Site

A central goal of SERP partnerships is to address partner districts' problems in a way that is scalable to other districts. Accomplishing this goal requires two things: solutions that are scalable and evidence that those solutions can work in other settings. Scalability requires that programs be designed so that others can and want to use them. SERP invested in building internal design capacity for this purpose, anchored by a director of media and design who had previously worked as a teacher and principal. To determine effectiveness in other locations required an effectiveness study in other districts. With the results from the quasi-experimental study, we secured funding for a larger scale randomized controlled trial (RCT) of Word Generation (IES Grant #R305A090555) that was conducted in 22 schools in three districts. Ultimately, the RCT replicated the impacts found in the quasi-experimental study regarding vocabulary but added new insight on the role of dosage and discussion quality as mediators of impact (Lawrence, Crosson, Paré-Blagoev, & Snow, 2015; Lawrence, Francis, Paré-Blagoev, & Snow, 2016). It also confirmed that LM students and recently reclassified English learners (ELs) showed larger gains (Hwang, Lawrence, Mo, & Snow, 2014; Hwang, Lawrence, Snow, & Collins, in press; Hwang, Lawrence, & Snow, 2016), but teachers consistently requested additional supports for using the program with ELs. While the RCT required very different relationships with districts, we nonetheless sought out opportunities to respond to this request.

One such opportunity emerged when we received funding from IES through the Center for Research on the Educational Achievement and Teaching of English learners (CREATE). The project supported a revision and evaluation of a subset of Word Generation units to address the needs of ELs, which demonstrated positive impacts. We also developed a set of supplementary supports for teachers of ELs tied to one of the three Word Generation series. The supports are referred to as Advancing Academic Language for All! (AALA; aala.serpmedia.org), since teachers have found them to be helpful with struggling students who are native English speakers as well. The CREATE revisions, as well as the AALA materials, were developed largely by experienced teachers.

Adapting to a Changing Environment

The four lines of work—Word Generation, STARI, RISE, and Internal Coherence—were all productively moving forward in BPS when the superintendent retired and an interim superintendent stepped in. With the departing superintendent's protective handoff, buttressed by well-established relationships with others in the central office and strong partnerships with a set of schools, the SERP work continued. However, uncertainty about future directions meant that no new work was undertaken, although existing commitments were maintained.

A year later, a newly appointed superintendent brought in an entirely new team. Having been briefed by the prior superintendent, the new superintendent was supportive of maintaining the SERP partnership but, while partnership meetings continued, relationships needed to be built anew. There were cases in which the goals of the SERP work already under way were at odds with the vision of the new cabinet. For example, the newly appointed director of research and accountability had plans to purchase an off-the-shelf reading assessment for middle grades students for district-wide use. Because the newly developed RISE assessment did not yet have well-established psychometric properties, the director did not consider it an acceptable alternative, even in a subset of schools where we proposed to continue collecting data in order to make progress on determining reliability and validity. Without trusting relationships with the entirely new team, there was no opportunity to pursue the issue further within BPS. A well-initiated and very promising line of work was threatened with extinction. SERP needed to adapt.

Fortunately, at this critical moment, a neighboring district that had been alerted to SERP's work sought out an opportunity to use the RISE assessment, as did a former BPS leader who had assumed a senior leadership position in another urban district. The RISE work in these two sites allowed for the development of solid psychometric properties (Sabatini, O'Reilly, Halderman, & Bruce, 2014b; Sabatini, Bruce, Steinberg, & Weeks, 2015), and the RISE assessment can now be administered through ETS in any location nationwide. Had the SERP team (including the ETS partners) not adapted, the RISE project would have been dead in its tracks.

Generating New Knowledge: Catalyzing Comprehension Through Discussion and Debate

Observations in Word Generation classrooms led the SERP research team to rethink the mechanisms and factors that promote reading comprehension. We noted the ways in which discussion motivated students to work at comprehending texts for purposes of making and defending arguments, as well as enhanced comprehension skills through consideration of classmates' alternative interpretations of texts. We noted that, while students discussed controversial topics, they were actively engaged in perspective taking and critical reasoning, both emergent capacities required for content area learning (Donovan & Bransford, 2005). When IES announced a major Reading for Understanding initiative that would provide up to $20 million for teams to test a theory of deep reading comprehension, develop interventions, and rigorously evaluate them, the SERP-BPS team was in a good position to respond. We hypothesized that there are three contributors to success with deep comprehension of content area texts in the middle grades that had been given little attention in the literacy community: academic language, perspective taking, and complex reasoning. We further hypothesized that discussion would motivate adolescents to engage in the disciplined work of developing these skills. As the NRC committee had predicted based on experiences in other fields (Donovan et al., 2003), the observations of practice led to new theory.

As the partnership team discussed the opportunity, BPS literacy leaders suggested that a program like Word Generation was needed for fourth and fifth grades. Evidence from middle school classrooms corroborated the need for strengthening literacy skills in these earlier grades. IES's focus on content area literacy also provided an opportunity to address a concern among some members of the partnership team that the standards for argumentation, as applied to discussion of perspectives on controversial social issues, are quite different from the disciplinary standards for argumentation in science and social studies. Developing more in-depth units for these two disciplines moved onto the agenda, with the benefit that teachers could spend more time on developing the Word Generation–related skills without skimping on required content. In science, we also proposed creating professional learning opportunities for teachers to directly address reading comprehension and argumentation challenges (http://serpmedia.org/rtls/). Thus, the growing emphasis in the literacy field on the need for instruction in disciplinary literacy converged nicely with the interests of BPS and of the SERP research team. The substantial expansion of Word Generation curricular resources would not have been possible without a convergence of factors, among them the positive views within BPS about the Word Generation approach and the history of productive collaboration with BPS practitioners.

Finally, BPS was encouraged that STARI students showed gains with the pilot program, but the feedback from teachers suggested the program was somewhat unwieldy. Students who are far behind in reading need very structured opportunities to develop the full array of reading and comprehension skills, and they need materials that are well calibrated to their specific reading levels. Many teachers found the volume of materials produced in order to meet these needs daunting. The teacher lesson plans were likewise voluminous. The proposal also included efforts to streamline STARI materials, to use design expertise to make the program more user-friendly, to bring it to professional standards so that it could be scaled, and to develop a second year of program curriculum.

When the project was funded almost a year later, we faced another change in the district. The chief academic officer (CAO) departed for a position at a major foundation. Building a new relationship takes time, particularly when the new appointee is from outside the district and must learn an entirely new context. While the SERP team's relationship with the new CAO was still developing roots, the new CAO resigned. When the next replacement also left the position before a year had passed, the partnership with the district weakened. Partnership meetings, which had previously been routine, became difficult to schedule as new appointees struggled to determine the lines of communication that would allow the work for which they were accountable to get done. The internal coherence work, which required trust between senior district leaders and principals, was put on hold because new district leaders did not yet have the working relationships with principals to move the work forward.

SERP needed to adapt yet again. While the district expressed interest in maintaining the partnership, it was not in a strong position to respond to the opportunity presented by the new grant. The grant requirements for large-scale RCTs of the newly developed or revised programs required that other districts be recruited, in any case, in order to generate sufficient power. Efforts to engage BPS to maintain the field site relationship continued, and the BPS leads in science and social studies vetted ideas for the in-depth units. Other districts, though, became more central to the development and testing of the expanded Word Generation and STARI programs. When the second BPS superintendent retired and an interim superintendent was once again appointed, BPS participation in the work, which had initially been launched to meet that district's specific needs, became limited to only a few schools.

Partners and Participants

As a partnership organization, SERP approached districts to participate in the Reading for Understanding studies in the spirit of genuine collaboration. Typical RCTs place significant constraints on how teachers are to implement a program, in the interest of testing the impact of that program when implemented with fidelity. But the Reading for Understanding project condensed development and evaluation into a single-year grant period. The fact that the programs were still under development in the early years allowed for responsiveness to feedback from teachers and administrators. The varied district contexts led to relationships that ranged from enthusiastic partner to tentative participant. The study provided yet another opportunity to build knowledge of conditions supportive of reading growth and to test the conjecture that an intervention developed in close partnership with educators could be useful and effective in other districts.

The Word Generation suite of programs was evaluated in a total of four districts (BPS and three others). The largest of the districts had engaged in a SERP study previously. Although the relationship was very positive, the district is located in a challenging urban environment that experiences exceptionally high turnover of teachers and administrators—a challenge for any new program. A change in district leadership, as well as civil unrest during the study period, added to the climate of uncertainty and decreased the level of engagement with the SERP team.

Two additional, smaller districts were newly involved with SERP. These districts were characterized by relatively high levels of organizational coherence and strong leadership. However, in one of these smaller districts, there were no district-employed individuals specifically committed to supporting the program. SERP coaches provided PD—a standard practice in RCTs. No one in this district assumed primary responsibility for nurturing or overseeing either the relationship or the implementation of the programs, and requests for meetings would go unanswered, or participants from the district would cancel at the last minute. In this case, a robust partnership relationship never developed.

In the second smaller district, the superintendent was very responsive, and the literacy coach embraced both Word Generation and STARI eagerly. In a mutually beneficial agreement, she became employed part-time as a project coach to support implementation. Because the channels of communication were so robust, this district generated multiple suggestions for additions and modifications that were incorporated into the program. The coach returned to full-time employment by the district at the project's end and continues to support the implementation of both programs district-wide.

Generating Evidence

The Catalyzing Comprehension Through Discussion and Debate project confirmed our hypothesis regarding contributors to deep reading comprehension. With newly developed instruments to measure academic language, perspective taking, and critical reasoning, the study documented their independence as constructs and their significant relationships to reading comprehension.

Program impacts were somewhat variable across the participating districts and schools, for reasons that could be traced back to implementation challenges (LaRusso, Donovan, & Snow, 2016). Nonetheless, Word Generation was successful in promoting growth in academic vocabulary, hypothesized mediators of reading comprehension, and reading comprehension itself (Jones et al., under revision).

The revised and expanded STARI curriculum was also tested in four districts, two of which overlapped with Word Generation. STARI showed significant gains on the RISE assessment in word recognition, morphological awareness, and efficiency of basic reading comprehension (Kim et al., 2017). More surprisingly, it showed gains on a measure of deep comprehension, the GISA assessment (Sabatini, O'Reilly, Halderman, & Bruce, 2014a), with a population of students for whom gains in comprehension have been exceedingly difficult to achieve (a goal that had been central in the proposal).

Thus, the funding opportunity provided by the IES Reading for Understanding initiative allowed for major progress on the program of work initiated in response to specific and local problems identified by BPS leadership. It allowed instructional programs to be honed, improved, expanded, and brought to the point where evidence for their effectiveness could be collected through rigorous evaluations. It also provided the funding to bring those materials to professional standards.

Going to Scale

Word Generation materials made available for download on the SERP website were updated and expanded as the new materials became available. Since the programs are freely downloadable, no revenue to publicize the programs has yet been generated. Yet, hundreds of districts and schools have been discovering the program via the internet, word of mouth, or other channels. A year after the full suite of programs was made available online, the number of registrants surpassed 20,000. Note, however, that registration is not required to access the materials, and a registrant can represent an individual, a school, or a district.

The STARI materials have been made available only recently through an "early adopter" registration. More than 1,500 have registered as of January 2017, and new registrations are received daily. We conjecture that the uptake of these programs by practicing teachers reflects the value-add of teacher input in their design and adaptation; they are recognizably designed in ways that are both usable by teachers and highly engaging to students.

In some cases, districts have requested SERP support for professional development when introducing Word Generation or STARI. This was the case, for example, with the approximately 100 schools that are part of the New York City Department of Education's Middle School Quality Initiative. This initiative has implemented Word Generation continuously since the 2012–2013 school year and began using STARI in the 2015–2016 school year. Many users of Word Generation and STARI, however, have received no direct support from SERP, perhaps relying on the guidance available through website resources and through the teacher guides. All SERP programs and online resources are intentionally designed to maximize the chance that teachers and students will benefit from the programs when used independently, even though we believe initial implementation support would bolster their effectiveness, especially for STARI.

Continuing to Respond to the Needs of Practice

Although the major Catalyzing Comprehension Through Discussion and Debate grant has ended, interest in the work continues to grow. As the number of teachers using Word Generation and STARI has increased, so have requests for additional supports for ELs (recall that AALA was for a small subset of Word Generation units only). Exploring the nature and widespread usability of Word Generation enhancements for second language learners would produce new knowledge while solving local problems of practice. Understanding how members of different linguistic and cultural groups function in U.S. schools is one of the great challenges facing educators in an immigrant society. Studying the varied responses of students from these groups to an academic language and literacy program is also a mechanism to learn more about the processes of language and literacy development in general. Yet, to be responsive to the practitioners' requests would once again require resources, and our efforts in this regard have not yet been successful.

In 2016, IES contracted with two research firms to conduct an independent evaluation of the impact of academic language programs on the literacy development of fourth and fifth graders, particularly those who are disadvantaged or have limited English proficiency. WordGen Elementary was the program chosen by IES and the research firms for the evaluation. The study will provide the SERP team with an opportunity to further develop the supports for coaches and teachers who will be spread across widely dispersed districts.

Discussion

The SERP program of work originally launched with BPS has achieved several of the central goals for which the SERP organization was established—goals that are not accomplished in more traditional models of research. The work was responsive to the BPS-defined problem of practice, and the focus on the needs of practice was maintained throughout. We attribute the uptake of the programs in other districts to the responsiveness of the SERP model (and to other DBIR models) to the realities of the classroom as defined by practitioners rather than as imagined by researchers. The program of work followed the contours of the problem over time: It responded initially to the district's need for student reading profiles and for an approach to addressing weaknesses in academic vocabulary but expanded to encompass an internal coherence project and the development and testing of an adolescent reading intervention. The sequence displays an integrated approach to problem solving that optimizes coherence across an array of new programs and problem solutions (Donovan et al., 2013). The products of the work have successfully scaled to other districts, with uptake steadily expanding.

The SERP partnership with BPS achieved other research-related goals as well. The program of work successfully generated and tested new theory, developed new research instruments, and provided evidence regarding contributors to implementation challenges and program impacts. As the NRC report predicted, the structured partnership was of value to federal agencies. It allowed SERP and BPS to respond to IES's ambitious vision to rapidly advance our knowledge of reading comprehension and its improvement and to provide programs to enact that knowledge in practice. The postulated theory around which the proposal was constructed was rooted in observations of practice in Word Generation classrooms, and the confidence to propose a major curriculum development effort (and presumably of reviewers to take that proposal seriously) was rooted in prior years of experience building close and productive working relationships among researchers, designers, and practitioners.

We attribute the successes of the work on middle grades reading comprehension to the partnership model. Without the initial commitment of BPS leaders to working closely and persistently with the SERP-recruited research team, without the opportunity for researchers to explore current practice and observe teachers and students engaging with new materials, without the willingness of teachers to pilot materials and provide critical feedback, without designers' skillful reshaping of researchers' curricular content into materials that teachers found usable, and without the intentional commitment of all parties to listen to and place a high value on the contributions of every member of the partnership, the accomplishments from the decade of work would not have been realized.

The NRC panel's original vision was of an infrastructure of field sites distributed across the country that would create stable, fertile ground for the work of RPPs so that coherent programs of problem-solving research and development would become the norm. Without incentives built into the system to support districts as sites for ongoing problem-solving research and development, however, success at following the contours of a problem to work toward scalable solutions will likely be the exception. Challenges to the model required that we adapt, sometimes in ways that altered essential features, including the long-term partnership commitment. The partnership initially survived the churn in leadership that is a common feature in major urban school districts, but when the rate of churn became too high and the uncertainty that accompanies change persisted for too long, the partnership frayed. There are no fingers to be pointed; on the contrary, district leaders themselves were working exceedingly hard to manage through periods of change and uncertainty. As one mid-level district leader explained during the most difficult transition period, the reluctance to continue partnership meetings was not a judgment on the value of the partnership; it was simply an artifact of uncertainty about who from the district had sufficient decision-making authority to be at the table.

Similarly, while the RISE work was stopped in its tracks when a new district leader chose an off-the-shelf assessment, he can hardly be faulted for insisting that assessments used in the district have established psychometric properties. He simply did not share the purpose of the prior superintendent, who asked for a new assessment that would provide reading profiles. In addition, the reluctance of the new superintendent to override a member of her cabinet whom she had just recruited to the district in favor of a research partnership to which she had been newly introduced is not only understandable but sensible from a management perspective.

These district leaders' job descriptions did not include prioritizing a research and development agenda in order to generate the knowledge and tools to improve education practice. The ongoing work of SERP and other problem-solving RPPs attests to the fact that there are many district leaders and other practitioners who greatly value what an RPP can offer. Yet, continuity within a district would require the consecutive appointment of leaders who value an RPP's maintenance—an outcome that is highly unlikely without high-level agreements and incentives designed specifically for that purpose.

The coherence of the program of work described here is likely to be an exception for another critical reason: The funding opportunities were atypical. Through the Reading for Understanding initiative, IES made a one-time investment in a major program of work, allocating more than $100 million to this single initiative. The agency faced criticism for making such concentrated investments in major programs of work by a few teams at the expense of small research studies by many teams. Still, the concentrated investment is precisely what was needed to carry the program of work to a point at which the promise of the partnership model could be realized with respect to generating the knowledge and tools for improvement.

In the absence of district incentives for continuity and funding for a program of work rather than a single study, long-term RPPs will be dependent on the ability of the partnership team to adapt to rapidly changing circumstances in districts and to engage in nearly continuous grant development. Adaptation can be a good thing. To the extent that funding and partnership opportunities signal values and priorities that deserve responsiveness, it is entirely appropriate for partnership organizations to adapt, but some adaptations come with considerable costs. When a partnership is maintained over time, productivity is enhanced, and the cost of time-consuming relationship building is reduced as interactions become more routine. When it becomes necessary to move the work to another site, the prior capacity developed for collaborative work with the district and the knowledge of context is sacrificed. Costlier still, spreading pieces of the work across different sites means that the power of the multi-component approach is not tested. The four lines of work initiated in BPS were never implemented as a package because the district's engagement had waned by the time all four had been brought to completion.

The NRC report that launched SERP called for a public-private partnership to provide sustained funding for long-term partnerships. Commitments from school boards and superintendents to protect the partnership work, even during periods of transition, was to be incentivized by the resources brought to a field site district. Although design-based partnerships are becoming more popular, support has thus far been for a short duration and on a scale that is too small to warrant the sustained attention of district leaders and school boards. This is not to diminish the contributions of partnerships, particularly their relevance and responsiveness to the needs of practice. Rather, it is to note that the work of building an infrastructure to sustain coherent programs of work in practice settings, in order to systematically build and continuously improve the knowledge and tools for educational practice, still lies ahead.

Acknowledgments

The work described was funded in its various stages by the William and Flora Hewlett Foundation, the Spencer Foundation, the Carnegie Foundation, the Leon Lowenstein Foundation, and the U.S. Department of Education, Institute of Education Sciences, through grant number R305A090555, *Word Generation: An Efficacy Trial* (Catherine Snow, Principal Investigator), and grant number R305F100026, *Catalyzing Comprehension Through Discussion and Debate*.

References

Abelman, C., Elmore, R. F., Even, J., Kenyon, S., & Marshall, J. (1999). *When accountability knocks, will anyone answer?* Philadelphia, PA: Consortium for Policy Research in Education.

Bryk, A., & Schneider, B. (2002). *Trust in schools: A core resource for improvement.* New York: Russell Sage Foundation.

Donovan, M. S., & Bransford, J. D. (2005). *How students learn: Science in the classroom.* Committee on How People Learn: A Targeted Report for Teachers National Research Council. Washington, DC: The National Academies Press.

Donovan, M. S., Snow, C., & Daro, P. (2013). The SERP approach to problem-solving research, development, and implementation. In B. Fishman, W. R. Penuel, A. Allen, &

B. H. Cheng (Eds.), *Design-based implementation research: Theories, methods, and exemplars* (pp. 400–425). National Society for the Study of Education Yearbook, 112(2). New York: Teachers College, Columbia University.

Donovan, M. S., Wigdor, A. K., & Snow, C. (Eds.) (2003). *Strategic education research partnership*. Washington, DC: National Academy Press.

Edmondson, A. (2002). The local and variegated nature of learning in organizations: A group level perspective. *Organization Science, 13*(2), 128–146.

Fishman, B., Penuel, W. R., Allen, A., & Cheng, B. H. (Eds.) (2013). *Design-based implementation research: Theories, methods, and exemplars*: National Society for the Study of Education Yearbook. New York: Teachers College, Columbia University.

Forman, M. L., Stosich, E. L., & Bocala, C. (forthcoming). *The internal coherence framework: Creating the conditions for continuous improvement in schools*. Cambridge, MA: Harvard Education Press.

Goddard, Y. L., Goddard, R. D., & Tschannen-Moran, M. (2007). A theoretical and empirical investigation of teacher collaboration for school improvement and student achievement in public elementary schools. *Teachers College Record, 109*(4), 877–896.

Hwang, J. K., Lawrence, J. F., Mo, E., & Snow, C. E. (2014). Differential effects of a systematic vocabulary intervention on adolescent language minority students with varying levels of English proficiency. *International Journal of Bilingualism, 19*(3), 314–332.

Hwang, J. K., Lawrence, J. F., & Snow, C. E. (2016). Defying expectations: Vocabulary growth trajectories of high performing language minority students. *Reading and Writing, 30*(4), 1–28.

Hwang, J. K., Lawrence, J. F., Snow, C. E., & Collins, P. (in press). Vocabulary and reading performances of reclassified fluent English proficient students. *TESOL Quarterly*.

Jones, S. M., LaRusso, M., Kim, J., Kim, H. Y., Selman, R., Uccelli, P., . . . Snow, C. E. (under revision). Experimental effects of Word Generation on vocabulary, academic, language, perspective taking, and reading comprehension in high poverty schools. *Journal of Research on Educational Effectiveness*.

Kaestle, C. F. (1993). Research news and comment: The awful reputation of education research. *Educational Researcher, 22*(1), 23–31.

Kim, J. S., Hemphill, L., Troyer, M. T., Thomson, J. M., Jones, S. M., LaRusso, M., & Donovan, S. (2017). Engaging struggling adolescent readers to improve reading skills. *Reading Research Quarterly, 52*(3), 357–382.

Lagemann, E. C. (2002). *An elusive science: The troubling history of education research*. Chicago, IL: University of Chicago Press.

LaRusso, M. D., Donovan, S., & Snow, C. (2016). Implementation challenges for tier one and tier two school-based programs for early adolescents. In B. Foorman (Ed.), *Challenges to implementing effective reading intervention in schools: New directions for child and adolescent development, 154* (pp. 11–30).

Lawrence, J. F., Capotosto, L., Branum-Martin, L., White, C., & Snow, C. (2012). Language proficiency, home-language status, and English vocabulary development: A longitudinal follow-up of the Word Generation program. *Bilingualism: Language and Cognition, 15*, 437–451.

Lawrence, J. F., Crosson, A. C., Paré-Blagoev, E. J., & Snow, C. E. (2015). Word generation randomized trial: Discussion mediates the impact of program treatment on academic word learning. *American Educational Research Journal, 52*(4), 750–786.

Lawrence, J. F., Francis, D., Paré-Blagoev, E. J., & Snow, C. E. (2016). The poor get richer: Heterogeneity in the efficacy of a school-level intervention for academic language. *Journal of Research on Educational Effectiveness*. Advance online publication. doi:10.1080/19345747.2016.1237596

Newmann, F. M., King, M. B., & Youngs, P. (2000). Professional development that addresses school capacity: Lessons from urban elementary schools. *American Journal of Education, 108*(4), 259–299.

Ravitch, D. (1985). Major trends in research: 22 leading scholars report on their fields. *The Chronicle of Higher Education, 31*(1), 14.

Roderick, M., Easton, J. Q., & Sebring, P. B. (2009). *The consortium on Chicago school research: A new model for the role of research in supporting urban school reform.* Chicago, IL: Consortium on Chicago School Research.

Sabatini, J. P., O'Reilly, T., Halderman, L. K., & Bruce, K. (2014a). Broadening the scope of reading comprehension using scenario-based assessments: Preliminary findings and challenges. *International Journal Topics in Cognitive Psychology, 114*, 693–723.

Sabatini, J. P., O'Reilly, T., Halderman, L. K., & Bruce, K. (2014b). Integrating scenario-based and component reading skill measures to understand the reading behavior of struggling readers. *Learning Disabilities Research & Practice, 29*(1), 36–43.

Sabatini, J. P., Bruce, K., Steinberg, J., & Weeks, J. (2015). SARA reading components tests, RISE forms: Technical adequacy and test design. *ETS Research Report Series, 2015*(2), 1–20.

Snow, C., Lawrence, J., & White, C. (2009). Generating knowledge of academic language among urban middle school students. *Journal of Research on Educational Effectiveness, 2*, 325–344.

4

FIGURING IT OUT TOGETHER

A Research–Practice Partnership to Improve Early Elementary Mathematics Learning With Technology

Josephine Louie and Pamela J. Buffington

Many school districts across the country struggle to help students in early elementary grades build a strong foundation in mathematics. The adoption of one-to-one digital devices (i.e., one device per student) is a strategy that growing numbers of districts are using to try to improve student learning (Penuel, 2006; Zheng, Warschauer, Lin, & Chang, 2016). In Auburn, Maine—a small city where a majority of students qualify for free or reduced-price lunch—educators faced low mathematics achievement in the early elementary grades. In 2011, district leaders implemented a one-to-one iPad initiative with the hope that the devices would support more customized student instruction and improve achievement. After three years of implementation, the Auburn School Department recognized that the introduction of mobile devices and associated professional learning had not been sufficient to take full advantage of the technologies and to promote high-quality mathematics learning and teaching.

With a team of education researchers from Education Development Center (EDC) and mathematics education faculty from local Maine universities, Auburn formed a research–practice partnership (RPP) in 2014 to help investigate the one-to-one mobile technology improvement effort and try to improve mathematics learning in the technology-rich early elementary classrooms. The improvement process was complex and faced a variety of challenges, but within a year of the partnership's inception, teachers and researchers together developed a hypothesis about a digital strategy that might help improve students' mathematical thinking and discourse. The group also committed to ongoing classroom testing and co-investigation of this strategy.

Within a semester of co-investigation, the partners began to observe substantial shifts in students' mathematical understandings and communication. At the same time, educators displayed shifts in their own views of how to support classroom learning. Researchers immersed themselves in participating classrooms and gained new insights into how research-based practices could be enacted in technology-rich early elementary environments. By the second year, enthusiasm among Auburn educators helped expand the partnership to additional teachers in the district, and teacher leaders emerged to spread the work beyond the district. This chapter describes the strategies the original team employed to form and develop the partnership, the preliminary outcomes that emerged, and how the partnership is continuing to evolve.

Forming and Developing a Research–Practice Partnership in Auburn, Maine

Auburn is a small city and former mill town in west-central Maine. Students who attend public schools in Auburn come primarily from working-class families; a preponderance (85%) of students are White, and a majority (54%) qualify for free or reduced-price lunch (NCES, 2015). In early 2014, Pam Buffington (second author), a director of science and mathematics programs at EDC, reached out to Auburn school leaders to explore the formation of an RPP to help the district address its struggles in mathematics education and technology integration. Under the auspices of the Research + Practice Collaboratory (RPC) project, funded by the National Science Foundation (NSF), and through the RPP with Auburn, EDC hoped to test a key research conjecture of the RPC project: When researchers and educators work together to identify important problems of practice, develop and test solutions, and study how solutions can be implemented in different contexts, the partners are more likely to generate innovations that are relevant and responsive to the realities of practice and will lead to lasting improvements in educational outcomes.

Buffington had previously worked as a teacher and administrator in Auburn and had strong connections with district administrators. She recognized the potential for a partnership because EDC researchers and Auburn educators brought overlapping strengths and experiences. At EDC, project team members had expertise in mathematics learning and teaching, integrating digital technology tools into education, and education research. Buffington was a "boundary crosser" (Penuel, Allen, Coburn, & Farrell, 2015): As an education researcher with decades of experience teaching and leading professional learning efforts in mathematics and science, she was familiar with navigating between the worlds of research and STEM educational practice. In Auburn, district leaders valued education research and had many years of experience working with outside researchers on multiple education reform initiatives. In addition, a senior Auburn district leader and a school administrator each had doctorates in education and thus were also familiar with navigating the two cultures of research and practice. As in other successful partnerships, boundary crossers supported the work from both sides of the research-practice "divide" (Penuel & Gallagher, 2017).

The project encountered both challenges and opportunities while launching and building a sustainable RPP that could serve the goals and priorities of all partners. The following sections summarize the strategies the partnership adopted to engage in this collaborative effort while navigating the complexities of an educational system committed to change and improvement.

Emphasizing Alignment and Building on Trust

One of the first challenges the team faced was to situate the RPP within the district's existing priorities. Testing research conjectures about partnerships was not of foremost interest to the district. Instead, district leaders were focused most on improving mathematics learning in early grades. In addition, Auburn's public schools were already engaged in multiple school improvement initiatives, and the superintendent regularly received offers from respected organizations to test new learning programs and educational reform approaches. For district leaders, engaging in a new initiative with an unfamiliar partnership approach risked drawing energy and time away from existing efforts and overloading educators with competing demands.

Several factors helped district leaders decide to make room for a partnership with EDC. First, the superintendent consulted with and attained the willing participation of several elementary school principals in her district. These principals were open to the partnership because it focused on one of the district's key priorities of improving achievement in early elementary mathematics. The partnership approach also fit with the district's existing effort to promote "distributed professional development," or ongoing professional learning opportunities that are supported by many contributors (Muir, 2013). In addition, the history between Buffington and district leaders was beneficial. District leaders felt that Buffington listened to them and was willing to adapt the work of the partnership to help meet district goals. In an interview with a team researcher during the second year of the partnership, the superintendent recounted the factors that led her to form an RPP with EDC. She said, "We trust Pam, because we know her . . . and I know she knows us." The superintendent emphasized that she wanted the work of the partnership to align with other major district initiatives: "It cannot be seen as something different." She also told Buffington that the work must support iPad use with students: "If you don't support the iPad, don't bother." Having received the buy-in of key school principals, the superintendent agreed to the partnership because Buffington was "flexible . . . [and] she said she was willing to do all that . . . and I trusted she would."

Forging Agreement on Principles and Processes

The EDC team knew that Auburn educators wanted help to improve early mathematics education with one-to-one iPads, but team members did not come to the partnership with a preset intervention or solution. Instead, consistent with the principles of design-based implementation research (DBIR; Penuel, Fishman, Haugan Cheng, & Sabelli, 2011), EDC proposed that project researchers and professional learning experts work as co-equal partners with district educators to systematically study classroom needs and design and test solutions collaboratively. Buffington explained the project's approach to Auburn's district superintendent: "We don't have a program, we don't have an answer. . . . We're going to figure this out together."

The co-investigative approach that EDC proposed was completely new to the district and risked misunderstandings about mutual roles and responsibilities. Buffington therefore worked with Auburn district leaders to draft and sign a formal memorandum of understanding that made explicit the underlying values of the partnership and the obligations of each partner. Groups involved in RPPs recommend that partners create such formal agreements, clarifying topics such as partner goals, governance, operating principles, and time frames (Coburn, Penuel, & Geil, 2013; Tseng, 2012).

Addressing the broad principles behind the partnership, the memorandum of understanding stated that partners would aim for "bi-directional exchange and partnership between and among practitioners and researchers so that the knowledge and skills of all parties can inform and strengthen the work," and the partnership would be "built upon the shared understanding that we can each benefit from working together." Regarding specific activities, the memorandum of understanding stated that teams from EDC and Auburn would collectively "explore and identify persistent problems in mathematics in technology-rich, early elementary classrooms" and jointly "discuss and establish a research plan, identify data sources, design strategies/an intervention, and engage in interactive cycles of implementation, study, refinement and further testing." EDC and Auburn district leaders agreed that a group of more than a dozen administrators, content leaders, STEM specialists, and classroom teachers from the three lowest performing elementary schools in Auburn would participate most actively in the partnership's work. In addition, a small group of four core district and school leaders would meet regularly with EDC and university researchers as part of a "design team" to support partnership needs. Such support included information about concurrent district initiatives and access to meeting spaces, classrooms, and student data. A separate agreement outlined the specifics of data sharing between EDC and Auburn.

Setting Up the Partnership for Current and Future Work

EDC brought NSF funding to support the RPP with Auburn, but the funding could support only a small EDC project team and would last just a few years. The EDC team therefore decided to seek strategic relationships with additional partners that could continue and potentially expand the RPP after NSF funding ended. Buffington reached out to two local university faculty members involved in mathematics education to join as partners. One was a professor from the University of Maine in Farmington, and the other was from the University of Southern Maine. Both were well versed in current research on best practices in mathematics education but less familiar with research related to using digital technology to promote mathematics learning.

The faculty members saw the partnership with Auburn as an opportunity to build ties with a local district, observe current mathematics education practice in nearby classrooms, connect their preservice teachers with local mathematics improvement efforts, and engage in research to learn more about effective ways to support mathematics education with digital technology. They also valued the opportunity to meet, collaborate, and learn about each other's work. From EDC's perspective, the two faculty members brought additional mathematics research and education expertise to the partnership, and their local involvement increased possibilities for some form of research–practice collaboration to continue after the end of the project grant.

District leaders in Auburn welcomed the expanded collaboration because they felt the additional capacity aligned with district priorities to support teachers' professional learning. In addition, the teacher education programs at both universities provided the district with student teachers and new teachers. District leaders hoped that professional learning supported by the partnership would benefit both Auburn's practicing educators and preservice educators who might join the district in the future.

Building Relationships With Key Stakeholders Throughout the District

The team at EDC believed it was important from the start to build relationships with Auburn educators who had different roles in the district. After Auburn's superintendent and key school principals agreed to work with EDC and local university faculty, the partnership needed buy-in from teachers and other district leaders. To build interest and support, EDC and the two university faculty members organized a meeting in early spring 2014 with over 30 early elementary teachers and administrators across all six elementary schools in Auburn. The purpose of the meeting was to hear educators' views of the root causes underlying low mathematics achievement in Auburn's early elementary grades, and—following a core principle of DBIR—to work toward identifying a persistent problem of practice to address together.

The meeting sparked thoughtful observations among Auburn teachers and school leaders, who welcomed the opportunity to discuss challenges they faced in early mathematics learning and teaching with one-to-one iPads in the classroom. The meeting also revealed, however, that teachers and school leaders did not have a clear understanding of the major contributors to low mathematics achievement among Auburn's early elementary students. They also did not share with researchers the same language to articulate the types of struggles their students encountered when working through the district's mathematics curriculum, *Everyday Mathematics* (The University of Chicago School Mathematics Project, 2016). Although the teachers and school leaders clearly strived to support students in developing numerical fluency, they were not able to articulate the specific developmental stages students move through, where a particular student might be in that development, and what the student needed to progress. From these conversations, researchers saw an opportunity to explore key issues with student mathematics learning and to introduce concepts and frameworks from the research literature that could help teachers make sense of these issues, diagnose where students were in their development, and suggest possible paths forward.

By the end of the meeting, participants identified the following general problems as most critical: (1) weak number skills among students in early grades and (2) unclear understandings among teachers of what effective mathematics instruction looks like, both with and without iPads. The EDC team felt that ongoing conversations and collaboration could potentially help all partners come to a shared understanding of what teachers meant by "weak number skills" and identify a focus within the broad realm of mathematics instruction that the partnership could tackle.

Developing a Shared Language and Common Vision of Desired Outcomes

To gain deeper insight into the problems that Auburn educators faced, members of the EDC team spent time observing mathematics lessons in early elementary grades, interviewing key district and school leaders, and analyzing student test score data. EDC team members learned that few teachers or school leaders had received any professional development in mathematics instruction in recent years. They noticed that in the majority of classrooms they visited, students used iPads during mathematics lessons typically by themselves, wearing headphones, for supplemental drill-and-practice activities. Even as teachers shared their frustrations with low levels of problem-solving skills among students, EDC team members observed that students did not have many opportunities to engage in rich problem-solving activities in the classroom.

Based on these observations, the EDC team felt that the partners needed to develop a shared language to describe and discuss students' mathematics struggles, as well as a common vision of high-quality learning and teaching in mathematics with mobile devices in early elementary classrooms. To do so—in consultation with district leaders, school principals, and the two local university faculty partners—the EDC team led a 35-hour professional learning experience in the summer of 2014, organized as a series of full- and half-day workshops over a two-month period. Participants from Auburn included seven teachers in grades K–2, an elementary math coach, four elementary school principals, and five district administrators.

EDC designed the experience as a set of activities in which partners studied and discussed relevant research on the mathematics learning of young children and effective uses of technology to support such learning. Because educators in Auburn had said they needed help to connect the learning approaches in their mathematics curriculum with the learning opportunities offered by mobile devices, EDC researchers compiled resources describing research on young children's developmental pathways in mathematics and research on effective uses of technology in classrooms. The EDC team thought such research could provide frameworks to support teachers in situating students' learning needs within a landscape of mathematical learning goals and help them select among digital and nondigital support strategies to move students toward these goals.

The specific research the partners studied included Young Mathematicians at Work (Fosnot & Dolk, 2001) and research briefs written by EDC researchers that summarize literature by Clements and Sarama (2014) on early learning trajectories for the development of numeracy skills. To develop a shared understanding of what high-quality mathematics learning and teaching could look like in early grades, the group watched video clips of mathematical discussions among young learners facilitated by skilled instructors (Cameron, Hersch, & Fosnot, 2004; Fosnot & Uittenbogaard, 2007). The group also learned about the Standards for Mathematical Practice from the Common Core State Standards, focusing on MP3 ("Construct viable arguments and critique the reasoning of others"), MP4 ("Model with mathematics"), and MP5 ("Use appropriate tools strategically") (National Governors Association Center for Best Practices & Council of Chief State School Officers, 2010). These three practices were particularly relevant to Auburn's teachers, given the district's interests in boosting early elementary students' problem-solving skills and teachers' effective use of one-to-one iPads during mathematics instruction. The group examined resources to connect these practices to classroom instruction, including the websites *Illustrative Mathematics* (Illustrative Mathematics, 2015) and *Inside Mathematics* (Charles A. Dana Center at the University of Texas at Austin, 1997).

To learn how digital tools might support students' mathematical problem solving, the group read research on best practices for technology use in schools and in mathematics (Lewis Presser & Busey, 2016). Participants explored online mathematical modeling apps (The Math Learning Center, n.d.) and screencasting tools, such as Explain Everything, which allow students to make audiovisual recordings of themselves solving mathematics problems using a digital whiteboard on their iPad. The EDC team encouraged all partners to use these apps not for student drill, practice, remediation, or tutoring, but to help students represent what they know and engage in critical thinking about mathematics problems (Jonassen, 2000; Soto, 2015; Soto & Ambrose, 2016). Some, if not all, of the ideas and tools were new to most partners, which helped everyone take on the role of learner.

By studying new resources together, the group was able to come to common understandings of important mathematical concepts and practices to promote in early grades and how a variety of tools and strategies—such as open number lines (Ashlock, 2010; Bramald, 2000; Klein, Beishuizen, & Treffers, 1998) or a Math Congress (Fosnot & Dolk, 2001)—might support such learning.

Supporting Shifting Needs

The EDC team initially took a strong leadership role in designing and delivering the summer professional learning experience to launch the partnership's work. Because the EDC team was bringing a collaborative approach that was new to the district, EDC shouldered much of the initial planning and group facilitation work. Based on classroom observations and needs expressed by Auburn educators, the EDC team also felt that this period of foundational work—reviewing research on early mathematics learning and effective uses of technology—was necessary before the partners could jointly identify a focused problem of practice to address. EDC team members had the expertise to identify relevant research and resources to help the group get started.

As the summer unfolded and as the partnership's work moved into the academic year, however, Auburn educators became more active in discussing what they wanted to learn and explore. With a commitment to valuing the insights and experiences of educators, and with the goal of promoting a truly equitable collaboration between researchers and practitioners, EDC team members tried to solicit and respond to educators' expressed needs much more than they had done in prior projects. For example, teachers noticed similarities between the idea of a Math Congress, described by Fosnot and Dolk (2001) as an opportunity for students to share and defend their ideas, solutions, and conjectures with one another in a whole-group discussion, and the workshop model they had earlier started to institute for literacy learning. In response, EDC team leaders developed written resources and devoted a later summer workshop session to deepen understanding and support implementation of Math Congresses in early elementary grades. In the fall, when the partnership began to convene in monthly professional learning community (PLC) meetings, teachers shared difficulties they faced in creating a discourse-rich mathematics community among their students. In response, EDC and the university partners introduced research about promoting mathematical communication and the affordances of "open" versus "closed" mathematics tasks. Teachers expressed such strong interest in the topic that EDC and the university partners assembled and developed resources to help them design and implement open tasks for use at the group's next PLC meeting.

By supporting Auburn educators in steering the direction of the group's professional learning activities, EDC researchers sometimes felt the focus of the joint work followed a meandering path. EDC and the university partners could not always anticipate what questions or needs the Auburn educators would voice with great interest or urgency. Unable to plan far in advance, the EDC and university partners were challenged to assemble resources and supports that could be helpful to Auburn educators in timely ways. Yet, meeting this challenge seemed critical for remaining responsive to teachers and for scoping out the problem space where a rich research question might lie.

Identifying a Shared Hypothesis and Research Question to Explore

After completing the initial summer professional learning experience, the partners embarked on an extended effort to co-investigate how teachers might implement new strategies and iPad tools they had learned over the summer and their possible impacts on student mathematics learning. In September 2014, the group embarked on a "toe-in-the-water" phase in which teachers agreed to try one new strategy with their students each month. Because teachers carried different levels of technical and content expertise, this approach allowed them to explore new strategies in ways that fit their comfort levels and needs. Teachers agreed to document in an online log each strategy they used, how the strategy worked, and what they might do differently the next time. During monthly PLC meetings, the entire RPP group discussed strategies that appeared particularly promising.

EDC researchers hoped that within a couple months of active classroom exploration, the group would arrive at a common hypothesis about a core problem underlying students' struggles with mathematics and a promising solution. The initial exploration phase turned out to be longer and bumpier than anyone expected, however. Some teachers were slow to test new strategies and iPad tools with their students, due to competing classroom demands and discomfort with technology-based strategies. Other teachers felt the level of effort involved in strategy testing efforts (including strategy planning, implementation, observation, reflection, and online documentation), in addition to data gathering for other district improvement initiatives, was burdensome. Over a period of four months, the partners met monthly to discuss their prior month's experiences and findings, but many teachers felt that developing a group hypothesis to investigate was difficult and was not advancing their own professional learning.

To address these concerns, the partners worked together to provide more guidance for teachers who needed help using and managing new iPad tools during mathematics lessons. In consultation with teachers, EDC researchers streamlined data collection forms. In addition, the group agreed that their monthly PLC meetings would be restructured to include a portion dedicated explicitly to professional learning that could support teachers' immediate mathematics learning and teaching needs.

To help the group arrive at a shared hypothesis for collaborative investigation, EDC researchers in early 2015 collected statements from all participating teachers about specific strategies the teachers believed held great promise for promoting students' mathematics learning. Multiple teachers observed that students were highly engaged when using a screencasting app to make audiovisual recordings of themselves solving mathematics problems. Students not only enjoyed recording and hearing their own voices but also noticed their own errors and independently self-corrected and rerecorded their explanations. These teachers proposed the following hypothesis: If students in early grades regularly use a screencasting app, such as Explain Everything, to record explanations of their thinking when solving mathematics problems, they will likely show improvement in their mathematical problem-solving skills and communication.

The teachers had generally found the process of developing a group hypothesis unfamiliar and challenging, but because they had begun to see positive student responses to the new tools and strategies they were testing in the classroom, most of them were ultimately excited to test the hypothesis that the group devised. They agreed that starting in February 2015, they would ask their students at least twice a month to use screencasting to explain, record, and review their explanations when solving a mathematics task. Extending the routine established in the fall, they agreed to document how they used the strategy with students (e.g., in small groups, in pairs, or individually) and students' responses to their methods of implementation. Then, each month, the teachers would spend part of the PLC meeting sharing student screencasts and discussing their observations.

Iterative testing of the group strategy continued through the end of the school year. Three teachers left the partnership the next year because they continued to feel the level of effort too burdensome, but the other four teachers remained. The group added a new cohort of nine teachers from two other Auburn elementary schools, and the partnership continued iterative testing of the strategy through the subsequent academic year, 2015–2016.

Emerging Changes in Learning and Practice

Within the first year of joint work, the RPP in Auburn began to yield signs of strong shifts in the knowledge, practices, and views of all partners, including students. Data providing evidence of these shifts include teachers' online log entries, partner surveys, monthly PLC meetings' group sharing, classroom observations, student screencasts, email correspondence between teachers and EDC or university faculty partners, and interviews with 17 key participants. With the input of Auburn teachers and principals, EDC and the university researchers created coding schemes for the qualitative data to identify major themes that emerged in the group's early analyses.

Deeper Insights Among Project Researchers of "What Works" to Promote Educational Change

The EDC team came to the partnership with deep experience working collaboratively with educational stakeholders in a wide variety of settings. Participating in the RPC project, however, pushed the EDC team to work with Auburn educators to truly "figure things out together." The approach led to some of the highest levels of teacher engagement that team members have experienced. A second-grade teacher shared that "the collaboration has been one of the best professional development experiences I have had" (Maislen, 2016). The district superintendent observed, "The way [EDC] designed [the work] really had [the teachers] feel ownership in it. . . . They were investigating things together in a safe environment. . . . You could see the confidence in those who participated" (interview, June 17, 2016). These types of responses have helped EDC team members and the university partners come to believe that mutualistic collaborations have the potential to facilitate powerful changes in the professional practice of school educators.

Altered Views Among School Leaders of Ways to Promote School Improvement

Interviews with school leaders suggest that the partnership has had profound effects on their views of mathematics learning and how schools should approach educational improvement. One school principal described the iterative cycle of "giving us some information [and] then setting up the process of implementing [a strategy] and talking about it and really picking it apart" as more valuable and empowering than traditional professional development approaches (interview, February 1, 2016). She observed that "because you guys certainly don't have all the answers either," having classroom educators examine student work and teacher practice with researchers "has been really what brings [our work] to that next level." She also stated that even after project funding ends, "the whole process is something we could always continue." Another principal came to believe that schools and researchers must work in partnership for educational improvement to occur:

> I've been in education a long time. When I first started we really relied on the "experts" to tell us what we needed to do. And it's really clear to me now that moving forward we have to work collectively in partnerships such as this one to figure out how to best use technology and how to maximize learning for students. . . . There's so much now to know and you really need to bring together all of the experts together. We're all experts in what we do.
> *(interview, March 11, 2016)*

Shifts in Confidence, Knowledge, and Classroom Practices Among Teachers

Project data suggest that the teachers who participated most actively in the partnership's work developed a stronger understanding of the research process and greater confidence in their abilities to serve as co-creators of research knowledge.

A second-grade teacher said she had an "epiphany" once project team members began to present group findings at regional and national conferences: "You actually couldn't do what you do if it wasn't for us" (interview, March 2, 2016). A first-grade teacher said that the partnership inspired her to become a math coach. She stated that, prior to joining the partnership, "I don't think I would have [considered] a role as a math coach," but she found that "the co-investigative model was so valuable." She realized, "We could do this with all teachers. I don't have to be the expert, but I now have this pool of resources and information that I could help share with others, and [we could] really be a collaborative group [examining] what's working, what's not working. And modeling that kind of situation with other staff" (interview, January 27, 2016).

Project data also indicate that the teachers in the partnership developed new understandings of how to support mathematical thinking among young students. Classroom observations revealed that, over time, teachers stopped asking students to use iPad apps for drills and instead encouraged students to choose visual modeling apps as aids for mathematical problem solving. Once the group began to test its screencasting hypothesis, teachers stopped asking students to use their iPads quietly with headphones and instead encouraged them to record and share their mathematical thinking with teachers and peers. The work of the partnership appeared to build teachers' appreciation for having students engage in mathematical discourse, as reflected in the words of a kindergarten teacher:

> Honestly, in the past, I'd never really thought about how important it is to have [students] explain what they're doing, what they're thinking. . . . It's really been an eye-opener, and a changer, in how I teach my kids.
> *(interview, February 25, 2016)*

A second-grade teacher reflected on her shifting practices:

> I'm trying harder to be less at the front of the classroom giving the instruction and trying to be more of a facilitator as students work through strategies. I'm finding myself trying to . . . talk less to allow the students to talk more. . . . Students can really learn a lot from each other and that's valuable.
> *(interview, February 2, 2016)*

Shifts in Mathematical Learning Among Students

As the partnership progressed, Auburn educators described transformations in mathematical communication patterns, conceptual understandings, and problem-solving abilities of students. A second-grade teacher noted that by using iPad tools and discourse strategies to promote standards of mathematical practice, her students became more articulate in solving mathematics problems. "In the past, my kids have said, 'Well, this is how I did it.' Or, 'I just knew it,' and they don't discuss anymore. This year, they're having discussions and talking about their thinking and responding to others" (interview, January 26, 2016). Multiple teachers observed that during screencasting, students displayed more agency in their learning. The math coach observed that "when they're doing their work and recording, and then they go back and listen . . . [they will] be reflective in the sense of self-correcting, like 'Oh, wait a minute, I meant this' . . . [and] may clarify a misunderstanding they may have had" (interview, January 27, 2016). The strategy also appeared to help students feel safer making mistakes and exploring mathematical ideas.

One of the strongest outcomes appeared to be greater equity of student mathematics learning opportunities. A second-grade teacher reported that regular screencasting "forces everyone to engage in [the] problem and everyone to talk," and "creating the videos requires *all* students to think" (interview, February 4, 2016; log, January 23, 2016). Another second-grade teacher reported that screencasting was a particularly strong scaffold for students with varied learning needs:

> With my English language learners, sometimes they don't have the language and the ability to write down what they're thinking. But if they can use this recording tool and an app, they can show it and can talk about what they've done a little more easily than if it was pencil/paper.
>
> *(interview, January 26, 2016)*

An administrator observed that when teachers use screencasting, "all of the students are equal participants. And all of the students' ideas are equally valued" (interview, March 11, 2016).

The Evolving Partnership

Consistent with a core principle of DBIR, the EDC team endeavored from the start to build the capacity of participants to help lead partnership activities. Early in the collaboration, the two university faculty members facilitated professional learning components at the monthly PLC group meetings; as time went on, they led presentations and developed publications summarizing partnership findings for mathematics educator audiences. During the second year of the partnership and as NSF funding began to wind down, the faculty partners wrote grant proposals with Auburn administrators to continue the partnership work and to explore collaboration opportunities between preservice teachers and Auburn teachers. Other local faculty members in mathematics education have expressed interest in working with the partnership to expand the work to other high-needs Maine districts.

Based in part on the initial successes of the partnership work in Auburn, in early 2017, the Maine Department of Education awarded EDC funds to expand the mathematics professional learning approach developed in Auburn to 11 new districts and 22 additional schools across the state. To help lead this work, four teachers from Auburn are spreading their learning to new cohorts of teachers. The efforts that EDC researchers and the local university faculty employed to build the capacities of teachers in Auburn to support early elementary mathematics learning with iPads has helped this core group of teachers develop the confidence to share their new knowledge with others. Empowered by their experiences, these teachers are collaborating with EDC and university researchers to create and publish resources to support national audiences of educators interested in promoting early mathematics learning in technology-rich environments.

Acknowledgments

This material is based upon work supported by the NSF under grants DUE-1238253 and DRL-1626365. Any opinions, findings, and conclusions or recommendations expressed in this material are those of the authors and do not necessarily reflect the views of the NSF.

References

Ashlock, R. B. (2010). *Error patterns in computation: Using error patterns to help each student learn*. Boston: Allyn & Bacon.

Bramald, R. (2000). Introducing the empty number line. *Education 3–13, 28*(3), 5–12. Retrieved from https://doi.org/10.1080/03004270085200271

Cameron, A., Hersch, S. B., & Fosnot, C. T. (2004). *Addition and subtraction minilessons, grades preK–3: Facilitator's guide*. Portsmouth, NH: Heinemann.

Charles, A. Dana Center at the University of Texas at Austin. (2017). *Common core resources: Mathematical practice standards*. Retrieved March 5, 2017, from www.insidemathematics.org/common-core-resources/mathematical-practice-standards

Clements, D. H., & Sarama, J. (2014). *Learning and teaching early math: The learning trajectories approach* (2nd ed.). London: Routledge.

Coburn, C. E., Penuel, W. R., & Geil, K. E. (2013). *Research–practice partnerships: A strategy for leveraging research for educational improvement in school districts*. New York: William T. Grant Foundation. Retrieved from http://learndbir.org/resources/Coburn-Penuel-Geil-2013.pdf

Fosnot, C. T., & Dolk, M. (2001). *Young mathematicians at work: Constructing number sense, addition, and subtraction*. Portsmouth, NH: Heinemann.

Fosnot, C. T., & Uittenbogaard, W. (2007). *Minilessons for extending addition and subtraction: A yearlong resource*. Portsmouth, NH: Firsthand/Heinemann.

Illustrative Mathematics. (2015). *Practice standards*. Retrieved March 5, 2017, from www.illustrativemathematics.org/practice-standards

Jonassen, D. H. (2000). *Computers as mindtools for schools: Engaging critical thinking*. Upper Saddle River, NJ: Prentice Hall.

Klein, A. S., Beishuizen, M., & Treffers, A. (1998). The empty number line in Dutch second grades: Realistic versus gradual program design. *Journal for Research in Mathematics Education, 29*(4), 443. Retrieved from https://doi.org/10.2307/749861

Lewis Presser, A., & Busey, A. (2016). *Mobile technology and mathematics learning in the early grades* (Research + Practice Brief). Education Development Center. Retrieved from http://interactivestem.org/wp-content/uploads/2016/07/Mobile-Technology-and-Math-Learning-in-the-Early-Grades.pdf

Maislen, P. A. (June 30, 2016). *Maine grade 2 teacher flourishing in research + practice context* [Blog post]. Retrieved from http://interactivestem.org/blog_relnei/maine-grade-2-teacher-flourishing-in-research-practice-context

Muir, M. (November 24, 2013). *The need for a quality, distributed professional development system* [Blog post]. Retrieved from https://multiplepathways.wordpress.com/2013/11/24/the-need-for-a-quality-distributed-professional-development-system/

National Center for Education Statistics [NCES]. (2015). *Common core of data*. U.S. Department of Education. Retrieved from http://nces.ed.gov/ccd/elsi/

National Governors Association Center for Best Practices & Council of Chief State School Officers. (2010). *Common core state standards for mathematics*. Washington, DC: Author. Retrieved from www.corestandards.org/assets/CCSSI_Math%20Standards.pdf

Penuel, W. R. (2006). Implementation and effects of one-to-one computing initiatives: A research synthesis. *Journal of Research on Technology in Education, 38*(3), 329–348.

Penuel, W. R., Allen, A. R., Coburn, C. E., & Farrell, C. (2015). Conceptualizing research–practice partnerships as joint work at boundaries. *Journal of Education for Students Placed at Risk (JESPAR), 20*(1–2), 182–197. Retrieved from https://doi.org/10.1080/10824669.2014.988334

Penuel, W. R., Fishman, B. J., Haugan Cheng, B., & Sabelli, N. (2011). Organizing research and development at the intersection of learning, implementation, and design. *Educational Researcher, 40*(7), 331–337. Retrieved from https://doi.org/10.3102/0013189X11421826

Penuel, W. R., & Gallagher, D. (2017). *Creating research–practice partnerships in education*. Cambridge, MA: Harvard Education Press.

Soto, M. (2015). Elementary students' mathematical explanations and attention to audience with screencasts. *Journal of Research on Technology in Education, 47*(4), 242–258. Retrieved from https://doi.org/10.1080/15391523.2015.1078190

Soto, M., & Ambrose, R. (2016). Making students' mathematical explanations accessible to teachers through the use of digital recorders and iPads. *Learning, Media and Technology, 41*(2), 213–232. Retrieved from https://doi.org/10.1080/17439884.2014.931867

The Math Learning Center. (n.d.). *Free math apps*. Retrieved from https://www.mathlearningcenter.org/resources/apps

The University of Chicago School Mathematics Project. (2016). *Everyday mathematics* (4th ed.). New York: McGraw-Hill Education.

Tseng, V. (2012). *Partnerships: Shifting the dynamics between research and practice*. New York: William T. Grant Foundation.

Zheng, B., Warschauer, M., Lin, C. H., & Chang, C. (2016). Learning in one-to-one laptop environments: A meta-analysis and research synthesis. *Review of Educational Research, 86*(4), 1052–1084.

5

THE EVOLUTION OF A MULTI-STAKEHOLDER RESEARCH–PRACTICE PARTNERSHIP ON EQUITY IN SCHOOL DISCIPLINE

Yolanda Anyon, Jessica Yang, Katherine Wiley,
Eldridge Greer, Barbara J. Downing,
Ricardo Martinez, and Daniel Kim

Studies of school disciplinary practices have revealed racial disparities in exclusionary outcomes for more than 50 years. Black, Latino, and Native American youth—particularly young Black men—are significantly more likely than students of other backgrounds to be referred to school administrators for disciplining and to receive out-of-school suspension or expulsion as punishment (Skiba, Mediratta, & Rausch, 2016). These exclusionary discipline sanctions often have adverse implications for students' academic and life trajectories, pushing them out of school and into the criminal justice system (Skiba et al., 2016). Although this issue has caught the attention of national media outlets and federal agencies in recent years (e.g., Lhamon & Samuels, 2014), only a small number of districts have voluntarily responded to the problem of racial discipline gaps with robust policy reforms (The White House, 2016).

Denver Public Schools (DPS), the largest urban school district in Colorado, stands as an exception to these national trends. In response to a multi-year educational justice campaign led by community and youth organizers from Padres & Jóvenes Unidos (Padres), the Denver board of education passed a major discipline policy reform in 2008. The goal of the new policy was to reduce suspensions and expulsions, eliminate racial disparities, and increase the use of approaches such as restorative practices and therapeutic interventions in response to rule-breaking behavior.

Three years later, Padres released an accountability report evaluating the impact of discipline policy reforms in Denver (Padres & Jóvenes Unidos, 2011). It recognized the district's success in sustaining reductions in suspension and expulsion rates for students of all backgrounds, but it also highlighted the persistence of racial discipline gaps as an ongoing problem. In closing, the report called on DPS to increase resources that would support stronger implementation of nonpunitive and nonexclusionary interventions, particularly in schools with high suspension rates.

Around the same time, broad agreement was emerging across regional and local stakeholder groups about the need to disaggregate and analyze school discipline data to monitor reform implementation and improve equity. The passage of Colorado Senate Bill 12-046 in 2012, known as the Smart School Discipline Law, also spurred by Padres organizing, signaled statewide support of efforts to document and disrupt discipline disparities. At the federal level, several initiatives were encouraging educators to use culturally responsive and restorative practices to mitigate racial disparities in exclusionary outcomes (e.g., United States Department of Education, 2011).

As many of these processes were getting under way, the lead author joined the faculty at the Graduate School of Social Work (GSSW) at the University of Denver (DU). With a background in university–community partnerships (Anyon & Fernández, 2007) and racial equity in education (e.g., Anyon, 2009), she pursued an opportunity with faculty colleagues to develop a research–practice partnership (RPP) with DPS. Simultaneously, she was also building relationships with Padres because of her admiration of their youth-led campaigns to end the school-to-prison pipeline and her background in facilitating youth voice programs. After separate relationship-building meetings with each stakeholder group, it was clear that there was an interest in locally relevant research using the district's administrative datasets. The work moved forward in part because the research team members were perceived as having the personal values, academic expertise, and professional experiences that were credible to both central office administrators and community organizers.

With initial interest secured from key players, an RPP between the Division of Student Equity and Opportunity at DPS and GSSW at DU was established in the fall of 2012. Guided by interdisciplinary models for bridging the gap between research and practice through iterative and nonlinear inquiry, dissemination, and implementation cycles (e.g., Wandersman et al., 2008), the purpose of the RPP was as follows:

1. Conduct rigorous and relevant research on school discipline and racial disparities in exclusionary practices.
2. Collaborate with policymakers, administrators, educators, and other local stakeholder groups to identify research questions, interpret results, and disseminate findings.
3. Strengthen and sustain efforts to connect research with local policy reforms and advocacy efforts.

Research–Practice Partnership Design

In Denver, as in other cities around the country, there is vast disagreement about the root causes of educational inequities such as school discipline disparities. Yet, few would contend with the statement that these inequities are the result of complex interactions between individuals and institutions over hundreds of years. Such deeply rooted problems have not been solved through quick or narrowly focused interventions or fragmented initiatives led by different research, practice, and advocacy organizations. Our RPP was therefore grounded in a shared belief that multi-year reforms reflecting the expertise of educators, students and their families, community members, and researchers have great potential to generate the knowledge, capacity, and motivation necessary to reduce disparities (Skiba et al., 2016). We felt scholars needed to understand how practitioners, administrators, and advocates make sense of problems of educational equity in order to generate information that has the potential to shift attitudes and beliefs that are barriers to change. Without this type of cross-sector collaboration, it seemed unlikely that researchers would adequately be able to *see* the relevant factors that shape racially disparate outcomes in schools, or that evidence-based recommendations would actually be taken up in local educational systems.

Indeed, the literatures on RPPs, research use in school district policymaking, and prevention science frameworks for dissemination and implementation suggest these initiatives typically address the knowledge and beliefs of stakeholder groups at multiple stages through facilitated data inquiry (see, e.g., Coburn, Penuel, & Geil, 2013; Honig & Coburn, 2008; Wandersman et al., 2008). Our RPP was designed to create opportunities to identify local explanatory frameworks for discipline disparities and understand how they sustained, or minimized, racial injustice in schools. We aimed to ensure that interventions designed to reduce disparities would be understood as compatible with—and responsive to—local norms, needs, and historical contexts.

The blueprint of our RPP also reflected consensus from studies in this area that social ties and trust are critical resources in successful efforts to bridge research and practice (Honig & Coburn, 2008; Wandersman et al., 2008). We enlisted local advocacy groups, building-based educators, and central office administrators to engage in an iterative research process that involved explicit relationship-building activities, evolving research questions, and changing sources of data. The inclusion of multiple stakeholder groups also reflects evidence that alignment between policy efforts at multiple levels supports data-driven decision-making in schools and districts (Honig & Coburn, 2008). As a result, the evolution of our long-term RPP was equity oriented and community engaged from the start.

The Evolution of a Long-Term Partnership on Equity in School Discipline

With this literature in mind, it is important to note that before our RPP began, several threshold conditions were in place that ultimately helped sustain the partnership and its impact over time. First, there was an existing venue for professional learning through which research findings could be communicated to practitioners.

Second, there was strong support among DPS stakeholders, influenced by local, regional, and federal policy initiatives, to use data in discipline decision-making. Finally, DPS partners had very clear and specific questions they wanted to answer, and DU researchers had the methodological skills, content knowledge, and personal interest in these priority topics. These conditions were ripe for an RPP that could engage in significant and focused work to address racial disparities in discipline practices.

We also want to highlight again that our partnership's inquiry and action cycle has been an iterative and nonlinear process that has involved defining a problem of interest, examining related risk and protective factors, assessing implementation conditions for promising interventions, translating research findings for practitioner audiences, and leveraging results to change attitudes and build capacity for equity-oriented practices. This process is presented in the following sections as a discrete set of phases, but in fact, they were overlapping and had more breadth than what is described here.

Phase 1: Address Beliefs and Assumptions About School Discipline

Addressing Local Narratives About the Problem of Practice Through Facilitated Data Inquiry

Initial meetings between university and district partners included three central office administrators occupying director-, manager-, and coordinator-level roles in the Division of Student Equity and Opportunity. Two were trained as psychologists, and the other had a background in teaching and school administration. Together, these individuals were responsible for developing policy and data systems related to school discipline, allocating division resources to schools, and designing professional development opportunities for building-based staff. The initial research team included one junior, senior, and clinical faculty member, supported by a doctoral student, who collectively had expertise in mixed methods research, school-based prevention and intervention programs, and racial disparities in education.

Early conversations among the RPP team focused on understanding the district's research questions and the data necessary to answer them. Two working hypotheses were defined: (1) Black and Latino students' increased likelihood of suspension would not be fully explained by poverty, the nature of their offenses, or disability, and (2) students who receive therapeutic or restorative interventions would be less likely to be suspended from school after accounting for other contributing factors such as the type and number of their discipline incidents.

The topics were selected because they addressed competing ideas held by practitioners and administrators in the district about the root causes of discipline disparities. Many school-based and central office staff members believed that racial disparities in suspension and expulsion were actually reflections of racial differ-ences in behavior, eligibility for special education, or free or reduced-price lunch status. This dominant narrative was captured in conversations about the "bad kids" who ruin the learning environment for a majority of students. Others were skeptical that the alternative discipline approaches encouraged by the new disci-pline reform policy had much worth. Yet, our district partners were convinced by national publications, particularly Losen and Gillespie's (2012) report, that both sets of beliefs were unfounded. Our initial research agenda combined these two hypotheses by aiming to identify the key risk and protective factors for exclusion-ary discipline outcomes that persisted when controlling for confounds such as poverty, disability status, and type of discipline incident.

With our questions clearly defined, the university research team wrote appli-cations to the review boards of the district and university for approval to access identifiable student data. While the requests were being processed, the lead author participated in a variety of discipline policy reform activities, such as community, school, and parent forums, in order to understand how the issue played out in local contexts. These meetings illustrated that competing explanatory frameworks for the problem of racial discipline gaps existed beyond district walls. In contrast to narratives expressed by some educators, parents and community members usu-ally pointed to race as the determining factor in discipline decisions. These stake-holders also found suspension to be an unnecessarily punitive response to what were perceived as minor infractions by students. Almost unanimously, parent and community representatives argued that restorative and therapeutic interventions should be used in lieu of exclusionary approaches like suspension or expulsion.

These tensions among different stakeholder groups generated greater resolve among the RPP team to directly address these implicit hypotheses and spend a fair amount of time disseminating conclusive results before moving on to other topics. Moreover, because of the contentious nature of the problem of practice, the researchers agreed to a confidentiality agreement that allowed the district to ultimately decide if, when, and with whom research findings would be shared. (Of note, in the five years that the partnership has existed, the RPP team has only once been in disagreement about the audience for study results.) The RPP team also created a formal authorship agreement that outlined the types of con-tributions (including partnership meetings where research questions and methods were collaboratively determined) that made one eligible for authorship and how author order would be determined. These documents served the function of building trust by cultivating a sense that all types of expertise would be valued in the products that came out of the partnership. They also provided assurances that the district would not be embarrassed unnecessarily and that the partnership would not be endangered, although it was also understood that professional codes of ethics would supersede any of these interests.

Once the lead investigator received district data, we began meeting regularly to conduct validity checks by reviewing descriptive trends in order to surface substantial cleaning, coding, and/or entry errors. This work was fairly time-intensive and required creative problem solving on both sides before all were confident that the final dataset was accurate. Although this took several months, these meetings were essential for building relationships between members of the partnership team and for assuring district partners that our findings would be credible. Given the degree to which there were competing narratives about this relatively controversial problem, the district team was understandably concerned about potential errors, such as duplicative counts of disciplined students or incorrectly coded office disciplinary referral reasons. For example, due to intercorrelations among some study variables (e.g., race and other student demographics or referral reasons and suspension outcomes), a coding error could meaningfully impact study findings about the salience of race in discipline decision-making and the promise of alternatives.

At this stage, we were also worried that our analyses might not provide decisive evidence about our hypotheses of interest. Mixed findings—for example, in which race might be a large predictor of discipline outcomes but not statistically significant—would make it challenging to communicate results to stakeholders. In other words, if trends went in a clear direction, but were only due to chance (statistically speaking), the ability to accurately interpret findings would require more technical knowledge of mathematical probability, leading to more complexity in joint meaning-making. Fortunately, findings were conclusive, and we decided as an RPP to release the results in a report (Anyon et al., 2013) that was a public-facing document relying on language and visuals that could be used by community and district stakeholders. Additionally, we further explored the following findings in a peer-reviewed academic journal article (Anyon, Jenson, et al., 2014):

- Clinically meaningful and statistically significant racial disparities in office disciplinary referrals, out-of-school suspensions, and referrals to law enforcement persisted across all four years of data, even after accounting for student characteristics such as disability, family income, and discipline offense type, along with school demographic composition. Specifically, Black students experienced greater risk than their White peers for every type of exclusionary discipline outcome, but this pattern was less consistent for Latino youth.
- The influence of race decreased as students moved through the discipline process: Student racial background had the strongest effect on office disciplinary referrals but was not a statistically significant predictor of expulsion decisions.
- Racial disparities in out-of-school suspension across the district worsened over time, which primarily reflected larger declines in suspensions among White students compared to students of color. Disparities were especially pronounced in elementary and middle schools. In contrast, suspension gaps in high schools decreased over time and were not statistically significant in the final year of the analysis.

- Students who participated in restorative interventions (RIs) or were assigned in-school suspensions were at lower risk for out-of-school suspension. However, students who received behavior contracts (in which adults identify the root causes of a student's discipline incidents and create action steps) as a consequence for office referrals were at greater risk of out-of-school suspension.

Guiding Sense-Making and the Search for Solutions

With compelling findings in hand, we discussed the best strategies for disseminating key results among practitioners. The partnership team worked together to share findings through presentations at district-level discipline team meetings and interdepartmental "priority" gatherings. Even though the district already had a stated vision for racial equity, validating it with research that also challenged backroom conversations allowed central office administrators to accelerate their commitment to discipline reforms, as reflected in conversations during senior leadership team meetings.

In order to directly address educators' beliefs about the salience of racial disparities and the promise of alternative approaches to discipline, research partners presented study findings at the district-led monthly trainings for discipline building leaders, then facilitated a conversation about their relevance to, and implications for, practice. To enhance the credibility and utility of study findings with educators, GSSW faculty continued to work with the district facilitator for the rest of the school year to develop and implement activities related to themes from that initial discussion: developing upstream interventions, understanding classroom-based restorative practices, teaching code switching strategies, and building partnerships with mental health and youth development organizations. Ongoing and direct contact with the partnership team increased the relevance of our research by allowing building-based practitioners to have their unique questions or concerns about our findings answered immediately. These activities also served to strengthen relationships that proved to be useful in terms of uptake of recommendations and future participation in our RPP studies.

Participants reported that this deep dive into the data helped them understand the richness of why racial discipline gaps exist and the need to look for alternatives to suspension, providing a stronger motivating rationale for district reforms.

Supporting Community Engagement with Key Findings

Research findings also served as starting point for conversations with Padres about how the partnership's work could add value to its advocacy and accountability efforts. The organization had been deeply engaged in community advocacy and mobilization to support district-wide and statewide school discipline reform. Transparency with discipline data was a defining feature of Padres' reform agenda, and study results supported their claims about racial disparities and the need to increase the implementation of restorative practices. These early discussions were promising enough that Padres agreed to co-sponsor an event to draw the attention of educators, parents, and community members to key research findings and the issue of discipline disparities. A nationally known scholar was selected for a one-day consultation and public lecture. His itinerary involved meetings with central office staff, senior district leaders, building-based educators from a network of middle schools, organizers from Padres, and the DU-DPS partnership team, followed by a free talk and reception at DU. The Division of Student Equity and Opportunity covered his consulting fees, GSSW provided event space and food, and Padres publicized the lecture and mobilized its members to attend. Over 300 people participated in the events of the day. Several invited members from the local teachers' union, the Denver Classroom Teachers Association (DCTA), who had created a working group to document problems with school discipline reforms, also attended.

Afterward, GSSW faculty members invited representatives from DPS, Padres, and DCTA to participate in an impromptu debrief of the day's events. There was broad, if tentative, agreement that a variety of stakeholders were engaged during the visit and many were exposed to evidence that challenged their beliefs about discipline. At the same time, the events highlighted successes in Denver and connected local reforms to national initiatives, effectively conveying a message to participants that their work had value locally and beyond. The success of the visit was also a sign that collaboration between district, community, and university leaders could add value to each organization's mission. Historically, relationships between the district, Padres, and DCTA had been strained and characterized by conflict, with tensions fueled by perceptions of competing agendas. In contrast, GSSW faculty were seen as neutral conveners and credible experts. Building on the positive energy and momentum of the events, representatives from each organization agreed to meet one month later to identify additional opportunities for collaboration.

Phase 2: Assess Intervention Impact and Implementation Status

Building a Stronger Evidence Base for Restorative Practices Through Implementation and Outcome Analyses

At this stage of the RPP, we now had some interest and buy-in to the problem of racial disparities and the potential solution of restorative interventions (RIs). We wanted to pivot to a focus on equitable and scalable strategies that educators and community members could use to address the issues highlighted in our first set of analyses. Our research therefore aimed to generate stronger evidence about the impact of RIs and identify how often, and with whom, they were being used in the district. Analyses, shared in a second annual report (Anyon, Yang, et al., 2014) and published in an academic journal (Anyon, Gregory, et al., 2016), revealed the following key findings:

- The use of restorative practices in DPS schools steadily increased after the passage of the district's reform policies in 2008, even though the policy included no new funding for school sites. That year, just 3% of disciplined students in the district participated in RIs, a rate that increased to 25% by the 2014–2015 school year. However, there was great variability in implementation between schools; the percentage of students who received RIs ranged from 0% to more than 87%, with an average rate of 18%.
- In statistical models that accounted for confounding variables, students who were Black or Latino were *more* likely than their peers to receive an RI.
- Longitudinal analyses indicated that disciplined students who received an RI in the fall semester were much less likely to have another office discipline referral or be suspended in the spring semester. This negative association between first-semester participation in an RI and second-semester discipline incidents was stronger in schools that used the approach more often. To illustrate: in a school with an average implementation rate, a disciplined student who did not participate in an RI in the first semester had a 72% chance of returning to the discipline system. Disciplined students who received an RI at a school with a higher implementation rate had only an 18% chance.
- Unfortunately, these practices did not seem to translate into the elimination of suspension gaps. Black students' odds of suspension compared to their White peers remained essentially unchanged after accounting for student participation in RIs and their use schoolwide.

Shifts in Policy and Practice to Encourage Restorative Interventions

In response to the finding that RIs had positive results in reducing students' likelihood of entering the discipline system or being suspended from schools, district leaders decided that schools would be allowed to use funds from their mental health expansion grants to pay for positions specializing in restorative practices. (This funding stream was previously limited to services provided by psychologists and social workers.) These grants were allocated to schools with the highest needs, operationalized using student demographic characteristics. Around this time, district partners also reworked the discipline "ladder" and "matrix" so that restorative practices were explicitly named at each level of offense and stage of intervention. Finally, to support increased implementation, the district made it easier for whole staff teams to participate in trainings on restorative practices by offering them during new teacher induction training and making them available during staff meetings or professional development days on-site, in addition to existing district-level offerings in a centralized location.

Expanding Community Engagement and Formalizing the Involvement of Multiple Stakeholder Groups

The university research team began holding meetings with Padres, DPS, and DCTA in February 2014. After several sessions, it became clear that although each organization had different priorities, they actually shared several interests: (1) additional partnership research on the implementation and impact of restorative practices; (2) ongoing opportunities for students, parents, and teachers to have a voice in setting the partnerships' research agenda; (3) training for school leaders and staff members on the requirements of the reformed discipline policy and restorative practices; and (4) additional human and financial capital for highly impacted schools.

The group committed to meeting on a monthly basis to work toward these collective objectives through grant-writing, advocacy, and data analysis. We called this group the Denver Collaborative on Racial Disparities in School Discipline (the Collaborative) and viewed it as an informal advisory board to the RPP. The primary purposes of the group were to further strengthen relationships between DU, Padres, DCTA, and the district; generate research questions of interest to all parties; and engage in collective interpretation of partnership study findings. The research team designed these meetings to be a space to build trust and shared responsibility across these organizations, thereby strengthening the social ties that could facilitate the incorporation of research findings into leaders' decisions. Since the data also seemed to indicate that racial discipline gaps were not being reduced, the partnership team selected a second scholar with expertise in culturally responsive practices to visit Denver, meet with stakeholders, and deliver a public lecture. DCTA—along with Padres, GSSW, other departments and initiatives at DU, and DPS—also co-sponsored the event this time, leading to more participation among teachers. There was greater turnout at these events than at the first scholar's visit, which helped sustain participation in the Collaborative.

Phase 3: Identify Conditions and Strategies That Strengthen Promising Practices

Introducing Qualitative Inquiry Into the Research to Increase Its Trustworthiness to Stakeholders

With evidence that RIs protected students from reentering the discipline system and were being delivered to students with the highest needs, but had been implemented unevenly across schools, the Collaborative became interested in the conditions that supported high-quality, widespread implementation of restorative practices and other allied nonpunitive and nonexclusionary approaches to addressing misbehavior. However, using only quantitative administrative data sources, we were unable to identify many school-level factors that were associated with increased rates of RI implementation, suggesting the need for original data collection. The partners therefore decided to pursue two new qualitative studies, involving interviews and focus groups, to document strategies employed at (1) schools that had low suspension rates, or (2) schools that had been identified by multiple stakeholders as exemplary models of schoolwide restorative practices.

The aims of these two studies were parallel: to identify promising practices from successful schools so that these strategies could be quantified and disseminated to practitioners throughout the district. Our initial focus on studying schools that had met district goals and highlighting "what works" was strategic; we wanted to generate goodwill and social capital that could be leveraged to propose a more rigorous experimental study of restorative practices. Indeed, school leaders were enthusiastic about sharing what worked in their schools and eagerly welcomed the chance to share their strategies for success. The positive focus of this phase of our work, on successful practices in schools, also strengthened the resolve of Collaborative members who work in policy environments where, typically, the emphasis is on what schools are doing wrong.

Together, these studies identified the following key factors that strengthen schoolwide delivery of restorative practices and allied approaches:

- Inclusive and tiered protocols for responding to misbehavior that start with universal classroom-based strategies such as co-constructing and modeling expectations or affective statements; then connect consistently misbehaving students to additional supports through modalities such as peace circles, mediation, or counseling; and, finally, rely on punitive and exclusionary discipline only as a last resort.
- Full-time, site-based coordinators who specialize in restorative practices, school culture building, and/or social-emotional learning.
- Universal professional learning, training, and coaching that strengthen staff members' awareness of restorative practices, classroom management, racial inequalities, and implicit bias.
- Emphasis on relationship building between students and all school adults through strategies such as home visits, advisory periods, greetings, and classroom-based, grade-level, or schoolwide morning meetings.
- High ratio of support service providers to students, including social workers, psychologists, counselors, youth development workers, and family liaisons.
- District resources such as policy frameworks that encourage the use of therapeutic and RIs in response to perceived misbehavior, consultations with central office coordinators of school discipline and restorative practices, and the provision of professional development units on restorative practices, equity, and culturally responsive instruction.

Results from each study were described in two public reports (Anyon, 2016; Anyon, Wiley, et al., 2016) and a manuscript currently in press (Wiley et al., in press). Building upon these findings, the partnership team is currently leading a study involving qualitative participant observations at a smaller number of schools. We aim to synthesize findings from each phase of our partnership to develop a user-friendly tool that practitioners and researchers can use to assess readiness and implementation quality of the interconnected schoolwide approaches most utilized in the district.

Expanding Resources for Restorative Practices in the District

In addition to providing more support for ongoing strategies such as school-based professional development on restorative practices, phase 3 partnership research supported several new policies and practices. First, findings were incorporated into trainings of social workers and psychologists. Results were also integrated into electronic training modules on school discipline for new discipline building leaders. In 2016, the district secured $15 million through a local mill levy for social-emotional learning and restorative practice coordinators, among other support services highlighted in the Spotlight on Success report. Most recently, the district was awarded an Expelled and At-Risk Student Services grant from the Colorado Department of Education to strengthen and expand restorative practices in DPS schools, for which the lead author serves as a consultant.

Community Engagement in Efforts to Secure More Resources for the Partnership

The Collaborative worked together to write several federal grant proposals that would strengthen the RPP and support expansion of restorative practices district-wide. Although the proposals were not funded, they provided the conceptual foundation for what is now known as the Denver School-Based Restorative Practices Partnership, which includes DPS, Padres, DCTA, the National Education Association, and the Advancement Project. GSSW faculty and students serve as the partnership's evaluation team as part of the broader partnership research agenda. The mission of this coalition of racial justice, education, labor, and community groups is to ensure widespread and high-quality implementation of restorative practices in Denver and beyond through the creation of an implementation guide for schools, a national visitation program, and a local school mentoring initiative. This initiative involves three schools in Denver with a long-standing history of being restorative that are also committed to addressing issues of equity in education (these schools constituted the sample for the Anyon 2016 report) mentoring three other sites that want to strengthen their implementation of the approach.

Discussion: Lessons and Tensions

Like other place-based partnerships, the RPP in Denver aimed to be mutually beneficial to both researchers and practitioners (Coburn et al., 2013). Three additional factors uniquely contributed to the sustainability and impact of our work:

luck, the characteristics of collaborators who represented diverse interest groups, and the mixed blessing of receiving only internal funding.

Reciprocity

The partnership was mutualistic and reciprocally beneficial for all parties involved. On the district and community side, working with a university partner granted legitimacy to advocates' and central office administrators' efforts with building-based educators. Researchers provided a voice for ideas that were not always taken seriously when espoused by district officials or Padres organizers (echoing a partner's belief that "you can't be a prophet in your own land"). Having information available to complicate and challenge the myths that were persisting in the district around student misbehavior, alternatives to suspension, and the potential for school improvement proved to be powerful. Surprisingly for the research team, the ability to refer to peer-reviewed articles that were specific to the district was especially useful for maximizing the credibility of some district initiatives. Moreover, our RPP was able to acknowledge strengths and accomplishments, in addition to challenges or problems, thus rejuvenating—and showing respect for—practitioners who are regularly asked to change their behavior. In several ways, the evidence we gathered provided credibility for good practices rather than just undermining negative approaches, as is often the case when studying equity issues.

The research partners benefited in that they gained access to large administrative datasets that are favored by many peer-reviewed journals, with variables that were of theoretical and empirical relevance to the field. (However, junior faculty on the team had to be willing to compromise publication timelines on a tenure clock—the time from acceptance of an assistant professorship to the tenure application—and a more easily fundable research agenda for the sake of meeting the needs of the RPP. Both were especially difficult to justify without external resources.) The partnership was also fertile training ground for Ph.D. students in conducting community-engaged research, from generating strategies for diplomacy when working with multiple stakeholder groups to addressing concerns about practitioner-friendly language in public dissemination of research methods and findings. Such a focus allowed students who did not necessarily share substantive areas of interest with the lead faculty member to remain interested and invested at different stages of the partnership. Finally, the involvement of master's level students allowed them to see how research can inform policies and practices that may improve the lives of students throughout the school district, particularly in the context of a turbulent political landscape. Students reported that this experience was more fulfilling than typical research assistantships because they learned how scholarship can be a tool for promoting social justice, which ultimately led several students from underrepresented groups to consider research careers for the first time.

Kismet

Introductions between partnership team members were essentially serendipitous and generally the result of existing personal relationships. The first introduction was facilitated by a new clinical faculty member from GSSW who had previously worked in DPS, attended a lecture by the lead author, and identified overlapping research interests. The partnership also happened to be addressing discipline gaps during a time (2012–2017) when related issues of racial profiling and police brutality were taking center stage in national conversations about racial equity, and thus resonated with many of us at an emotional level as well as intellectual and programmatic levels.

Characteristics of Collaborators

Partnership team members shared several key attributes, including a common sense of urgency, passion, and commitment to eliminating racial disparities in school discipline, that may help explain the emerging successes of the partnership. These characteristics supported an unusual willingness to stretch outside of traditional roles, take risks, and persist in the face of setbacks such as unfunded grant applications. For example, given the politically charged nature of racial equity issues in education, district partners were remarkably unafraid of airing the district's "dirty laundry" in terms of disparities in exclusionary discipline practices. They reported that their jobs were not to make the district look good, to obscure internal fissures, or protect their positions; instead, it was to fight for the mission of educational justice. Our partners felt this was an issue of integrity and accountability; just as students have learning objectives, the district had a mandate for data-driven decision-making. The superintendent publicly stated his interest in transparency and a desire not to "hide from the data," so our partners' value on research was certainly supported by central office norms. Still, above and beyond ideas about evidence-based policy was a recognition that fear constrains one's ability to think creatively and, as co-author Eldridge Greer remarked, "If you're going to lose your job, it should be for something that makes a difference."

Likewise, the RPP and the Collaborative were opportunities for the research team to live their values and commitment to public service scholarship. Fortunately, faculty members' involvement in the partnership was consistent with DU's strategic initiatives to become a great private university dedicated to the public good through community-engaged teaching, research, and service. On the community side, advocates had to show willingness to engage with district officials in new ways that were not always consistent with traditional community organizing tactics. Building trust with the targets of their campaigns could call into question where they stood in the movement; instead, they profited from these relationships, leveraging them to fundraise and otherwise advance their organizational profiles and missions. In particular, the Collaborative revealed the possibility that groups politically at odds with one another can come together, sitting side by side to guide our research agendas.

Other personal attributes that proved invaluable to the functioning of the RPP and the Collaborative were genuine curiosity, a desire to learn and understand, and an openness to new ideas or ways of thinking about a problem. A partnership that involved a variety of stakeholder groups was essential toward this end: community members, district officials, and researchers all had different perspectives and ways of knowing that had to be negotiated in order to be successful. Indeed, this is a central benefit of RPPs. Without the distinct roles of each partner or collaborator, there is a tendency to speak only to niche audiences that are within each one's existing professional networks. Furthermore, though our partnership may mirror others in terms of having multiple types of organizations involved, it also proved critical that we had individuals at multiple levels of each organization at the table: the executive director and director of youth organizing, in the case of Padres; coordinator, managerial, and director-level staff from the district; and the president and field organizers from DCTA. The inclusion of individuals reflecting different levels of leadership ensured that conversations about our research were never too far removed from those working in school buildings, nor would their implications be unsupported by those in administration.

The Double-Edged Sword of Funding

Lack of external funding (the partnership did benefit from several internal awards that had rapid response timelines) was a challenge for the partnership on several fronts. Without it, intervention research, randomized trials, and extensive qualitative research were not possible. It also created challenges to sustainability. All RPPs require extraordinary effort in order to have an impact: researchers have to communicate their methods and theoretical frameworks in new ways, whereas practitioners must be willing to help scholars make sense of complex policy and data systems. Without additional funding, everyone on the partnership team or in the Collective had to essentially volunteer their time in kind, as the possibility of "buying out" teaching or practice time was precluded.

However, our financial independence was also a source of agility. The process of building an authentic community-university partnership should fundamentally be an organic one, yet most federal and private funding streams (even those focused on RPPs) require the articulation of well-specified research questions, methods, and goals many months before implementation. Such structures do not allow for the kind of dynamism necessary to rapidly respond to new findings, relationships, and political contexts. The abilities of a partnership team to bring together historically opposing stakeholders, or to teach each partner to find value in one another's strengths and contributions, is not valued by funding agencies to the same degree as methodological rigor. Flexibility on the part of all parties can allow for creativity and innovation to take hold, which can create new trajectories for partnership efforts that may produce unanticipated positive results, such as qualitative research in our case. More flexible and nontraditional funding mechanisms are needed, particularly in the context of partnerships between universities that are not research intensive, where faculty have relatively high teaching loads, and urban districts under local control where central office administrators are responsible for hundreds of schools, the majority of which serve low-income students and are sorely under-resourced.

Conclusion

The overall trajectory of this RPP was to begin by examining dominant narratives about the problem of practice, then to identify a promising intervention and assess the stages of its implementation, and finally, to highlight the conditions under which implementation was strengthened. With a focus on both challenges and opportunities, our collective efforts grew over time and were sustainable without external funding. This sustainability was largely due to the involvement of individuals at multiple levels, from multiple stakeholder groups, who held an unwavering commitment to educational equity and were embedded in institutions whose cultural norms were consonant with the values of RPPs.

The trajectory of our partnership is consistent with much of the literature on RPPs but also suggests a need for RPPs to increase their community engagement in order to expand their reach and impact, especially when focused on equity issues. In Denver, when we expanded the number of community collaborators involved in our partnership, we began to witness measurable impacts of our work on local policies. It should not come as a surprise that complex problems of practice require multifaceted partnership arrangements that involve a variety of stakeholders in order to be impactful. However, these complicated power dynamics require extra attention to competing local beliefs and constantly shifting relationships. Researchers who wish to engage in this work should focus on identifying partners who are passionate about the topic at hand and willing to collaborate without external funding, at least initially. Funders who wish to support this work would be wise to provide resources to longer standing partnerships that have a track record of community engagement and are willing to invest time in trust-building activities that go well beyond the scope of traditional research.

References

Anyon, Y. (2009). Sociological theories of learning disabilities: Understanding racial disproportionality in special education. *Journal of Human Behavior in the Social Environment*, *19*, 44–57.

Anyon, Y. (2016). *Taking restorative practices school-wide: Insights from three schools in Denver, CO:* Denver School-Based Restorative Justice Partnership.

Anyon, Y., & Fernández, M. A. (2007). Realizing the potential of community-university partnerships. *Change, 39,* 40–45.

Anyon, Y., Gregory, A., Stone, S., Farrar, J., Jenson, J., Greer, E., Downing, B., & Simmons, J. (2016). Restorative interventions and school discipline sanctions in a large urban school district. *American Educational Research Journal, 53*, 1663–1697.

Anyon, Y., Jenson, J., Altschul, I., Farrar, J., McQueen, J., Greer, E., Downing, B., & Simmons, J. (2014). The persistent effect of race and the promise of alternatives to suspension in school discipline outcomes. *Children and Youth Services Review, 44*, 379–386.

Anyon, Y., McQueen, J., Jenson, J., Altschul, I., Farrar, J., Greer, E., Downing, B., & Simmons, J. (2013). *School discipline trends in Denver public schools: 2008–2012.* Denver, CO: Division of Student Equity and Opportunity, Denver Public Schools.

Anyon, Y., Wiley, K., Yang, J., Pauline, M., Grapentine, J., Valladares, G., . . . Pisciotta, L. (2016). *Spotlight on success: Changing the culture of discipline in Denver public schools.* Denver, CO: Office of Social and Emotional Learning, Division of Student Equity and Opportunity, Denver Public Schools.

Anyon, Y., Yang, J., Farrar, J., McQueen, J., Jenson, J., Greer, E., Downing, B., & Simmons, J. (2014). *Denver public schools accountability report: Update on racial disparities in school discipline.* Denver, CO: Division of Student Equity and Opportunity, Denver Public Schools.

Coburn, C. E., Penuel, W., & Geil, K. (2013). *Research–practice partnerships: A strategy for leveraging research for educational improvement in school districts.* New York: William T. Grant Foundation.

Honig, M. I., & Coburn, C. E. (2008). Evidence-based decision making in school district central offices: toward a policy and research agenda. *Educational Policy, 22*, 578–608.

Lhamon, C., & Samuels, J. (2014). *Dear colleague letter on the nondiscriminatory administration of school discipline.* Washington, D.C.: U.S. Department of Education Office of Civil Rights & U.S. Department of Justice Civil Rights Division.

Losen, D. J., & Gillespie, J. (2012). *Opportunities suspended: The disparate impact of disciplinary exclusion from school.* Los Angeles, CA: The Civil Rights Project.

Padres & Jóvenes Unidos. (2011). *A community analysis of the implementation of the 2008 Denver school discipline policy.* Denver, CO: The Advancement Project.

Skiba, R. S., Mediratta, K., & Rausch, K. (Eds.) (2016). *Inequality in school discipline: Research and practice to reduce disparities.* E-book: Palgrave Macmillan.

Wandersman, A., Duffy, J., Flaspohler, P., Noonan, R., Lubell, K., Stillman, L., . . . Saul, J. (2008). Bridging the gap between prevention research and practice: The interactive systems framework for dissemination and implementation. *American Journal of Community Psychology, 41*, 171–181.

The White House. (2016). *The continuing need to rethink discipline.* Retrieved from www.whitehouse.gov/sites/default/files/docs/school_discipline_report_-_120916.pdf

United States Department of Education. (2011). *Secretary Duncan, Attorney General Holder announce effort to respond to school-to-prison pipeline by supporting good discipline practices* [Press release].

Wiley, K., Anyon, Y., Yang, J., Rosch, A., Valladares, G., Cash, D., . . . Pisciotta, L. (in press). Looking back, moving forward: technical, normative, and political dimensions of school discipline. *Educational Administration Quarterly.*

PART III
Expanding Models of RPPs

6

RETHINKING "THE COMMUNITY" IN UNIVERSITY–COMMUNITY PARTNERSHIPS

Case Studies From CU Engage

Ben Kirshner, Jennifer Pacheco, Manuela Stewart Sifuentes, and Roudy Hildreth

Community engagement has become a floating signifier—benign enough to be acceptable to anyone, vague enough to mean anything. Universities and school districts tend to have offices for community outreach and engagement, but who or what gets counted as "community" and how "engagement" gets put into practice vary considerably. In this chapter, we complicate our views of community and argue for an approach to research–practice partnerships (RPPs) that invites people directly affected by educational injustices to participate in analyzing their root causes and generating strategies to address them. This approach challenges paternalistic views of young people and deficit-based narratives about low-income communities of color, seeks to broaden who participates, and is attentive to issues of power.

The participatory approach we describe overlaps with key elements of RPPs, such as their effort to broaden participation in educational research, their emphasis on relationship building for successful partnerships, and their commitment to producing research that is relevant to practice (Coburn, Penuel, & Geil, 2013; Gutiérrez & Penuel, 2014). Our approach elevates the democratic potential of RPPs through its emphasis on reaching beyond those with professional credentials when identifying problems of practice. RPPs are about more than just technical improvement; they represent a moral commitment to expand who gets to be in the room to define consequential decisions about policy and practice.

To advance our argument, we draw on community engagement and organizing scholarship that critiques traditional patterns of university outreach and offers alternative approaches. We then illustrate efforts to put these approaches into practice with three examples from our work with the University of Colorado Boulder's CU Engage: Center for Community-Based Learning and Research. We share what we have learned about a critical participatory method for engagement that seeks to develop partnerships with those adversely affected by inequality.

Theorizing Equitable University–Community Partnerships

Critical Perspectives on Outreach and Service

University-based community outreach and engagement efforts have a troubled history (Fine, 2012; Hill-Jackson & Lewis, 2011; Patel, 2016; Tilley-Lubbs, 2009). When framed in terms of a university–community binary, the word *community* tends to flatten and homogenize those whom outreach aims to serve (Cruz & Giles, 2000). This becomes problematic when universities position a non-profit executive director as capable of speaking for their membership or when universities assume homogeneity in a population that is in fact quite diverse (Gutiérrez & Rogoff, 2003). The university–community binary can also be distancing for university staff and students because it implies that universities are not themselves communities and are not a part of the surrounding community. Such a framing can reinforce the notion that universities are not complicit in the broader systems of relations that construct certain neighborhoods as impoverished or gentrifying.

A closely related problem in discourses of community engagement is the unstated premise that people in "the community" lack something or are in need of help. Although a helping impulse may be some people's starting point for socially engaged work, it can quickly become poisonous if saturated with deep-seated racist ideologies prevalent in the United States (Bonilla-Silva, 2014). Deficit thinking about Black and Latino/a families is particularly common in education partnerships focused on achievement or parent involvement (Valencia, 2010). Myths about parents' lack of interest in their children's education or their alleged inability to provide adequate guidance to their children get reproduced in everyday discourse among social service providers and educators (Park, 2005; Riojas-Cortez & Bustos Flores, 2009; Volk & Long, 2005). Too often, university outreach treats the symptoms of complex problems rather than their deeper systemic causes (Butin, 2003; Ginwright & Cammarota, 2002; Marullo & Edwards, 2000; Mitchell, 2008).

Another problem identified in the literature is that, despite the best of intentions, outreach efforts often fail the test of reciprocity and mutuality in their work with community partners (Holland, 2005). For instance, the literature on parent engagement has produced long-standing findings about problems that arise for family-school partnerships when institutional agents do not adjust meeting times or locations to accommodate the daily routines of working families (Souto-Manning & Swick, 2009). Modes of discourse and language use, if not carried out in a participatory or inclusive way, can alienate or marginalize (Booker & Goldman, 2016; O'Connor, Hanny, & Lewis, 2011). Scheduling can be a problem when students or faculty are only available during the university semester, which may not correspond to the work cycles of community groups.

Promising Approaches

In recognition of the limitations of university outreach efforts described in the previous section, scholars and activists have increasingly sought alternative approaches to community engagement. Community-based participatory research (CBPR), perhaps most common in the public health field, offers a set of principles and practices for research partnerships that co-construct knowledge in solidarity with those struggling against education inequality or institutional racism. Community organizing, with origins in the civil rights movement and other social change movements, emphasizes strategies for addressing issues of power, self-interest, and coalition building.

Community-Based Participatory Research

CBPR engages researchers and community members in working collaboratively to identify questions, gather and analyze data, and generate social change strategies, recognizing that each party has a unique set of strengths to contribute (Fals-Borda, 1987; Wallerstein & Duran, 2008). CBPR projects bring people together with varied training and expertise, working collectively in mutually beneficial ways, on research studies that address public challenges (Strand, Marullo, Cutforth, Stoecker, & Donohue, 2003). This approach underscores a larger public vision of universities as devoting some portion of their research activities to understanding, explaining, and helping solve challenges and needs identified with community members. In the field of public health especially, CBPR is viewed as an effective strategy for gathering data relevant to addressing structural issues that contribute to health disparities (Israel et al., 2010).

CBPR is also a promising method in education contexts, particularly for extending the RPP methodology to a broader range of stakeholders, such as youth and parents. (We use CBPR here as an umbrella term that also includes participatory action research, which tends to be more common in education; e.g., Cammarota & Fine, 2008.) This approach is consistent with sociocultural theories of learning that build on family funds of knowledge and critical race theory perspectives that emphasize the multiple kinds of capital and expertise that exist in communities of color (Gonzalez, Moll, & Amanti, 2005; Ladson-Billings, 2000; Yosso, 2005).

Community Organizing

Community organizing represents a tradition going back to Ella Baker, Myles Horton, and other civil rights and labor rights organizers to build power in marginalized communities (Kwon, 2013; Warren & Mapp, 2011). Although varied in their orienting strategies and principles, organizing groups share a commitment to mobilizing excluded or marginalized populations in campaigns that challenge injustice, build collective power, and hold public institutions accountable (Su, 2009).

Although centers housed in public universities experience institutional constraints on the kinds of organizing they do, several insights and practices are relevant to community engagement work. First, community organizing groups typically have a clear-headed analysis of how power shapes public interactions and the uptake of research evidence. Research adoption is not merely a technical decision based on impartial weighing of evidence, especially when it confronts entrenched interests or requires those with power to give up privileged opportunities (Renée, Welner, & Oakes, 2010). This is why it is important for RPPs to have broad participation from stakeholders, including teachers, families, and students, who can advocate for their interests and goals when it comes to the way research is utilized. A second insight pertains to the notion of self-interest. Organizers are critical of the savior mentality sometimes found in service learning (Smith, 2011). They work *with*, not *for*. Membership campaigns begin with in-depth relational meetings that not only build trust but also try to surface people's dreams for themselves and their families and the barriers that get in their way. Universities, too, need to be transparent about their self-interests, such as those associated with producing research, as they enter into and maintain partnerships.

CU Engage: Center for Community-Based Learning and Research

Launched in July 2014, CU Engage supports programs and initiatives that work collaboratively with community groups to address complex public challenges, guided by values of democracy, equity, and reciprocity. CU Engage is based in the School of Education and serves the whole CU Boulder campus. It represents the campus's effort to coordinate and sustain its various community engagement efforts in one academic unit.

Because CU Engage is a community engagement center at a predominately White research university located in a county with stark income inequalities, staff have proceeded with awareness of the problems associated with efforts by universities to "improve" communities or "solve" public problems. CU Engage has sought to draw on the insights described in the prior literature. This means, for example, embracing a broader and more democratic conception of knowledge production found in CBPR, which values the insights and experiences of people outside university walls. It also means drawing on notions of participatory democracy and community organizing, which recognize people's rights to participate in decisions that affect their lives (Freire, 1970; Levine, 2013). CU Engage seeks to cultivate and sustain partnerships that enable those most directly impacted by injustice or inequality to participate in identifying causes and solutions to problems of practice.

Cases

We discuss CU Engage's approach to partnerships in three short cases. Each reflects a different part of the broader ecosystem in which CU Engage works, with shared commitment to broadening who is defined as part of the community and co-producing knowledge in democratic or dialogic spaces. The first two cases discuss partnerships with members of the university community. The third reflects our efforts to respond to evidence of education disparities in the surrounding communities through work with Latino/a parents.

Participatory Action Research With Undergraduate Students

In its early days as a center, CU Engage sought to avoid the problematic tendencies associated with service learning, such as being uncritical about the risks of saviorism or being inaccessible to students whose multiple jobs limited their time for community-based activities. We also suspected that many students of color and students from low-income families engaged in their communities, such as returning home on weekends to volunteer with their church, but this work went unrecognized because it occurred outside typical structures at the university. We did not want to reproduce existing dynamics of power and privilege with regard to community engagement opportunities on campus. This, then, was a *problem of practice* that we faced as a new center: How do we deepen the culture of community engagement on campus and design programs that are accessible and inviting to a broader population of CU students? How might we make visible and consequential the diverse forms of public service that students perform?

Consistent with the ethos of CBPR, we sought to develop a collaborative research partnership with students who might have special insight into this issue by virtue of their experiences on campus. Ben Kirshner (first author), who initiated the project, sought to recruit people who participated in organizations serving students of color or students from marginalized groups, who were not already active in current civic engagement programs, and who showed interest in issues of leadership, inclusion, or community. This effort to go beyond existing service learning students meant reaching outside existing networks. Ben met the student who ended up being a lead organizer of the participatory research team, for example, while waiting for a bus to the airport: it just so happened that a group of student members of the African Students' Association were heading to another university for a conference. The association's president expressed interest in the project and signed on. Soon after that, she recruited new members with interests in social justice and community engagement.

Students showed interest in this topic, and the initial group, together with a graduate student research assistant, wrote and secured an Undergraduate Research Opportunities Program grant that provided modest stipends for students, offered institutional legitimacy, and enabled students to gain research experience. The composition of the group evolved over time, starting with an initial team of three, expanding to six, and then contracting to four after two students graduated.

The project was facilitated by a graduate student who took time to build trust in the group and develop democratic routines and practices. Meetings typically began with personal check-ins that left room for open discussions of experiences on campus. An especially powerful meeting took place the morning after the Ferguson, Missouri, grand jury decision not to indict police officer Darren Wilson in the shooting of African American teenager Michael Brown. The group suspended its agenda to process members' emotions about what was happening in Ferguson and how it related to their experiences on the campus. Creating democratic practices was also essential. For example, the group rotated facilitators, guided by the graduate advisor who met in advance to coach students on how to design an agenda and facilitate meetings. This collaborative approach led to participants redefining the focus of the study as they started developing research questions—rather than just focusing on opportunities for civic engagement on campus, they shifted toward researching issues of campus climate in general, across a range of student co-curricular programs.

After interviewing peers through a snowball sampling method, the group analyzed data over multiple meetings and identified several findings and recommendations, which they presented to a packed room of campus leadership, faculty, and student peers. Student researchers shared evidence about varied types of student civic engagement, features of safe and unsafe spaces, and strategies for building on community cultural wealth. Evidence of "spotlighting," for example, in which instructors or peers placed unwanted attention on a student of color during class discussions, resonated with people in the audience and elicited follow-up questions and comments. As important as the findings themselves are, we also attribute the enthusiastic response from people in the packed room to the fact that students were leading the conversation about problems with campus climate and how to change it. The positive reception fueled further work on a report, titled "Students of Color Are Motivated Agents of Change: Why Aren't We Joining Your Programs?" (Arreola Pena et al., 2015). In addition, through their own networking, students organized presentations for two campus student support services groups. These student-initiated efforts led to an invitation from the university's Ethnic Minority Affairs Committee to organize a campus-wide event on racial and ethnic inclusion, which received positive feedback and informed subsequent campus diversity training for faculty and staff.

This project offers an example of how CU Engage, in its first year, sought to redefine *community* by starting with students on the CU campus from marginalized groups. The group sought to shift the narrative about civic engagement and student leadership on campus by generating insight and knowledge from those whose experiences and achievements had been excluded from that narrative. By using research as a primary method, the approach was aligned to the core mission of the university, which may have helped the project gain traction with staff and faculty.

CU Dialogues

The presence of a blue-collar workforce, operating in the shadows and often silent, is taken for granted on many college campuses. At our university, people of color and recent immigrants serving meals, cutting the grass, or cleaning the restrooms stand out in contrast to the relatively small numbers of people of color on the faculty or in senior leadership. In their work with residential academic programs, instructors Ellen Aiken and Karen Ramirez learned that custodial staff worked in residence halls with students, but had little means to build community with those students. For Aiken and Ramirez, this became an issue of equity. How could custodial staff be more effectively included in the university community? How might dialogues improve workplace conditions for staff and student learning through better relations between custodians and students?

CU Dialogues was founded in 2007 in part to address these questions. The mission of the program is to "enhance the educational experience at CU-Boulder by engaging diverse communities within the University in open conversation with one another" (www.colorado.edu/cudialogues/about-us). Dialogues bring together diverse groups to discuss issues such as immigration, gender identity, income inequality, and diversity and inclusion. Dialogues in residence halls also address what it means to live together and how student behavior can impact the work of custodial staff. Building a partnership with the Housing Facilities Services (HFS) staff has been instrumental in bringing more voices into the conversation. Participation by staff is voluntary; supervisors facilitate participation by giving staff paid "release time" to participate.

The success of the Dialogues program, measured in terms of demand from varied campus units and survey responses from dialogue participants, has led to more stable funding and institutional support. Dialogue has become incorporated into the university's "action plan" for fostering cross-cultural understanding and, in 2013, the CU Dialogues program received the President's Diversity Award.

The partnership with HFS, however, is not without tensions and challenges. A tension exists, for example, between CU Dialogues' open-ended, long-term goals of building mutual understanding and the goals of some custodial staff for the dialogues to reduce disrespectful behavior by students in the short term. Because dialogues are often one-time events, even if the student participants shift their understanding and recognition of the custodial staff as members of their residential community, this may not fundamentally change the culture of the residence hall, resulting in cleaner bathrooms and less vandalism, for example.

Power dynamics in the classroom have presented additional challenges for ensuring that community participants are treated and viewed equitably. Addressing issues as they arise has been an important part of the process. Dialogues staff work intentionally to disrupt these power imbalances by holding regular conversations with the custodial staff. Program Coordinator and Facilitator Pilar Prostko attends HFS staff meetings to build relationships, discuss upcoming dialogues, and hear staff suggestions for topics. The relationships she developed have been essential for staff interest and therefore sustainability of residence hall dialogues. As a result of the meetings, some suggestions from staff included holding dialogues where they work and not only in "student spaces," using name tags for all participants, wearing clothing other than work uniforms, and attending to unequal levels of "risk" for custodial staff during dialogues. Practical costs of participation, such as sometimes having to make up work missed while participating in dialogues, were also brought up as tensions.

The role of custodial staff has been further refined through the assessment and evaluation process. Staff surveys are given after each dialogue; yearly surveys are filled out during the appreciation luncheon, and interviews surface important feedback. During the fall of 2015, Dialogues program staff interviewed five HFS staff members, two supervisors, and one administrator about what was working well and what needed to change. Staff responses revealed that an academic agenda had begun to drive the design of the dialogues. Staff felt that when professors chose topics to enhance their curriculum or meet the learning needs of their students, this didn't always take into account the needs of the staff. Staff wanted more of a role in determining topics and directing conversation. In response, CU Dialogues facilitators worked with staff in a number of ways, such as finding strategies to enable staff to attend dialogues on topics of interest to them, distributing participation more evenly across work teams, and including supervisors in dialogues. Facilitators also worked with HFS staff to develop a new list of topics to be offered during the 2016–2017 school year.

This Dialogues case offers an example of redefining *community* to include custodial staff and approaching the work in ways that are attentive to power relationships and people's different goals for participation. As the program evolves, at its heart remains a commitment to creating opportunities for all members of the university community to take more public roles in campus life and planning. This began with dialogic encounters between students and staff aimed at humanizing both parties for each other and has led to new initiatives at the unit level. As part of the university's Inclusive Excellence initiative, dialogues have been held solely for grounds and custodial staff with the purpose of building understanding about differences. Though not a formal mechanism for policy formation, it represents a beginning step toward including broader participation in workplace and campus culture.

This case underscores the importance of self-evaluation and being reflexive about whether the partnership is meeting everyone's needs. By conducting internal evaluations with custodial staff, Dialogues found that some aspects of the program had drifted from an initial goal of improving workplace relations between staff and students. This active seeking of feedback created opportunities for program revisions and renewed mutuality.

Parent Engagement Through CBPR

The City of Lafayette is the third largest municipality in Boulder County with a population of 28,278 (City of Lafayette, 2016). Approximately 39% of students in Lafayette schools are Hispanic/Latino, and 20% are English language learners (ELLs). Over 41% of students in Lafayette schools qualify for the free or reduced-price lunch program, compared with 20% for the district as a whole (Colorado Department of Education, 2015). The University of Colorado, including CU Engage, has been active in Lafayette schools, particularly those that have higher populations of Latino/a students and students from low-income families. Programs include afterschool tutoring, youth empowerment, and mentoring. In recognition that even high-quality programs were not designed to address systemic disparities in opportunities to learn, CU Engage sought to cultivate new kinds of partnerships with parents from diverse Latino/a communities. This parent engagement project is still in its early stages, focused on building relationships with residents who might be interested in joining a CBPR project.

The first step was to get to know the area and the people in it in a more personal and humanizing way. Jennifer Pacheco (second author) spoke with Latino/a parents about their experiences in schools and institutions. Pacheco's conversations revealed various themes that parents identified as concerning, such as ESL tracking, not feeling welcome in their children's school, and the underrepresentation of their children in Advanced Placement classes and the International Baccalaureate program. Building on these relationships, as well as those cultivated by Manuela Stewart Sifuentes (third author), CU Engage's Director of Community Partnerships, Jennifer and Manuela began inviting Spanish-speaking Latino/a immigrant parents to explore the idea of a CBPR project addressing systemic barriers to Latino/a, undocumented, and/or first-generation students' successful participation in schools. Such a project would offer the chance to learn from the knowledge that already resided within networks of Latino/a parents and families. Further, the schools and school district had been seeking new ways to involve immigrant and Spanish-speaking parents, and we saw a potential future role in supporting that effort.

Manuela and Jennifer started by using the format of a *cafecito*, an informal gathering with coffee and cookies to build relationships and explore possible project ideas. In planning and running these cafecitos, which are still under way as of this writing, we've sought alternatives to typical professional norms for meetings. For example, we schedule the cafecitos at times that work best for the parents, which is often Friday evenings. We meet after-hours at a community center—as opposed to the library or a coffee shop—to provide privacy for parents to share their experiences. The meetings are held in Spanish and avoid academic jargon whenever possible. In addition to this commitment to flexibility and responsiveness to parents' daily work and family routines, we also have continued to prioritize steady and deliberate relationship building rather than rushing quickly into a project.

Despite—or perhaps in response to—our emphasis that this project be parent-led, at the third cafecito, one of the parents expressed confusion about what CU Engage was aiming to get out of the project. This question about CU Engage's aims evoked the issue raised in the community organizing literature about the importance of articulating self-interest and the risks of claiming to do things *for* others. It prompted conversations on our team about what our motives were and how to articulate those in authentic ways with our research partners at subsequent meetings. As we write this chapter, we are working with parents to decide on the best next steps for a CBPR project.

This case, which is still in its formative stages, shows that we sought to redefine who or what counts as "the community" by connecting with parents outside of an existing nongovernmental organization, school committee, or civic structure. This decision, although posing some logistical and organizational challenges, reflected a need that we perceived to invite new voices into the conversation about educational access and equity and center the research on local knowledge. It also reflected an effort to complement more conventional university outreach efforts, such as service learning or academic support in schools, with participatory research that has more of a policy and systems focus. Such work becomes more explicitly "political" as it gets into issues of power and education policy. This is a place where the university may be able to play a role as catalyst and broker for important and critical conversations that lead to policies that are more just and responsive to the goals and needs of marginalized families.

Discussion

We shared three examples of community partnerships—participatory action research with undergraduate students, dialogues, and parent engagement—that define *community* in different ways. These projects reflect an effort to inject precision into the term *community* for theoretical, practical, and ethical reasons. We want to encourage universities and school districts engaged in community partnerships to adopt more expansive and layered conceptions of community that emphasize cultural funds of knowledge and seek out the perspectives of those most adversely affected by inequalities. This effort is important not just because it offers a more accurate description of the people who make up communities but also because of its practical value for working with those whose daily experiences position them to be experts in defining and addressing complex public challenges. At the same time that we see practical value, we caution that participatory approaches are not always more efficient, nor should their justification rest primarily on instrumental reasons. We also see an ethical imperative for fostering partnerships that honor people's right to participate in public decisions that affect their lives.

In this final section, we name core themes that cut across the case studies and that we believe offer practical guidance for RPPs, particularly those that aim to broaden their reach to communities struggling against structural inequality.

Emergent Principles

Go Beyond the Usual Suspects

The three cases showed efforts to seek partnerships with specific types of stake-holders who were not already part of defining problems of practice at the university. CU Dialogues offers a particularly valuable example of what it looks like to redefine community. Rather than locating community outside of the university in a way that creates distance and detachment, CU Dialogues sought to expand who is recognized as a member of the campus community. Similarly, the recent parent engagement work aimed to develop a new collective outside of existing channels, such as PTAs or NGOs, in order to reach out to parents who were not already part of decision-making or policy advocacy networks.

Embody Democratic Practices

Each of the three projects sought consistency between aspirations around partici-patory democracy and the conduct of the group. If the goal is to broaden who participates in policy decisions, then the place to start is with the practices that govern the group itself. We hoped to foster partnerships that had transparent and clear decision-making practices, allowed room for disagreement and dissent, and valued practices of listening and openness. In participatory action research with students, for example, this meant rotating facilitators and creating visible decision-making routines that offered room for changes in direction. CU Dialogues, simi-larly, offered a clear structure that enabled people to hear and be heard across lines of difference.

Critical Perspectives

A key theme across the cases is an effort to denaturalize or question existing patterns of privilege and marginalization (Fine, 2012). This critical perspective started by asking questions about why certain norms or patterns exist and chal-lenging assumptions about what counts as engagement or who counts as part of the community. It also included an effort to focus on systems rather than individ-ual people or programs (Ginwright & Cammarota, 2002). The CBPR work with parents, in particular, intentionally focuses on systemic disparities in opportunities to learn along lines of race, language, and immigration status, rather than solely focusing on the empowerment or learning of individual parents. Fixing systems, not people, is a guiding principle.

Work With Systems and Coalitions

At the same time that a participatory approach needs to take a critical look at systems as a whole, we see value in building toward institutional change. CU Engage can leverage its role to foster participation and communication across or within institutions. The student participatory action research project, for example, gained traction by leading workshops for campus advisors and linking its agenda to broader institutional change goals. So, too, with the parent engagement project. Although it is still in its early stages, we hope to leverage the status associated with the university to create opportunities for parents to present research findings and engage in discussions with key decision-makers. As we pursue this work, we are mindful that certain changes may require external pressure and community organizing (Renee et al., 2010).

Tensions

We have described these themes as principles rather than how-to procedures because they invariably encounter dilemmas and tensions that call for flexible situational thinking (Flyvbjerg, 2001). The imperative to work democratically and seek out new partners, for example, can run into challenges related to goal-setting and process. It can be hard to get people excited about a project that is not defined, which can cause false starts and present challenges to keeping people involved. Such ambiguity makes it even more important that university partners clarify their self-interests and address power relationships in emergent groups.

A closely related second tension is in people's different time horizons for taking action. Collaborative public work, such as CBPR, is often slow. This stands in tension with the real desire of parents or students to solve problems sooner rather than later. Working collaboratively requires a degree of faith that the efforts to build a democratic group will pay off in the end. Although the research phase of CBPR is a form of action, it does push the possibility of new policies or practices into the future. This tension has emerged in conversation with some of the parents we have met with, who seek quicker action to enhance educational opportunities for their children or friends' children. It has also emerged for some staff participants in the Dialogues program who seek changes to culture and climate that do not require starting over with new incoming classes of students each year.

Last but not least is a tension between taking a critical stance and working within systems. We have sought to anchor our work in an acknowledgment of structural inequality and racism, which has led us to cultivate relationships with people adversely affected by these issues and marginalized from the centers of power. We also, however, see value in trying to work within complex systems to create possibilities for meaningful change, which means engaging policymakers and institutional leaders. This vision rests on the belief that institutions can serve constituents if and when they live up to democratic ideals of mutual respect, openness, and inclusivity. Expanded participation is not a panacea; issues of power and privilege will persist. Public institutions have many different priorities and may resist collective efforts toward change. Tensions will be ongoing in the collective work to address structural inequality and institutional racism. But engaging with these tensions is central to work that fosters learning, participation, and more just public systems.

Acknowledgments

We would like to acknowledge and thank the following people, who contributed valuable feedback on earlier drafts of this chapter: Melissa Arreola Peña, Yohannese Gebremedhin, Susan Jurow, Becca Kaplan, Nurta Mohamed, Katie Raitz, and Karen Ramirez. We also appreciate the thoughtful feedback and guidance from the editors of this volume, Bronwyn Bevan and William R. Penuel.

References

Aiken, E., & Ramirez, K. (2014). Scaling up dialogues to boost engaged learning. *Academic Exchange Quarterly, 18*(4). Retrieved from www.rapidintellect.com/AEQweb/547814.pdf

Arreola Peña, M., Gebremedhin, Y., Kadima, G. K., Kaplan, R., Kirshner, B., & Raitz, K. (2015). *Students of color are motivated agents of change: Why aren't we joining your programs?* Boulder, CO: CU Engage: Center for Community-Based Learning and Research.

Bonilla-Silva, E. (2014). *Racism without racists: Color-blind racism and the persistence of racial inequality in the United States* (4th ed.). New York: Rowman & Littlefield.

Booker, A., & Goldman, S. (2016). Participatory design research as a practice for systemic repair: Doing hand-in-hand math research with families. *Cognition and Instruction, 34*(3), 223–235.

Butin, D. W. (2003). Of what use is it? Multiple conceptualizations of service learning within education. *Teachers College Record, 105*(9), 1674–1692.

Cammarota, J., & Fine, M. (Eds.) (2008). *Revolutionizing education: Youth participatory action research in motion.* New York: Routledge.

City of Lafayette. (2016). *Demographics.* Retrieved from www.cityoflafayette.com/369/Demographics

Coburn, C. E., Penuel, W. R., & Geil, K. E. (2013). *Research–practice partnerships at the district level: A strategy for leveraging research for educational improvement in school districts.* New York: William T. Grant Foundation.

Colorado Department of Education. (2015). *School dashboard demographics* [Data file]. Retrieved from www2.cde.state.co.us/schoolview/dish/schooldashboard.asp

Cruz, N., & Giles, D. E., Jr. (2000). Where's the community in service-learning research? [Special issue]. *Michigan Journal of Community Service Learning, 7*, 28–34.

Fals-Borda, O. (1987). The application of participatory action-research in Latin America. *International Sociology, 2*(4), 329–347.

Fine, M. (2012). Critical civic research. In D. Harward (Ed.), *Civic provocations* (pp. 35–41). Washington, DC: Bringing Theory to Practice Monographs.

Flyvbjerg, B. (2001). *Making social science matter: Why social inquiry fails and how it can succeed again.* Cambridge: Cambridge University Press.

Freire, P. (1970). *Pedagogy of the oppressed.* New York: Continuum.

Ginwright, S., & Cammarota, J. (2002). New terrain in youth development: The promise of a social justice approach. *Social Justice, 29*(4), 82–95.

González, N., Moll, L. C., & Amanti, C. (2005). *Funds of knowledge.* Mahwah, NJ: Lawrence Erlbaum Associates.

Gutiérrez, K. D., & Penuel, W. R. (2014). Relevance to practice as a criterion for rigor. *Educational Researcher, 43*(1), 19–23. Retrieved from https://doi.org/10.3102/0013 189X13520289

Gutiérrez, K. D., & Rogoff, B. (2003). Cultural ways of learning: Individual traits or repertoires of practice. *Educational Researcher, 32*(5), 19–25. Retrieved from http://doi.org/10.3102/0013189X13520289

Hill-Jackson, V., & Lewis, C. W. (2011). Service loitering: Service learning in an underserved community. In T. Stewart & N. S. Webster (Eds.), *Problematizing service-learning: Critical reflections for development and action* (pp. 295–324). Charlotte, NC: Information Age Publishing.

Holland, B. A. (2005). Reflections on community-campus partnerships: What has been learned? What are the next challenges? In P. A. Pasque, R. E. Smerek, B. Dwyer, N. Bowman, & B. L. Mallory (Eds.), *Higher education collaboratives for community engagement and improvement* (pp. 10–17). Ann Arbor, MI: National Forum on Higher Education for the Public Good.

Israel, B. A., Coombe, C. M., Cheezum, R. R., Schultz, A. J., McGranaghan, R. J., Lichtenstein, R., . . . Burris, A. (2010). Community-based participatory research: A capacity-building approach for policy advocacy aimed at eliminating health disparities. *American Journal of Public Health, 100*(11), 2094–2102.

Kwon, S. A. (2013). *Uncivil youth: Race, activism, and affirmative governmentality.* Durham, NC, London: Duke University Press.

Ladson-Billings, G. (2000). Racialized discourse and ethnic epistemologies. In N. Denzin & Y. Lincoln (Eds.), *Handbook of qualitative research* (2nd ed., pp. 257–277). Thousand Oaks, CA: Sage.

Levine, P. (2013). *We are the ones we have been waiting for: The promise of civic renewal in America.* New York: Oxford University Press.

Marullo, S., & Edwards, B. (2000). From charity to justice the potential of university-community collaboration for social change. *American Behavioral Scientist, 43*(5), 895–912.

Mitchell, T. (2008). Traditional vs. critical service-learning: Engaging the literature to differentiate two models. *Michigan Journal of Community Service Learning, 14*(2), 50–65.

O'Connor, K., Hanny, C., & Lewis, C. (2011). Doing "business as usual": Dynamics of voice in community organizing talk. *Anthropology & Education Quarterly, 42*(2), 154–171.

Park, Y. (2005). Culture as deficit: A critical discourse analysis of the concept of culture in contemporary social work discourse. *Journal of Sociology and Social Welfare, 32*(3), 11–34.

Patel, L. (2016). *Decolonizing educational research: From ownership to answerability.* New York: Routledge.

Renee, M., Welner, K. G., & Oakes, J. (2010). Social movement organizing and equity-focused educational change: Shifting the "zone of mediation." In A. Hargreaves, A. Fullan, D. Hopkins, & A. Lieberman (Eds.), *International handbook of educational change* (2nd ed., pp. 153–168). New York: Springer International Handbooks.

Riojas-Cortez, M., & Flores, B. B. (2009). Sin olvidar a los padres: Families collaborating within school and university partnerships. *Journal of Latinos and Education, 8*(3), 231–239.

Smith, S. (2011). Organizing 101: Lessons I wish I'd learned on campus. In N. V. Longo & C. M. Gibson (Eds.), *From command to community: A new approach to leadership education in colleges and universities* (pp. 234–256). Medford, MA: Tufts.

Souto-Manning, M., & Swick, K. J. (2009). Teachers' beliefs about parent and family involvement: Rethinking our family involvement paradigm. *Early Childhood Education Journal, 34*(2), 187–193.

Strand, K., Marullo, S., Cutforth, N., Stoecker, R., & Donohue, P. (2003). *Community-based research and higher education*. San Francisco: Jossey-Bass.

Su, C. (2009). *Streetwise for book smarts: Grassroots organizing and education reform in the Bronx.* Ithaca, NY: Cornell University Press.

Tilley-Lubbs, G. A. (2009). Good intentions pave the way to hierarchy: A retrospective autoethnographic approach. *Michigan Journal of Community Service Learning, 16*(1), 59–68.

Valencia, R. R. (2010). *Dismantling contemporary deficit thinking: Educational thought and practice.* New York: Taylor & Francis.

Volk, D., & Long, S. (2005). Challenging myths of the deficit perspective: Honoring children's literacy resources. *Young Children, 60*(6), 12.

Wallerstein, N., & Duran, B. (2008). The theoretical, historical and practice roots of CBPR. In M. Minkler & N. Wallerstein (Eds.), *Community-based participatory research for health* (pp. 25–46). San Francisco, CA: Jossey-Bass.

Warren, M. R., & Mapp, K. L. (2011). *A match on dry grass: Community organizing as a catalyst for school reform.* New York: Oxford University Press.

Yosso, T. J. (2005). Whose culture has capital? A critical race theory discussion of community cultural wealth. *Race, Ethnicity and Education, 8*(1), 69–91.

7

MESSY, SPRAWLING, AND OPEN

Research–Practice Partnership Methodologies for Working in Distributed Inter-Organizational Networks

Rafi Santo, Dixie Ching, Kylie Peppler, and Christopher Hoadley

Research–practice partnerships (RPPs) increasingly operate within multi-organizational networks, a trend with important implications for how common RPP practices are structured and enacted. Such networks include collective impact efforts that span actors across sectors (Kania & Kramer, 2011) and informal STEM and digital learning ecosystems that involve collectives of out-of-school providers (Akiva, Kehoe, & Schunn, 2017; Ching, Santo, Hoadley, & Peppler, 2016; Penuel, Clark, & Bevan, 2016). Many such networks are organized as or participate in RPPs that operate differently from partnerships that focus on a single school, district, or community organization.

In this chapter, we offer methodological strategies for *distributed RPPs* that operate in such multi-organizational, nonhierarchical contexts. We draw on lessons from an RPP involving the Mozilla Hive NYC Learning Network, a collective of over 70 informal educational organizations committed to experimentation with digitally inspired pedagogies, and Hive Research Lab, a university group led by the authors of this chapter, researchers from Indiana University and New York University.

The chapter centers on key dynamics of distributed RPPs. We see distributed organizational networks as requiring specialized routines but also providing new ways to engage in joint work. We explore four aspects of RPPs as they play out in a networked context: (1) negotiating the focus of joint work, (2) *the nature of problems* addressed within joint work, (3) building collective orientation toward the focus of joint work, and (4) engaging in collaborative design and knowledge building around problems of practice associated with joint work.

Hive NYC: A Distributed Network of Informal Learning Organizations

Founded in 2009, Hive NYC was the first of several Hive learning networks stewarded by the Mozilla Foundation with funding from the John D. and Catherine T. MacArthur foundation. It describes itself as

> a city-wide laboratory for educators, technologists and mentors to design innovative, connected educational experiences for youth. . . . Together, they create an ecosystem of equitable and accessible education opportunities for young people to explore their interests and develop skills that prepare them for success in the digital information age.
>
> *(HiveNYC.org, March 2017)*

This description encompasses two functions used to describe Hive networks. On the one hand, they are *networks that learn*—organizations learn from and collaborate with one another in order to create new educational initiatives and collectively advance communal expertise around informal learning and digital media. On the other hand, they are *networks for learning*—part of a broad ecosystem of learning experiences made available to young people to support their long-term learning trajectories across multiple institutions.[1]

Hive NYC's more than 70 informal learning institutions are diverse in terms of their missions, organizational forms, size, expertise, and age. Members include cultural institutions such as the American Museum of Natural History and Carnegie Hall, the major library systems in New York City, grassroots community-based organizations, and other youth-serving nonprofits with specialized approaches to learning. Diverse pedagogical expertise is present in the network in areas such as informal science, maker education, web and game design, filmmaking, journalism, youth organizing and civic engagement, media and digital literacies, and computer programming and physical computing. This diverse collective of organizations shares a common interest in serving youth and experimenting with digitally oriented pedagogies. There is also a common focus on giving youth opportunities to engage in learning that is driven by interest; centers on creativity, tinkering, and production; and is accomplished collaboratively with peers and mentors, aligning broadly with ideas of connected learning (Ito et al., 2013) and constructionism (Papert, 1980).

Beyond the membership of the network, an important aspect of Hive NYC is its stewardship by the Mozilla Foundation. In 2010, the Mozilla Foundation, best known for designing the open-source Firefox web browser, launched an educational initiative focused on digital technology and, in particular, web literacy, which it sees as critical for maintaining the internet as an open public resource. Hive learning networks represent contexts for developing new approaches to achieving this mission of mobilizing educators around digital literacy.

Within Hive NYC, Mozilla staff facilitate a wide range of activities that bring network members together. Many of these are in-person events, such as community meetings, professional development workshops, happy hours, and all-day collaborative youth-facing learning events called *pop-ups*. Others are virtual— a community listserv where members and Hive staffers can share information and announce various opportunities, a public blog where both network stewards and members share reflections more publicly, an online member directory that contains points of contact and specialties, and an online portfolio space where organizations can document and share resources relating to specific youth-facing initiatives they've developed. Finally, for most of its history the network has had an associated funding body, a collaborative donor fund called the Hive Digital Media and Learning Fund, which was founded through the support of the MacArthur Foundation. The fund issues biannual requests for proposals to support collaborative initiatives among member organizations, an important aspect of the network that provided resources supporting experimental projects among network members. Opportunities to receive funding also created conditions necessary for institutional buy-in to the network so that members could participate, share, and learn across the Hive.

Distributed Inter-Organizational Networks as RPP Contexts

We characterize Hive NYC Learning Network as a *distributed inter-organizational network*, defined by Russell, Meredith, Childs, Stein, and Prine (2015) as

> an arrangement of public and private organizations, agencies, and departments that have been explicitly constituted to facilitate collective action . . . [in which] . . . at least a portion of the interactions among actors in the network are framed in terms of something other than superior—subordinate relations (as in traditional hierarchy), including fee-for-service contracts and voluntary partnerships.
>
> *(p. 93)*

In discussing distributed inter-organizational networks, we focus on several characteristics that we see as making these distinct as RPP sites. Most importantly, the context contains multiple organizations as opposed to a single organization. Additionally, there is not a centralized organizational hierarchy or explicit line of authority, accountability, and reporting among the actors in the network— participation is voluntary, as are partnerships formed between organizations within it. However, issues of power—and competition—do exist. For Hive NYC, funding opportunities available via network participation were a powerful motivator and created something of a hierarchy between funders and members. Still, we saw the network's power dynamics as flatter than those of schools and school districts, enabling more equal collaboration among partners with complementary expertise. Throughout this chapter, we will explore how these characteristics of a distributed RPP context intersected with the ways that joint work unfolded between researchers and practitioners in Hive NYC.

RPP Activities Reframed Within Distributed Inter-Organizational Networks

In this section, we describe how many of the core activities in which RPPs engage have played out in our partnership and how these reflect working in a distributed inter-organizational network. We address four areas relevant to RPPs: (1) negotiating the focus of joint work, (2) defining the nature of problems addressed within joint work, (3) building collective orientation toward the focus of joint work, and (4) engaging in collaborative design and knowledge building around problems of practice associated with joint work.

How Does a Distributed Network Decide on the Focus of Joint Work?

One of the central questions of RPPs is "What is it, exactly, that we should be doing together?" This issue is often framed in terms of negotiation and deliberation, since *partnership* implies that no single actor decides the focus of work. The commitment to mutualism (Coburn, Penuel, & Geil, 2013) and to focusing on persistent problems of practice from multiple stakeholders' perspectives (Penuel, Fishman, Cheng, & Sabelli, 2011, p. 332) means that moments when decisions are made regarding the focus of joint work must be engaged with care and intentionality, and ideally, use deliberate strategies that involve many actors.

In the context of distributed RPPs, approaching this task of negotiating joint work presented some unique challenges. Convening all members of the RPP was logistically intractable. We needed to expect that different members would have different degrees of engagement, and there was also the issue of how to solicit equitable representation and voice. Broadly, we were faced with questions of who decides the focus of joint work when stakeholders are spread across a large set of organizational and institutional contexts and how we might approach this issue, given that actors in this context were not organized by traditional hierarchies and decision-making routines.

An Example From Hive NYC: From Consensus to Counsel

We present an example of how our project determined the initial focus of joint work through a network field scan approach begun in the summer of 2012. At the time, Hive NYC had been in existence for a little over three years, and network stewards at Mozilla and funders at the Hive Digital Media and Learning Fund were beginning to consider how research might play a role in the Hive. They wanted to know what burning questions stakeholders had that, if answered, could improve work at various levels.

At the time, two members of the research team, both of whom had previously been members of the Hive network, were engaged in our doctoral studies. Each of us had maintained our relationship with the Hive, and we also had aligned research interests. We were thus approached by Mozilla with an open-ended request: to engage in a network-wide field scan to find out what member and stakeholder needs were and what role research might play in strengthening the network.

The field scan used a straightforward set of methodological tools. We conducted dozens of interviews with stakeholders, including members, stewards, and funders. We conducted field observations at network events and in members' youth-serving programs. We held open roundtables where members brainstormed research needs. Informed by these broader data collection events, we then designed a network-wide survey to find out where our research might have the greatest interest and impact.

We heard a wide range of desires and needs: What makes for a successful partnership between members? What were teens up to on social media that could impact mentorship and afterschool program design? What community-based issues should members address in their work? How does an organization sustain a new line of work after it's been catalyzed through network funding?

We identified dozens of potential lines of inquiry, serving different needs. Many concerns of network stewards and funders related to the network's impact on organizations and youth. They wanted to know whether it was accomplishing the goal of being an inter-organizational collective focused on experimentation. One network steward shared that he hoped that research could shed light on the Hive's ability to support both R&D and retail functions—the development of new and interesting educational approaches, but also the wide circulation of those approaches. Some members were mainly interested in the efficacy of their own programs, having research improve the usability of technologies they were developing or having it shed light on how teens were finding their programs and what participation in their programs led to for youth.

In our final field scan report, our team aimed to express the divergent interests we heard but also note areas where there was potential alignment. We outlined a set of research areas based on a thematic analysis of stakeholder perspectives, noted the degree of interest we heard for each area, and included recommendations for approaching both the content and structure of possible research efforts. The report was brought back to network leaders to consider but was also circulated back to members virtually as well as in the context of an open meeting for discussion and consideration.

Following its completion, the initial field scan served as the basis for the formation of the RPP. The network stewards and funders solicited a proposal from the research team, requesting that we develop a research plan rooted in what members and stakeholders voiced as important during the field scan, as well as what we understood, based on our position as learning scientists, as important scholarship that could impact theory and practice.

This process highlights one way to negotiate research questions within a broadly distributed, and logistically unwieldy network. From the perspective of questions of *who's involved* and *who decides*, the field scan process of actively soliciting stakeholder perspectives to guide the research team represents a counsel-based approach to collective decision-making (Blunden, 2016). Counsel-based approaches to decision-making stand in contrast to two other more common approaches to collective decision-making: consensus, where all actors involved must come to full agreement on a decision, and majority, where all actors vote and, if a certain quantifiable subset agrees on a decision, that subset determines the group's decision. In counsel-based approaches, an individual or small group of individuals is instead responsible for a decision that affects a collective, but they cannot make that decision until all involved have been consulted to voice their views.

In the context of the initial negotiation of joint work within the RPP, as a research team we actively engaged in seeking counsel from as many of the Hive NYC stakeholders as we could within a fairly long timeframe and a resource-intensive process. We then engaged in developing a focus of joint work with the aim of representing the practitioner needs we heard. We found research questions that, based on our understanding of the broader field, would represent important contributions to both research and practice. This meant that even though there was indeed a single moment when the small group of network funders decided that the set of research activities our team proposed was appropriate, that moment was the culmination of a months-long decision-making process, based in the practice of counsel, that deeply involved and aimed to represent all network stakeholders.

The Nature of Joint Work in Distributed Networks: From Common *Problems* to Commons *Problems*

Having looked at the *how* of getting to a focus of joint work, in this section we look at the *what* of an RPP's joint work in a distributed inter-organizational network. What kinds of problems of practice can a distributed RPP address? What distinctive features might these problems have? In our partnership, the distributed organization led us to emphasize *commons* problems over *common* problems.

Common problems can exist in multiple settings but don't necessarily require solutions that link together and require coordinated institutional action across those settings. *Commons* problems, within the context of our discussion, exist at the intersections of institutional settings; they are not necessarily within the current scope of any given institution's responsibility or capacity to solve, but they could be solved through coordinated activity across multiple institutions. Challenges that can only be addressed through collective action across organizations are the main justification for allocating resources to coordinate distributed actors through inter-organizational networks. We next describe examples of what this looked like in our RPP.

When we conducted the network field scan, we heard a mix of common problems and commons problems that stakeholders saw as important. Examples of a common problem was that some members saw research as a possible way to understand best practices for incorporating digital media production into youth development programs, to better develop pedagogies based on youth interests, or to increase usability of learning technologies they were developing. These issues aligned well with Hive NYC in terms of its pedagogical values and, if addressed, could be beneficial to practice and in some cases research as well. But these were problems that did not require a coordinated network to be solved. To address them, the research team could have studied completely unconnected organizations to, for example, look at how they leveraged youth interest in their programming, and then identify principles for doing so effectively.

To add value to the network, the team chose to address the kinds of problems voiced in the field scan that were distinctive to a networked context as these would be the areas of highest leverage for a distributed RPP. The areas of joint work we ended up focusing on had the dual aims of creating a stronger *opportunity commons* for young people and a stronger *knowledge commons* for organizations. Whose job was it to make sure that, after a young person ends an experience in an informal learning organization, there is a next opportunity for that young person to continue that line of learning? Whose job was it to make sure that there are rich information and broad practices for a given organization to learn from that exist beyond its walls? In a certain respect, the answer to these questions is both *everybody* and *nobody*, and thus these questions made good candidates for attention in an RPP in an inter-organizational network.

The focus of RPP work related to supporting youth learning in networks was framed around youth trajectories and pathways and addressed a desire to understand and support youth in a way that was both long-term (in terms of time scale) and cross-setting (in terms of institutions and contexts). Rather than looking at what a youth experience was within a given out-of-school program and asking about program efficacy or design, the pathways research looked at what supported youth to engage deeply in technology-related learning interests across time and across space, and how a networked approach could support that. Building on scholarship within the learning sciences that views learning as "lifelong, life-wide and life-deep" (Banks et al., 2007) and in digital learning that focuses on "geeking out" (Ito et al., 2009), we looked to understand interest-driven learning from an ecological perspective (Barron, 2006). As part of this, we engaged in basic research through longitudinal case studies tracking youth involved in Hive programs for six to 18 months. We focused on understanding how their technology-related interests, such as game design or filmmaking, were supported socially by individuals in different parts of their lives—friends, parents, teachers and, of course, Hive educators (Ching, 2016). This allowed us to see where breakdowns of coordination occurred across institutions, uncovering a persistent problem we called "post-program slump," wherein youth whose interests had been well supported while they were participating in a Hive program experienced a strong drop-off in support once that program ended (Ching, Santo, Hoadley, & Peppler, 2014). A clear understanding of such breakdowns provided an opportunity for the research team to come back to the network with a specific issue to focus on in terms of coordination across organizations—countering post-program slump.

Our second commons problem involved networked innovation; we aimed to address how the network could be leveraged to effectively circulate ideas across organizations, engage in collaborations, and build collective knowledge. We saw this as a commons issue since it was in the interest of all members to have a strong network context in terms of organizational learning—all organizations benefited from being situated in a strong knowledge ecology. Yet, though all members had a role to play in making the network strong in this respect, it was no single organization's job to do so.

In our research in this area, we looked at norms that Mozilla, as the network steward, had developed through its role in the free/open-source software community (Coleman, 2013). Building on fieldwork observations, we noted differences in the ways Mozilla approached problem solving, learning, and organizational innovation compared to the network's out-of-school organizations. Adhering to a set of practices called "working in the open" or just "working open" (Santo, Ching, Peppler, & Hoadley, 2014b, 2016; Santo, 2017), Mozilla staffers promoted learning practices that valued transparency and flexibility, sharing work in progress within public contexts and making the results available to anyone to remix.

Through our basic research, we could see that this was a potential approach to building a strong knowledge commons in the Hive—we saw that when organizations worked in the open, there was robust circulation of ideas and strong feedback on emergent projects, and members were more easily able to find others working on similar problems. At the same time, we also found that the somewhat fast, loose, and very public orientation of "working open" had tensions associated with it. The orientation toward sharing early-stage prototypes in large public contexts, for instance, played out very differently when youth from nondominant communities were involved in the design process, something not uncommon in informal learning organizations that emphasized youth leadership. Sharing work that might be seen as unpolished in front of large audiences at conferences had different implications when it came to youth safety. These kinds of findings provided an important entry point into supporting network members and stewards to think through mutually productive strategies for supporting cross-organizational learning in the network.

Sustaining Collective North Stars: Continual Tuning, Sense-Giving, and Relationship Building

Due to the distributed nature of Hive NYC, network actors varied in how tuned in they were to the joint work. There was variation in how much they understood the research priority areas as well as in their interest and ability to make connections to their own work. Naturally, stewards at Mozilla had a deep awareness and orientation to the RPP's focus. But the situation with network members was different. Network participation was voluntary, and different individuals from these organizations engaged in different contexts of network activity (e.g., network meet-ups, funded collaborations, online listserv participation). In order to carry out our work, the RPP team needed to make an effort to sustain the network's focus on collective north stars. To do so, we engaged in two strategies: (1) tuning, context setting, and formative knowledge sharing, and (2) ongoing relationship building.

Tuning involved creating a set of ongoing project narration approaches that were as open and public as possible as we engaged in the RPP's work. We created a blog where we regularly shared initial insights, open questions, and documentation of research activities. We released semi-regular briefs summarizing research, including our emerging findings, on topics of interest to the community such as the nature of social support for interest-driven learning or models of achieving scale within out-of-school organizations. Research briefs were five to 10 pages long, included empirical data, and were more formal in their layout, whereas practice briefs tended to be two or three pages, used more visual representations of ideas, and focused on practice recommendations. See Figure 7.1 for an example.

In network participation structures, such as community calls and network meet-ups, we shared reports and emerging findings, facilitated conversations around our research areas, and co-facilitated activities alongside Hive stewards. Across all these tuning activities—engaging in context setting, sharing formative knowledge, sense-giving around what we were seeing—we tried to create a sense of what the RPP work was about, along with ways to contribute to it.

We found that tuning efforts were particularly important at times when they could contribute to other activities going on within our RPP. For instance, shortly after we released a research brief detailing the phenomenon of "post-program slump" in social support around youth technology interests (Ching et al., 2014), we invited network members to a meeting to design potential solutions to the problem, as we'll discuss in the next section. Additionally, we found that no matter how often we engaged in project narration and tuning, we were never *done*. As work continued to unfold and implicate new actors at various levels within member organizations, recontextualizing where the RPP priorities came from remained essential to carrying out research and design activities.

The second approach that we took to sustaining collective orientation toward RPP priorities was to actively build and sustain relationships with network stakeholders. We acted as participant observers in the network, which helped us build relationships that provided our team with important perspectives about the network members' evolving concerns and aims while also giving us opportunities to share about the goals and activities of the RPP. For example, in the first six months following the inception of the research project, we shared offices with the Mozilla network stewards. Co-working in the same space gave us a deeper understanding of their daily routines and priorities, and it allowed us to informally share knowledge from our fieldwork that could inform network governance. We also engaged in three months of intensive fieldwork once the RPP was formally under way, and during this period, we interviewed many network members and conducted observations at their organizations. During these interviews, we were not only collecting data but also discussing the research questions and strategies the RPP was focused on, helping orient these members, who were often different from those who had participated in the field scan during the prior summer. Beyond these initial efforts to build relationships, we also regularly attended network convening spaces like meet-ups, grantee meetings, professional development events, and holiday parties. Through this work, we developed relationships that deepened our understanding of network culture while also creating opportunities to talk through ideas we were thinking about and engage in collective sense-making around them with network members.

The process of tuning is one that spanned both the social geography of the network (across actors) and the long-term unfolding of network activities (across time). What this meant practically was that in a given moment of tuning—say, giving a short presentation about a new report on a community call—some members might be getting updated on questions they were already aware were being pursued, while others were being introduced to those questions for the first time. This ongoing narration meant it was more likely that network members would be able to productively engage with our efforts and understand their development and the rationales associated with them. This issue is salient in many RPPs where high turnover means that active strategies must be developed to deal with the realities of maintaining lines of work over long periods of time.

We don't hold any illusions that we ever achieved any sort of *universal* understanding of the priorities of the RPP across all Hive members. We know from an independent evaluation, in fact, that a good portion of network members were at times unclear about the research team's relationship to network stewards and funders, as well as whether we were engaged in a more traditional program evaluation role (Davis with Ching & Santo, 2016). We see these as indicators that the efforts we made to tune the network toward the areas of focus in the RPP in an active and ongoing way were necessary and that achieving collective understanding of an RPP in a networked context is indeed an important challenge to attend to. At the same time, achieving universality in terms of understanding the focus of joint work was not always essential. In a certain sense, we valued achieving a more traditional research dissemination goal of having as many member organizations

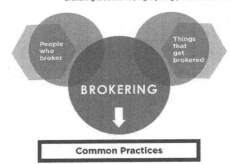

How can out-of-school organizations use brokering to support youth interest-driven learning pathways?

Dixie Ching, Rafi Santo, Chris Hoadley & Kylie Peppler

To download a copy of the Hive community-developed white paper, visit **http://bit.ly/brokering**

Being a Learning Broker supports youth pathways because it:

· **CONNECTS YOUTH TO MEANINGFUL FUTURE LEARNING OPPORTUNITIES** including events, programs, internships, individuals, and institutions that will support youth in continuing their interest-driven learning.

· **ENRICHES THEIR SOCIAL NETWORKS** with adults, peers, and institutions that are connected to/have knowledge of future learning opportunities.

Basics of Brokering: People, Practices, and Learning Opportunities

Brokering is about helping a young person make that crucial connection to a next learning opportunity.

· **PEOPLE WHO BROKER:** Brokers are everywhere in a young person's life. They include **family members** (parents, grandparents, aunts, uncles); **non-family adults** (educators, teaching artists, mentors); and **peers** (friends, significant others, students at school).

· **THINGS THAT GET BROKERED:** Learning opportunities are the building blocks of pathways. They might include **experiences** (programs, one-day events, classes, internships, fellowships); **social connections** (mentors, institutional gatekeepers, collaborative peers); **institutions** (colleges, companies, organizations); and **information sources** (websites, books, how-to guides).

· **COMMON PRACTICES:** Hive NYC community members have surfaced a range of brokering practices that can happen across the life cycle of a program (see page 3).

FIGURE 7.1 RPP Practice Brief Developed by the Research Team on a Key Practice: Brokering Future Learning Opportunities

as possible attend to our findings within their organizations, but we also valued other forms of engagement. From the perspective of having an RPP where we aimed to engage in joint work, we found that having a certain threshold of collective understanding across the network was enough to catalyze deeper forms of collaborative work with a smaller subset of network actors. This ability to

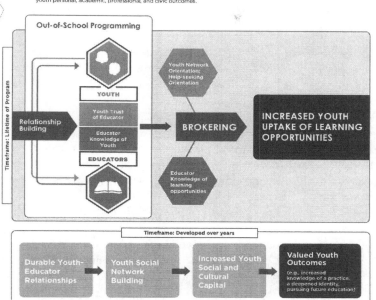

Conceptual model of social capital development through brokering

We propose a conceptual model for how brokering relates to social capital development leading to valued youth personal, academic, professional, and civic outcomes.

This model highlights an important route to supporting **increased youth uptake of learning opportunities**. Key to this process is the **relationship building** that occurs between educators and youth typically in the context of informal learning after school programs. We postulate that the environment afforded by these programs provides a promising context for two important outcomes necessary for effective brokering: the development of trusting, caring relationships between youth and educators (i.e, **youth trust of educator**) and a better understanding by educators of youths' interests, needs, etc. (i.e. **educator knowledge of youth**). As mentioned earlier, when educators know their youth and have close relationships with them, it is more likely that youth will take up future learning opportunities that these educators recommend. This allows for successful enactment of various **brokering** practices leading to increased youth engagement in learning opportunities.

FIGURE 7.1   (Continued)

draw on shared understanding of the RPP priorities—the results of our continual efforts to sustain collective north stars—was key to facilitating participation in joint work, as we'll explore in the next section.

Collaborative Creativity: Open Structures for Co-Design and Participatory Knowledge Building

So far, we've discussed a variety of issues related to engaging in RPPs within distributed inter-organizational networks—how the focus of joint work is determined, what kind of problems networks can focus on, and how to achieve and sustain orientation toward those problems. But what does actual engagement in joint work look like in a networked RPP context? In this section, we explore how two common outputs of RPPs—new designs and new knowledge—were produced in our partnership through collaborative joint work.

Design Charrettes: A Network Approach to Organizing Co-Design

Design research—an approach to iteratively developing and studying learning interventions in real-world contexts—is often utilized within RPPs, with practices of co-design (or collaborative design) being central, given the commitment to mutualism and focusing on problems relevant to both research and practice (Coburn et al., 2013; Penuel, Roschelle, & Shechtman, 2007). Although we won't focus on all the design research approaches we've utilized within our partnership, one aspect—how we went about convening network members to engage in co-design—is of particular relevance to working with networks.

After setting the stage through sharing formative insights with the network, we wanted to create a context to build on these and begin designing solutions. We didn't want a closed process, though, so we invited anyone in the network who wanted to participate to join what are called *design charrettes* (Howard & Somerville, 2014; Roggema, 2014), day-long sprints where members could learn more about issues, ideate potential solutions, and find new collaborators to bring these solutions to life. Creating open opportunities where any network members interested in the same issue, such as preventing post-program slump, could come together was important not only because it was democratic but also because our activities were focused on commons problems that sat at the intersection of institutions. Having multiple organizations in the same room meant that candidate solutions could leverage not just cross-organizational perspectives but distinct resources that different organizations could bring to bear.

In the case of a charrette focused on youth pathways, one member brought to the table an idea he'd been developing around creating Hive youth meet-ups, youth-centered events where youth leaders from across many member organizations could meet each other, share and give feedback on projects, make friends, and learn about opportunities across the network. As a sort of *connective tissue* within the network, the meet-up was the kind of design that sat at the intersection of multiple organizations to address a joint problem. The charrette created the opportunity for one member to share and refine an idea and to bring new organizations on board to make it a reality. Following the charrette, our team worked with a cross-organizational group formed during the meeting to prototype, test, and iterate the concept, and following this round of testing, the project eventually secured funding to continue its development.

Participatory Knowledge Building in Networked RPPs

The charrettes not only led to new designs but also catalyzed cycles of learning where the network could engage as a collective in participatory knowledge building (Santo, Ching, Peppler, & Hoadley, 2017)—processes of surfacing, synthesizing, and iterating on practice-linked insights that come from a wide range of actors through deliberative, community-based practices. An example of this occurred during the youth pathways charrette just described.

During the event, we engaged network members in a process where they collectively shared perspectives about youth pathways. They responded to prompts such as "What does a successful youth pathway experience look like?" and "What gets in the way of youth successfully having a pathway experience?" We built on their responses within group conversations that helped define the issue and created shared understanding that supported development of solutions.

In this process, a central practice—that of brokering future learning opportunities—was identified among the perspectives shared by members as an approach to supporting long-term, cross-setting learning pathways. The role of learning brokers had been previously discussed in the literature related to youth interest-driven learning pathways with technology (see Barron, 2006), but it hadn't been an active discussion within the network, despite the community's focus on pathways. The identification of brokering as a key pathway-supporting practice moved the collective frame from pathways (an outcome) to brokering (a practice supporting that outcome). This shift created a rich space for pedagogical exploration within the network.

Following the charrette, we combed through the ideas shared about brokering and began to develop a framework synthesizing the group's insights. In the months that followed, we engaged the network in a process of sourcing ideas, successes, tensions, and general knowledge around brokering practices. Practically, this meant working with network stewards to utilize the network's broader participation structures, such as community calls and meet-ups, as well as creating other structures with members, such as a working group, as spaces for participatory knowledge building. Through opening the conversation to the rest of the network, we were able to refine ideas around brokering learning.

After months of community sense-making around the concept of brokering, we developed a draft of a white paper (see Ching, Santo, Hoadley, & Peppler, 2015, 2016) in which we attempted to represent the network's thoughts, link them to our empirical research, and integrate insights from existing literature. The draft, in line with the broader participatory approach, was circulated to the network for feedback, with members making comments on the collaborative document (see Figure 7.2). This final round of participation in the knowledge-building process allowed us to not only clarify the core ideas but also reframe and add new ideas to create greater relevance to the realities of the network.

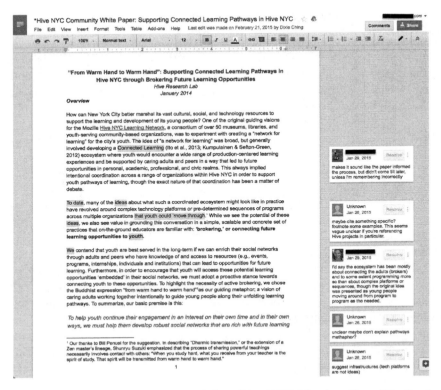

FIGURE 7.2 Collaborative Document Where Hive NYC Members Shared Feedback on an Initial Draft of a Community White Paper

By the end of the process, we'd engaged over 60 network stakeholders—members, network stewards, funders, and community allies—in the knowledge-building process. For some, participation was as simple as sharing an anecdote on a community call about a moment they attempted to connect youth to a new opportunity. Others were more deeply engaged, joining in working group meetings where we hashed out key definitions, meeting individually with our team to ideate and to refine practice recommendations, or digging into the white paper draft to give feedback to us researchers.

From the perspective of the RPP, engaging in participatory knowledge-building processes has important outcomes beyond the new knowledge represented in white papers or briefs. As is the case with design charrettes, participatory knowledge-building processes are key sites where shared language is developed and collective orientation around the RPP's north stars is deepened—part of the aforementioned tuning work that is central in network-based partnerships. Additionally, these processes position practitioners within the RPP as experts and foster a collective knowledge-building orientation through surfacing and representing their practice knowledge. Finally, through these processes, the focus of the joint work itself is further specified and iterated on, new areas of possible investigation are uncovered, and new, promising practices are clarified—all of which lays the groundwork for new initiatives and changes to practice within the network.

Discussion: "Working in the Open" as an Approach to RPPs in Distributed Inter-Organizational Networks

Mozilla's culture, which emerged from its role as a network steward with roots in the free/open-source software movement (Coleman, 2013), brought with it notable shifts to the work culture of these educational organizations. While the idea of code being open and remixable by anyone is central in this movement, another key aspect of this culture is that the process of production is open and collaborative by default—projects are run publicly such that anyone can join, participate in ways large and small, and contribute ideas and distinctive expertise. As mentioned earlier, we found that in Hive NYC, practices of "working in the open" (Santo et al., 2014b; 2016; Santo, 2017)—ways of organizing work and learning that emphasize public and iterative design processes, low barriers to participation in ongoing lines of work, and fostering active collaboration across many actors— were part of the DNA of the network's stewardship by Mozilla. What we didn't quite expect was that the methodological approaches of the RPP itself—our ways of structuring activities and engaging as research partners to the network—would also come to be influenced and characterized by this culture of "working open."

As the research partnership was initially taking shape, we asked ourselves what it meant to be researchers that could be useful in a context like the Hive NYC Learning Network. From the start, we aimed to design our research efforts in ways that were participatory and even democratic—we knew that taking a summative approach where we checked in once a year with an outcomes report wasn't in line with the open and experimental spirit of Hive. From the start, there was an assumption and a desire that the research team be in the mix of the network, rather than apart from it. As the work unfolded and we worked to create an RPP that was in line with the norms of the network, what eventually developed was a cultural hybrid. We utilized the kind of "working open" practices that guided Mozilla's network stewardship and integrated them with scholarly orientations toward principled inquiry, knowledge building, and development of practice-relevant insights in a way that we could not have envisioned before we initiated this collective work.

Given this, we're attendant to the fact that tensions we found in our basic research related to the network's open culture could also be at play within RPP activities that follow similar organizing principles. Our research on working in the open has shown that it's a mode of work that can privilege those in positions of power—for instance, those comfortable with sharing half-baked ideas and those less concerned with issues of closely guarding intellectual property. Participation in open work, be it in an RPP or not, also favors those with more resources to spare in terms of spending time in contexts where such work occurs, such as conferences, convenings, open calls, and various forms of online participation. Just as we think about equity-related issues concerning learning opportunities for youth, we see similar considerations as necessary for RPPs that engage youth and educators in seemingly open structures to avoid reinforcing inequities in opportunities to contribute to joint endeavors of the RPP.

The issues, insights, and practices we have shared in this chapter emerged from an RPP that took place in a distributed inter-organizational network. However, while the distributed nature of the Hive required our team to be especially attendant to certain issues that are particular to our community context, we see these issues as having salience to many RPPs, regardless of their context. How to decide on the focus of joint work in an equitable way, what kinds of problems to focus on, how to continually orient to ongoing research directions, how to involve stakeholders in collaborative activities—these are questions we believe all RPPs should consider. In offering examples from our partnership work, we hope to support others to reflect on theirs.

Acknowledgments

This work was made possible through the generous support of the Hive Digital Media and Learning Fund at the New York Community Trust and the MacArthur Foundation (through award #P13-000160), the Spencer Foundation (through award #201600113), Capital One Investing for Good, and through our ongoing partnership with the members and staff of the Hive NYC Learning Network. Truly, this work would not have happened without them. Additional thanks go to the volume editors, Bronwyn Bevan and William R. Penuel, for their feedback on the chapter.

Note

1 The framing of "networks for learning" and "networks that learn" for Hives was originally shared by Elyse Eidman-Aadahl of the National Writing Project.

References

Akiva, T., Kehoe, S., & Schunn, C. D. (2017). Are we ready for citywide learning? Examining the nature of within- and between-program pathways in a community-wide learning initiative. *Journal of Community Psychology, 45*(3), 413–425.

Banks, J. A., Au, K. H., Ball, A. F., Bell, P., Gordon, E. W., Gutiérrez, K., . . . Nasir, N. I. S. (2007). Learning in and out of school in diverse environments: Life-long, life-wide, life-deep. Seattle: The LIFE Center and the Center for Multicultural Education, University of Washington.

Barron, B. (2006). Interest and self-sustained learning as catalysts of development: A learning ecologies perspective. *Human Development, 49*(4), 193–224.

Blunden, A. (2016). *The origins of collective decision making.* Leiden: Brill.

Ching, D. (2016). *"Now I can actually do what I want": Social learning ecologies supporting youth pathways in digital media making.* Doctoral dissertation. New York University, New York.

Ching, D., Santo, R., Hoadley, C. M., & Peppler, K. (2014). *Hive research lab interim brief: Mapping social learning ecologies of hive youth.* New York: Hive Research Lab. Retrieved from https://hiveresearchlab.files.wordpress.com/2014/04/hive-research-lab-youth-trajectories-interim-brief-24.pdf

Ching, D., Santo, R., Hoadley, C., & Peppler, K. (2015). *On-ramps, lane changes, detours and destinations: Building connected learning pathways in Hive NYC through brokering future learning opportunities.* New York: Hive Research Lab. Retrieved from https://hiveresearchlab.files.wordpress.com/2015/05/hive-research-lab-2015-community-white-paper-brokering-future-learning-opportunities2.pdf

Ching, D., Santo, R., Hoadley, C., & Peppler, K. (2016). Not just a blip in someone's life: integrating brokering practices into out-of-school programming as a means of supporting youth futures. *On the Horizon, 24*(3), 296–312.

Coburn, C. E., Penuel, W. R., & Geil, K. E. (2013). *Research–practice partnerships: A strategy for leveraging research for educational improvement in school districts.* New York: William T. Grant Foundation.

Coleman, E. G. (2013). *Coding freedom: The ethics and aesthetics of hacking.* Princeton: Princeton University Press.

Davis, L., Ching, D., & Santo, R. (2016). *Hive research lab: Understanding research–practice partnerships in a distributed context. Highlights from an independent formative evaluation of 2013–2015 activities.* New York: Authors.

Howard, Z., & Somerville, M. M. (2014). A comparative study of two design charrettes: Implications for codesign and participatory action research. *CoDesign, 10*(1), 46–62.

Ito, M., Baumer, S., Bittanti, M., Cody, R., Stephenson, B. H., Horst, H. A., . . . Perkel, D. (2009). *Hanging out, messing around, and geeking out: Kids living and learning with new media.* Cambridge, MA: MIT press.

Ito, M., Gutiérrez, K., Livingstone, S., Penuel, B., Rhodes, J., Salen, K., . . . Watkins, S. C. (2013). *Connected learning: An agenda for research and design.* Irvine, CA: Digital Media and Learning Research Hub.

Kania, J., & Kramer, M. (2011). Collective impact. *Stanford Social Innovation Review, 9*, 36–41.

Papert, S. (1980). *Mindstorms: Children, computers, and powerful ideas.* New York: Basic Books.

Penuel, W. R., Clark, T., & Bevan, B. (2016). Designing and building infrastructures to support equitable STEM learning across settings. *Afterschool Matters, 24*, 12–20.

Penuel, W. R., Fishman, B. J., Cheng, B. H., & Sabelli, N. (2011). Organizing research and development at the intersection of learning, implementation, and design. *Educational Researcher, 40*(7), 331–337.

Penuel, W. R., Roschelle, J., & Shechtman, N. (2007). Designing formative assessment software with teachers: An analysis of the co-design process. *Research and Practice in Technology Enhanced Learning, 2*(1), 51–74.

Roggema, R. (2014). The design charrette. In *The design charrette: Ways to envision sustainable futures* (pp. 15–34). The Netherlands: Springer.

Russell, J. L., Meredith, J., Childs, J., Stein, M. K., & Prine, D. W. (2015). Designing inter-organizational networks to implement education reform an analysis of state race to the top applications. *Educational Evaluation and Policy Analysis, 37*(1), 92–112.

Santo, R. (2017). *Working open in the Hive: How informal education organizations learn, collaborate and innovate in networks.* Doctoral dissertation, Indiana University, Indiana.

Santo, R., Ching, D., Peppler, K. A., & Hoadley, C. M. (2014b). *What does it mean to "work open" in Hive NYC? A vision for collective organizational learning.* New York: Hive Research Lab. Retrieved from https://hiveresearchlab.files.wordpress.com/2014/12/what-does-it-mean-to-work-open-in-hive-nyc-hive-research-lab-october-2014.pdf

Santo, R., Ching, D., Peppler, K. A., & Hoadley, C. M. (2016). Working in the open: Lessons from open source on building innovation networks in education. *On the Horizon, 24*(3), 280–295.

Santo, R., Ching, D., Peppler, K., & Hoadley, C. (2017). Participatory knowledge building within research–practice partnerships in education. *SAGE Research Methods Cases.* London: Sage. doi:10.4135/9781473998933

PART IV

Designing for Equity in RPPs

8

FIVE EQUITY-RELATED TENSIONS IN PROJECT-BASED LEARNING

How Research–Practice Partnerships Can Spread and Sustain Deeper Learning

Angela Haydel DeBarger and Marc Chun

Walking into a project-based classroom, one might experience the exhilarating cacophony of students engaged in active learning. Students in one corner laugh and gesture wildly as they create artifacts, others focus intensely around a laptop, and still others install colorful student work on the classroom walls. But looking more closely, a number of challenges become clear. Some students might be analyzing migration patterns of a threatened bird species, while others are coloring a picture of the bird. Some work clearly addresses standards, while other work seems fun but has limited rigor or is disconnected from the flow of the larger learning objectives. Looking across multiple classrooms at the school, one might notice some teachers readily sharing project materials as part of a learning community but others preferring to keep their lesson plans to themselves. Administrators and principals may struggle with how best to support teachers and whether to focus on the innovators who pioneer this work or to encourage particular schoolwide project-based learning (PBL) practices (even for teachers outside of the coalition of the willing).

In this chapter, we seek to name these tensions, which can be easily overlooked. We start by making the case that, to ensure that all students graduate high school prepared for success in their career and civic lives, they must master a combination of competencies (dubbed *deeper learning*), which in turn requires a different approach to teaching and learning (such as PBL). However, the nature of effective PBL introduces particular equity-related challenges that, if not thoughtfully addressed, can exacerbate rather than ameliorate existing performance gaps.

The long-lasting success of progressive reforms requires partnerships that are committed to developing a collaborative learning culture among the adults seeking to support inclusive and engaging PBL for young people. Specifically, this chapter explores how research–practice partnerships (RPPs) involving multiple institutions (e.g., universities/research institutes, districts, charitable foundations) can address the challenges of deepening and scaling PBL. We describe problems of practice related to the design and enactment of PBL as a means to achieve deeper learning outcomes, including implementation variability as teachers adapt projects to meet the needs of their students. We argue that RPPs support evidence-based decisions in the localization of curriculum and develop sustainable communities of practice that foster a collaborative infrastructure for PBL. A shared learning agenda created and supported through an RPP can drive principled decision-making to address challenges and develop practices that work. This responsive approach may even result in a faster rate of adoption and sustainability of the innovative elements of PBL (Coburn, 2003; Rogers, 2003).

Project-Based Learning Develops Deeper Learning Outcomes

A growing body of literature (notably, Heller, Wolfe, & Steinberg, 2017; National Research Council, 2012a, 2012b) has made the case that, given the changing nature of work and civic life, K–12 education must emphasize a new set of competencies that enable students to apply what they have previously learned to solve novel problems—a process called *transfer*. Based on the framework presented by the National Research Council, transfer requires *deeper learning*, which is defined as an interrelated set of six learning outcomes that fall into three overlapping[1] domains: *cognitive* outcomes of (1) rigorous content and (2) critical thinking; *interpersonal* outcomes of (3) collaboration and (4) communication; and *intrapersonal* outcomes of (5) learning to learn and (6) academic/learning mindsets.

The American Institutes for Research conducted a quasi-experimental study and found that students attending schools focused on deeper learning had more opportunities to learn, higher standardized test scores (i.e., on cognitive outcomes), higher self-reports on interpersonal and intrapersonal competencies, and higher graduation rates, and they attended more selective institutions of higher education.[2] Educators who embrace a vision of deeper learning for all students create schools and classrooms where learning is focused on meaningful disciplinary ideas and practices, skilled professionals create caring and respectful communities that foster a culture of belonging and inclusion, and educators and students have access to the materials and resources they need to be ready to learn and to support learning (Mehta, 2014; Noguera, Darling-Hammond, & Friedlaender, 2015).

PBL is well recognized as a curricular approach and instructional practice to help students gain proficiency in all three domains of deeper learning (Condliffe, Visher, Bangser, Drohojowska, & Saco, 2016; Noguera et al., 2015; Peterson, 2012). Research in different disciplinary contexts has shown that PBL results in improvements on deeper learning cognitive outcomes. In mathematics, Boaler (1997) demonstrated that students who experienced PBL instruction outperformed students in classes that used a traditional approach to learning. Finkelstein, Hanson,

Huang, Hirschman, and Huang (2011) conducted a randomized controlled trial of a PBL economics curriculum and found significantly positive effects on economic literacy and problem-solving skills in economics. In a randomized controlled trial of PBL in sixth-grade science classes, Harris and colleagues (2015) found that students in the project-based science curriculum outperformed students in the comparison curriculum on assessments that addressed core science ideas and scientific practices.

PBL experiences also can develop students' deeper learning intrapersonal and interpersonal competencies. In one study, eighth-grade PBL students had more positive attitudes toward social studies than students in a traditional social studies class (Hernández-Ramos & De La Paz, 2009). Kaldi, Filippatou, and Govaris (2011) found that elementary-aged students had significantly more positive perceptions of experiential learning compared to traditional teaching and demonstrated greater motivation as well as positive attitudes toward peers from different ethnic backgrounds. Developing these relationships is a benefit of project-based experiences, and incorporating multiple opportunities for collaboration is a key feature of PBL (Krajcik & Shin, 2014).

The interactions through the enactment of projects drive the learning in PBL. Well-designed materials include educative features that support teachers in making choices about how to adapt materials; for example, to incorporate language strategies to engage English learners or to elaborate content connections and applications through multiple representations (e.g., Ball & Cohen, 1996; Davis & Krajcik, 2005; Zwiers et al., 2017). Professional development institutes coupled with planning and coaching meetings throughout the year also can facilitate shifts in teachers' knowledge and attitudes toward PBL (Dole, Bloom, & Kowalske, 2016).

Taken together, these studies serve as proof points that it is possible for PBL to develop deeper learning competencies. However, as is typically the case with any intervention, there can be great variability in implementation and questions about effective practice after the researchers and designers are no longer working with the teachers or school leaders.

Equity-Related Challenges in PBL

Attempts to scale the use of PBL to develop students' deeper learning competencies leads to two equity-related challenges: one is more macro, stemming from systemic patterns of education reform, and the other is more micro, related to the pedagogical requirements of PBL.

The macro issue arises from the nature of the larger education system and how reform typically occurs. Instructional practice to deliver on the set of deeper learning outcomes—like many other progressive education projects—has not been uniformly distributed throughout the system. Affluent communities have historically had greater access to deeper learning opportunities in line with professional careers, whereas students in higher poverty communities are more likely to be offered "rule-following" learning experiences that reflect factory and working-class jobs (Anyon, 1997; Mehta, 2014). Mehta (2014) adds: "To the degree that race mirrors class, these inequalities in access to deeper learning are shortchanging black and Latino students."

Bob Lenz of the Buck Institute of Education estimated that less than 5% of schools in the United States have received professional development to design and facilitate PBL (2017, private communication). A more equitable distribution, which moves PBL out of just a few classrooms or boutique settings, requires school and district systems to create the infrastructure needed to develop the human- and social-capital capacity to promote deeper learning. New forms of curricular materials and resources must be identified. Furthermore, for many teachers, PBL requires a challenging shift in pedagogical beliefs regarding their role and how students learn (Ertmer, 2005; Ertmer & Simons, 2006; Rogers, Cross, Gresalfi, Trauth-Nare, & Buck, 2011; Thomas, 2000). Professional development to improve students' deeper learning competencies also requires adjudication of questions about the new focus, how curricula should change, and for whom the reforms are first targeted (Chun, 2015). Unless implementation of PBL addresses both curricula and professional development, inequalities will inevitably result. Overall, it is clear that lower-resourced schools will have a steeper hill to climb to build this capacity.

From this macro, systems-level perspective, some equity questions emerge: How do we support a fairer distribution of opportunities for PBL across states, districts, and schools? What are effective distribution channels for curricula, professional development, and other resources?

At a more micro level, the nature of PBL makes such reform susceptible to implementation challenges that might exacerbate existing performance gaps. First, the core mechanism of PBL requires purposeful and authentic projects throughout the school year that address real-world challenges and require authentic disciplinary practices (Baines et al., 2017; Krajcik & Czerniak, 2013; Parker & Lo, 2016). In PBL, project activities ideally are relevant and connected to students' lived experiences, culture, and language, and encourage multiple pathways to learning.

This is where planning and enacting PBL become challenging (Thomas, 2000) and require a careful eye toward equity. Educators and school leaders—especially those who do not share the same cultural or demographic backgrounds as their students—must wrestle with questions such as these: How do we design projects that are relevant within and across classroom and school communities? If students from different backgrounds have unequal aspirational levels, how do we ensure that projects driven by individual student interests nevertheless lead to equal learning outcomes? How do educators support students in doing work that is authentic, even when the educator might have different forms of cultural capital? How do educators fairly support students who use different approaches to learning without privileging only one or a small subset of approaches?

Because PBL also expects students to participate in group-worthy tasks that include listening to and analyzing multiple perspectives, equity-related challenges also arise around questions such as these: How do teachers create classroom environments that promote equitable participation among students? How do projects incorporate language strategies to develop students' reading, writing, and discourse skills?

Given that PBL encourages intellectual risk taking, educators need to create supportive classroom cultures. Interactions must promote student agency. Furthermore, PBL also offers multiple ways for students to demonstrate growth. As a result, educators must consider equity-related implementation questions such as these: How do we invite students to shape the course of projects in the questions they pursue and the artifacts they create? How do we support teachers and district leaders in making adaptations that enhance the relevance of projects for students? How do we build learning communities for sharing best practices and productive adaptations that enhance the relevance of projects for students?

Using RPPs to Develop Equitable PBL Experiences

The aforementioned challenges and questions can be distilled into five critical tensions between macro- and micro-factors, as shown in Table 8.1. The first column presents the tensions. Two of these tensions focus on students (why students learn through PBL, what students experience through PBL), the next two focus on educators (where/when teachers learn about PBL, how teachers learn

TABLE 8.1 Five Critical Tensions Between Macro- and Micro-Factors in PBL

TENSION	*MACRO-FACTOR*	*MICRO-FACTOR*
WHY students learn through PBL *(rationale behind the learning goals)*	Rigorous learning goals	Relevant personal and community connections
WHAT students experience in PBL *(meaningful learning experiences)*	Coherent learning trajectory	Adaptations to enhance meaning
WHERE/WHEN teachers learn about PBL *(professional development to get started)*	At-scale, standardized institutes	Local or site-based customized sessions
HOW teachers learn about PBL *(degree of autonomy to achieve sustainability)*	Learn together, share with others	Learn alone, focus on own projects
WHO the primary implementers of PBL are *(building the culture)*	Focus on the larger structure	Support the local innovators

about PBL), and the last tension focuses on the overarching aspects of the culture (who the primary implementers of PBL are). The second and third columns indicate the macro- and micro-factors that constitute the tension; for example, with respect to why students should learn through PBL, there is a tension between how to maintain rigor and how to enable relevance. The resolution of this and the other four tensions has implications for equity. These tensions will not be resolved by moving to either extreme (e.g., extreme rigor at the expense of relevance, or complete relevance with no attention to rigor). Rather, to maximize equitable approaches to the learning, some middle ground needs to be found.

It is unlikely that any one actor can develop the infrastructure of support to navigate the complicated nature of these tensions. It would be difficult for practitioners alone to resolve these tensions because their positionality gives them a focused but limited view of the whole system, and they often aren't trained in the discipline of undertaking empirical research. By the same token, researchers are able to bring systemic and rigorous approaches to knowledge creation but often lack the lived experience in these school and district communities. Design-based RPPs may be uniquely positioned to consider these institutional, system-level factors as well as the transactional, classroom-level interactions. In addition to integrating the perspectives of multiple actors on persistent problems of practice, design-based RPPs create the *contexts*—through mechanisms intentionally organized to foster relationships and dialogue, frequently around data emerging through the partnership research—and the *processes* of iterative design, review, and redesign that can support reflection and refinement of improvement efforts at the center of these tensions (Bevan, 2017; Coburn & Penuel, 2016; Penuel & Gallagher, 2017). As each tension is further elaborated in the next sections, examples are included to demonstrate how RPPs can serve as resources for addressing the tensions.

Tension 1—Why Students Learn Through PBL: Designing Projects for Relevance While Maintaining Rigor

The work of creating PBL begins with articulating rigorous learning goals and crafting driving (or essential) questions that will be the focus of inquiry. Projects also should invite students to draw upon their personal experiences and use what they learn in projects to inform how they engage in the world outside of the classroom. The creation of each project's driving questions and the lessons that follow should be considered in relation to the communities and contexts within which the project will take place. Otherwise, the PBL efforts, though well-intentioned, could potentially widen any preexisting learning gaps between these schools. Looking at the whole system, how do educators make sure that the students in a more impoverished community (who might decide that the most real-world project they want to take on is to work to clean up an abandoned lot near their school) and students in a more affluent community (who might decide that they want to work with a nearby start-up company to develop a business plan for tech-enabled renewable energy sources) all have similar opportunities to develop core content knowledge?

Design-based RPPs can aid in iteratively developing and testing questions and lessons to address rigorous learning goals and incorporate local phenomena that are relevant to students. The Multiple Literacies in PBL project, for instance, involves a partnership among researchers and practitioners to create interdisciplinary (integrating science, literacy, and mathematics) PBL courses for the upper elementary grades (Krajcik, Palincsar, & Miller, 2017; Palincsar, Kucan, Fitzgerald, & Marcum, 2017). Together, the team brings deep expertise in science education, literacy development, mathematics, and elementary science teaching. To create PBL courses, the team first identifies rigorous learning goals for each project (e.g., based on the Next Generation Science Standards, Common Core State Standards, and research on social and emotional learning). They co-develop driving questions, and a small cohort of teachers tries out lessons. Teachers provide feedback on whether their students were interested in the project activities and how well the lessons' structures made designers' intentions explicit. The research team also collects extensive observations and field studies. Data from these "teaching experiments" inform minor refinements to projects (e.g., the addition of a formative assessment resource to help teachers attend to the different ways students may make sense of phenomena), as well as more extensive revisions (e.g., re-storyboarding a unit to adjust the flow and sequence of lessons). This intensive and iterative design process has resulted in rigorous and meaningful interdisciplinary PBL courses for third and fourth grades.

Tension 2—What Students Experience Through PBL: Supporting Adaptations While Enhancing Coherence

As with the spread of all educational innovations, PBL will involve communities of teachers who were not part of the original design team. Yet project-based lessons or investigations that were feasible in one setting may not be possible in other schools because of resource availability or levels of expertise. Furthermore, students from different neighborhoods may have different ideas that are meaningful and relevant from their perspectives. It can be empowering when teachers and students take ownership by adapting the course and lessons; however, this introduces the potential that adaptations will disrupt coherence in the original, research-based curriculum. If lessons are added to address new learning goals without careful attention to the driving question, or if supports reduce opportunities for language learning, adaptations can result in a more disconnected learning experience for students.

Coherence is essential to equitable PBL—projects are designed with a particular sequence of lessons and assessments across a number of weeks to ensure that students develop the resources to answer the driving question of the project (Shwartz, Weizman, Fortus, Krajcik, & Reiser, 2008). Curricula, however, also should be designed to support productive adaptations that maintain or enhance a balance between rigor and relevance (DeBarger, Choppin, Beauvineau, & Moorthy, 2013).

RPPs can provide guidance on how to adjust and implement lessons while maintaining the coherence of the projects and facilitate the systematic testing of adaptations. For example, a PBL partnership involving Stanford University, SRI International, and San Francisco Unified School District is engaged in a study to improve a sixth-grade PBL science course. Through piloting of the materials, the RPP is surfacing persistent gaps for students who are English learners. Drawing from research on language routines that work for English learners in mathematics (e.g., Aguirre & Bunch, 2012), the team agreed to incorporate language routines into the PBL science lessons. The research addresses the extent to which teachers use these and other practices to promote equitable participation of all students. Findings will result in revisions to this course and subsequent seventh- and eighth-grade PBL science courses in development.

Tension 3—Where/When Teachers Learn About PBL: Deploying At-Scale Professional Development While Supporting Customization to Initiate PBL Practices

Achieving equitable deeper learning through PBL is not likely to occur through curricular resources alone. Teachers need high-quality professional learning experiences to support enactment (Larmer, Mergendoller, & Boss, 2015). PBL requires new strategies for working with students (Tamim & Grant, 2013). Teachers may be familiar with only some deeper learning competencies (e.g., critical thinking, collaboration, and communication), and need professional development improve their practice on the others (e.g., learning how to learn or maintaining an academic/learning mindset).

Although centralized, at-scale professional development serves important practical needs (particularly when resources are constrained), teachers' learning needs differ, as do the experiences of their communities of students. Therefore, professional development must be customized, and the *when* and *where* of professional development needs thoughtful consideration. When PBL is first introduced, it can be more efficient to start with whole-group sessions followed by customized learning opportunities for smaller groups. In other words, a robust model of PBL professional development might couple initial centralized at-scale sessions about the purpose and goals of PBL with subsequent local in-person time for learning about and planning the projects, as well as coaching to address teachers' personal needs or school-based challenges (Lucas Education Research & Buck Institute for Education, 2017). Moreover, teachers are considering best practices and effective lessons *for whom* (particular students) and *under what conditions* (affordances and limitations of their school context and community). These learning goals also reflect a growth mindset for teachers, with the focus on progress and improvement, but not necessarily immediate attainment, of equitable deeper learning outcomes.

RPPs can be useful for iteratively testing and improving professional development, to think through questions of the *when* and *where* of their training, so that teachers are supported as they transition to PBL. For example, one collaboration among a PBL professional development provider and research team focused on how to design and improve a model of virtual coaching that supports teachers in developing expertise with project-based teaching (Krumm et al., 2016). Recognizing that teachers need one-to-one support while acknowledging the challenge with resources to visit each teacher in person, this study examined how coaches could effectively support teachers virtually by reviewing classroom videos and providing feedback in video conferences and in writing. The partnership identified coaching practices that were most effective by analyzing exchanges and interactions with teachers and coaches. In effect, the partnership used data in intentional ways to strengthen the trust and relationships among coaches and teachers, another important feature of RPPs. As a result of this RPP, the professional development provider now has an additional set of coaching strategies and tools to implement with teachers in the future.

Tension 4—How Teachers Learn About PBL: Building a Learning Community to Achieve Sustainability While Respecting Individual Private Experimentation

After a school or district adopts PBL, ongoing learning is required to achieve long-term sustainability. It can be a significant resource burden to sustain extensive professional development and personalized coaching for teachers at scale. Moreover, not all districts and schools have the resources to invest in professional PBL coaches, so teachers will need to rely on each other for guidance. To expand PBL, it becomes necessary to develop a community among educators who willingly share experiences and resources (e.g., PBL lessons and assessments) to improve their practice.

One major challenge in creating these professional learning communities for PBL is that the complexity of the practice can be daunting. In our own work, we have heard teachers express concerns that they are not sure their lessons are "good enough" or effective for students. They prefer to work privately until they are ready to share; for example, after completing a year of implementing a PBL course. For other teachers, the challenge is more systemic; teachers work in environments where they are not encouraged to share or do not have the necessary supports (e.g., time) to connect with colleagues.

RPPs can assist in several ways to develop vibrant communities of PBL educators who share effective tools, resources, and practices. First, RPPs can be structured intentionally to develop a learning community, including setting norms and practices for sharing within and beyond the partnership and creating mechanisms or routines that nurture collaboration. For instance, Lucas Education Research and the Institute for the Study of Knowledge Management in Education are examining how to promote more interaction among high school Advanced Placement PBL teachers; the research will help inform and refine facilitation practices to encourage greater teacher community engagement. Second, RPPs can explore more operational mechanisms that are supports for or barriers to community, such as the utility of openly licensing materials (e.g., as CC BY 4.0) to explicitly invite sharing and adaptation. Third, RPPs can support teachers in using practical measures that offer quick feedback about the effectiveness of new approaches (Bryk, Gomez, Grunow, & LeMahieu, 2015) and potentially increase teachers' confidence in sharing more readily.

Tension 5—Who the Primary Implementers of PBL Are: Creating a Supportive Infrastructure to Spread PBL While Encouraging Local Innovators

Literature on the diffusion of innovation describes the likelihood that different sub-populations will adopt a new practice or tool (Rogers, 2003). Innovators develop new practices, and early adopters are the first in line to use these new approaches, even before any evidence of efficacy is in place. The next adopters are the early and late majority, who will take on a practice or tool when valued opinion leaders provide a stamp of approval or when it's easier to do (than to not do) something new. "Laggards" are the last to come on board or, in some cases, they never will. It is rare for new practices to reach full market penetration, particularly progressive educational innovations such as equitable PBL; thus, PBL has been more prevalent in populations of teacher innovators and early adopters. This can be linked to a lack of attention to systemic support for capacity building in terms of providing curricular resources and comprehensive, sustained programs of practice to support significant changes in instruction (Cohen & Mehta, 2017).

For PBL to reach more students, administrators need to make headway in developing supportive infrastructures for PBL while acknowledging rather than avoiding the sometimes-conflicting demands or boundaries of the system. For example, accountability systems (e.g., state, district, or national assessments) do not necessarily promote the range of deeper learning competencies that are the focus of PBL. As a result, there are no systems drivers to motivate the early and late majority. Another challenge is the limited time that teachers are allotted for professional development; districts may have restrictions on the number of hours available for professional learning, leaving a majority of teachers unprepared to enact PBL effectively.

RPPs invite participation of district and school leaders so that competing demands can be acknowledged and negotiated. When challenges are within a local system (such as district-allotted time for professional development) and thus more difficult to change, RPPs can document the extent to which these limitations impact teaching practices and student engagement. These data can serve as evidence for PBL champions in the district to advocate for policy changes and can help move adoption from only the coalition of the willing to the whole system. Implied here is that the partnership involves a sustained long-term commitment among educators to discover challenges, gather systematic evidence, and mobilize levers that reduce barriers to participation. The field needs more examples of RPPs that demonstrate this evolution of evidence-based decision-making and approaches that leverage the work of early PBL innovators while creating supportive policies for PBL.

Conclusion

In this chapter, we discussed five equity-related tensions between the macro- and micro-factors of enacting equitable PBL—the why, what, where/when, how, and who of PBL that must be coordinated to develop, spread, and sustain deeper learning practices and outcomes. The intentional investigation guided by RPPs offers a promising, actionable approach to fostering a culture of learning and improvement to address these tensions. Importantly, these partnerships acknowledge that equity cannot be achieved at scale by simply replicating practices that worked in one context. They reflect a commitment to responsive pedagogy and research and anticipate that approaches will need to be adapted. RPPs encourage the community (e.g., district administrators, teachers, university researchers and educators, instructional designers, professional development designers/providers, and funders) to come together in a lasting partnership to ask questions about what works, what does not work, and why—to unpack problems of practice in their contexts and collect original data to iteratively improve PBL experiences and practices. RPPs focus on nurturing the partnership so that all stakeholders benefit and can build on the information learned. This community of practice coupled with the evidence base can increase the likelihood that innovations, such as PBL, can create at-scale, sustained, effective deeper learning opportunities for more students.

Notes

1   The overlapping aspect acknowledges that, for example, a competency such as adaptability might be located in both the interpersonal and intrapersonal domains, and continuous learning might be both intrapersonal and cognitive.
2   For more information, see www.air.org/project/study-deeper-learning-opportunities-and-outcomes.

References

Aguirre, J. M., & Bunch, G. C. (2012). What's language got to do with it? Identifying language demands in mathematics instruction for English language learners. In S. Celedón-Pattichis & N. Ramirez (Eds.), *Beyond good teaching: Advancing mathematics education for ELLs* (pp. 183–194). Reston, VA: National Council of Teachers of Mathematics.

Anyon, J. (1997). *Ghetto schooling: A political economy of urban educational reform*. New York: Teacher's College Press.

Baines, A., DeBarger, A. H., De Vivo, K., Warner, N., Brinkman, J., & Santos, S. (2017). *What is rigorous project-based learning?* (LER Position Paper 1). San Rafael, CA: George Lucas Educational Foundation.

Ball, D. L., & Cohen, D. K. (1996). Reform by the book: What is—or might be—the role of curriculum materials in teacher learning and instructional reform? *Educational Researcher, 25*(9), 6–14.

Bevan, B. (2017). Research and practice: One way, two way, no way, or new way? *Curator: The Museum Journal, 60*(2), 133–141. doi:10.1111/cura.12204

Boaler, J. (1997). *Experiencing school mathematics: Teaching styles, sex, and settings*. Retrieved from Google Books. Buckingham, UK: Open University Press.

Bryk, A. S., Gomez, L. M., Grunow, A., & LeMahieu, P. G. (2015). *Learning to improve: How America's schools can get better at getting better*. Cambridge, MA: Harvard Education Press.

Chun, M. (2015). Professional development and critical thinking: Influencing the how, who, and what of faculty practice. In T. Bers, M. Chun, W. T. Daly, C. Harrington, & B. F. Tobolowsky & Associates (Eds.), *Foundations for critical thinking* (pp. 71–86). Sterling, VA: Stylus Publishing.

Coburn, C. E. (2003). Rethinking scale: Moving beyond numbers to deep and lasting change. *Educational Researcher, 32*(6), 3–12.

Coburn, C. E., & Penuel, W. R. (2016). Research–practice partnerships in education: Outcomes, dynamics, and open questions. *Educational Researcher, 45*(1), 48–54. doi:10.3102/0013189X16631750

Cohen, D. K., & Mehta, J. D. (2017, April 17). Why reform sometimes succeeds: Understanding the conditions that produce reforms that last. *American Educational Research Journal*. doi:10.3102/0002831217700078

Condliffe, B., Visher, M. G., Bangser, M. R., Drohojowska, S., & Saco, L. (2016). *Project-based learning: A literature review*. New York: MDRC.

Davis, E. A., & Krajcik, J. S. (2005). Designing educative curriculum materials to promote teacher learning. *Educational Researcher, 34*(3), 3–14.

DeBarger, A. H., Choppin, J., Beauvineau, Y., & Moorthy, S. (2013). Designing for productive adaptations of curriculum interventions. In B. J. Fishman, W. R. Penuel, A-R. Allen, & B. H. Cheng (Eds.), *Design-based implementation research*. National Society for the Study of Education Yearbook, 112(2). New York: Teachers College Record.

Dole, S., Bloom, L., & Kowalske, K. (2016). Transforming pedagogy: Changing perspectives from teacher-centered to learner-centered. *The Interdisciplinary Journal of Problem-Based Learning, 10*(1), 1–14.

Ertmer, P. A. (2005). Teacher pedagogical beliefs: The final frontier in our quest for technology integration? *Educational Technology Research and Development, 53*(4), 25–39.

Ertmer, P. A., & Simons, K. D. (2006). Jumping the PBL implementation hurdle: Supporting the efforts of K–12 teachers. *Interdisciplinary Journal of Problem-Based Learning, 1*(1), 40–54.

Finkelstein, N., Hanson, T., Huang, C-W., Hirschman, B., & Huang, M. (2011). *Effects of problem-based economics on high school economics instruction*. Washington, DC: U.S. Department of Education, Institute of Education Sciences, National Center for Education Evaluation and Regional Assistance.

Harris, C. J., Penuel, W. R., D'Angelo, C., DeBarger, A. H., Gallagher, L. P., Kennedy, C. A., Chen, B.H., Krajcik, J. S. (2015). Impact of project-based curriculum materials on student learning in science: Results of a randomized controlled trial. *Journal of Research in Science Teaching, 52*(10), 1362–1385.

Heller, R., Wolfe, R., & Steinberg, S. (Eds.) (2017). *Rethinking readiness: Deeper learning for college, work, and life.* Cambridge, MA: Harvard Education Press.

Hernández-Ramos, P., & De La Paz, S. (2009). Learning history in middle school by designing multimedia in a project-based learning experience. *Journal of Research on Technology in Education, 42*(2), 151–173.

Kaldi, S., Filippatou, D., & Govaris, C. (2011). Project-based learning in primary schools: Effects on pupils' learning and attitudes. *Education 3–13: International Journal of Primary, Elementary and Early Years Education, 39*(1), 35–47.

Krajcik, J. S., & Czerniak, C. (2013). *Teaching science in elementary and middle school classrooms: A project-based approach* (4th ed.). London: Routledge.

Krajcik, J., Palincsar, A., & Miller, E. (2017). *Multiple literacies in PBL: Year 2 technical report.* Unpublished manuscript.

Krajcik, J. S., & Shin, N. (2014). Project-based learning. In R. K. Sawyer (Ed.), *The Cambridge handbook of the learning sciences* (2nd ed., pp. 275–297). New York: Cambridge University Press.

Krumm, A. E., Boyce, J., D'Angelo, C., Podkul, T., Feng, M., Christiano, E., & Snow, E. (2016). *Project-based learning virtual instructional coaching networked improvement community.* Final report. Menlo Park, CA: SRI Education.

Larmer, J., Mergendoller, J. R., & Boss, S. (2015). *Setting the standard for project-based learning: A proven approach to rigorous classroom instruction.* Alexandria, VA: ACSD.

Lucas Education Research & Buck Institute for Education. (2017). *Knowledge in action 2016–2017 professional development materials.* San Rafael, CA: George Lucas Educational Foundation.

Mehta, J. (2014). Deeper learning has a race problem. Learning Deeply Blog, *Education Week.* Retrieved from http:// blogs.edweek.org/edweek/learning_deeply/2014/06/deeper_learning_has_a_race_problem.html

National Research Council. (2012a). *Education for life and work: Developing transferable knowledge and skills in the 21st century.* Committee on Defining Deeper Learning and 21st Century Skills, J. W. Pellegrino and M. L. Hilton (Eds.), Board on Testing and Assessment and Board on Science Education, Division of Behavioral and Social Sciences and Education. Washington, DC: The National Academies Press.

National Research Council. (2012b). *Education for life and work: Guide for practitioners.* Board on Testing and Assessment and Board on Science Education, Division of Behavioral and Social Sciences and Education. Washington, DC: The National Academies Press.

Noguera, P., Darling-Hammond, L., & Friedlaender, D. (2015). *Equal opportunity for deeper learning. Students at the center: Deeper learning research series.* Boston, MA: Jobs for the Future.

Palincsar, A. S., Kucan, L. L., Fitzgerald, M., & Marcum, M. (April, 2017). *Designing and using texts in the context of project-based science instruction.* Paper presented at the annual meeting of the American Educational Research Association, San Antonio, TX.

Parker, W. C., & Lo, J. C. (2016). Reinventing the high school government course: Rigor, simulations, and learning from text. *Democracy and Education, 24*(1), 1–10. Retrieved from http://democracyeducationjournal.org/home/vol24/iss1/6/

Penuel, W. R., & Gallagher, D. J. (2017). *Creating research–practice partnerships in education.* Cambridge, MA: Harvard Education Press.

Peterson, B. W. (2012). Uncovering the progressive past: The origins of project-based learning. *UnBoxed: A Journal of Adult Learning in Schools, 8.* Retrieved from https://gse.hightechhigh.org/unboxed/issue8/uncovering_the_progressive_past/

Rogers, E. M. (2003). *Diffusion of innovations.* New York: The Free Press.

Rogers, M. A. P., Cross, D. I., Gresalfi, M. S., Trauth-Nare, A. E., & Buck, G. A. (2011). First year implementation of a project-based learning approach: The need for addressing teachers' orientations in the era of reform. *International Journal of Science and Mathematics Education, 9*(4), 893–917.

Shwartz, Y., Weizman, A., Fortus, D., Krajcik, J., & Reiser, B. (2008). The IQWST experience: Using coherence as a design principle for a middle school science curriculum. *The Elementary School Journal, 109*(2), 199–219.

Tamim, S. R., & Grant, M. M. (2013). Definitions and uses: Case study of teachers implementing project-based learning. *Interdisciplinary Journal of Problem-Based Learning, 7*(2), 71–101. Retrieved from http://doi.org/10.7771/1541-5015.1323

Thomas, J. W. (2000). *A review of research on project-based learning.* San Rafael, CA: The Autodesk Foundation.

Zwiers, J., Dieckmann, J., Rutherford-Quach, S., Daro, V., Skarin, R., Weiss, S., & Malamut, J. (2017). *Principles for the design of mathematics curricula: Promoting language and content development.* Retrieved from Stanford University, UL/SCALE. Retrieved from http://ell.stanford.edu/content/mathematics-resources-additional-resources

9

CONFIGURATIONS IN CO-DESIGN

Participant Structures in Partnership Work

Ashley Seidel Potvin,* Rebecca G. Kaplan,*
Alison G. Boardman, and Joseph L. Polman

Most practicing teachers in the second decade of the 21st century have experienced several waves of imposed silver-bullet reform efforts, resulting, for many, in reform fatigue. Too often, teachers are asked to enact curriculum designed by outsiders without their input. Many such curricula continue to subject students to prescriptive rote practices, in spite of advances from the field in understanding how people learn through active participation and interaction (Bransford, Brown, & Cocking, 2000). Likewise, professional development models aimed at supporting teachers in enacting new practices often rely on transmission models in which teachers "sit and get" procedural knowledge, in spite of research that points to active learning as a key component of successful teacher learning (Desimone, 2009).

In this chapter, we describe a partnership that set out to address these two connected problems of practice: curricula that rely on rote practices and top-down reform efforts delivered to teachers using outdated professional learning models. We approached these problems of practice by employing a co-design model for developing a project-based learning (PBL) curriculum for ninth-grade English language arts (ELA). Co-design provides a powerful context for strengthening connections between research and practice in ways that make the results more usable and sustainable in practice. Co-design is a common strategy for research–practice partnerships (RPPs; see Chapters 3–5, this volume) and can also operate to leverage and amplify teachers' voices and concerns in a wide variety of research and practice arrangements.

During our work together, we came to understand co-design as a process that mirrored the goals and values of PBL. PBL challenges students to address problems that matter to them and to others. Students work collaboratively to investigate essential questions and create consequential products or performances to share with public audiences. Thus, we designed the course using a co-design model grounded in PBL principles. Co-design, as an element of design-based implementation research (DBIR), engages teachers and researchers in designing, adapting, or testing curriculum materials together (Penuel, Fishman, Cheng, & Sabelli, 2011). Because co-design is adapted to the unique demands of the local context as well as the task at hand, specific functions and roles are locally constructed by members of the co-design teams (Penuel, Roschelle, & Shechtman, 2007). No matter the configuration of roles for participants, co-design is often a new way of working for many team members, creating both excitement and challenge as teams embark on generating new ideas.

Top-down reform efforts frame teachers and their capabilities as problems to solve, rather than as resources for the process of addressing problems (Cohen, Moffitt, & Goldin, 2007). As Fishman, Penuel, Allen, Cheng, and Sabelli (2013) have noted, DBIR can disrupt top-down reform if we "reconfigure the roles of researchers and practitioners [to bring] about systemic change" (p. 137). Reconfigurations can create learning communities of teachers and researchers working together to solve mutually agreed-upon problems of practice.

Long-term partnership work involving educators and researchers in curriculum co-design requires thoughtful consideration. In the sections that follow, we explore how the organization of co-design processes affected teacher engagement in the co-design process and ultimately adaptation and uptake of the products produced. Specifically, we describe how two group configurations emerged. These co-design teams included ninth-grade ELA teachers and university-based educators and researchers (faculty members and doctoral students).

Theoretical Framing

Our approach to understanding work in co-design teams is sociocultural (Vygotsky, 1978; Wertsch, 1991), with critical attention paid to power, authority, and agency. We utilize the notion of participant structures (Philips, 1972) to make sense of how teams of university-based researchers and practicing teachers take on roles. Herrenkohl and Guerra (1998) applied Philips's notion to classroom interactions aimed at transforming traditional active teacher and passive student roles to reconfigured roles more in line with a community of learners (Rogoff, 1994) approach. The traditional positioning of teacher and students that they sought to disrupt is similar to positioning found in traditional professional development sessions where teachers "sit and get" ideas, tools, and methods from active outside agents or experts. In contrast, a community of learners "is based on the premise that learning occurs as people participate in shared endeavors with others, with all playing active but asymmetrical roles" (Rogoff, 1994, p. 209) appropriate to the situation. As Penuel et al. (2007) state, in co-design,

> teachers are expected to play active, if not equal, roles in the design process. Teachers help construct the key problems co-design must address, help

frame the vision for what is to be created, test the innovation in their class-rooms, and provide input as changes and refinements are made.

(p. 55)

Further, Cornelius and Herrenkohl (2004) examined how relations of power are reified in classroom participant structures through expectations for who is expected to act in particular ways and what authority they are deemed to have. In co-design, facilitators of the process engage in "persuasive dialogue" in which multiple interlocutors co-construct action, with shared power (Wertsch, 1991). This contrasts with design that is driven by researchers who engage in "authorita-tive" or "monologic" discourse (Bakhtin, 1981) when speaking with educators, where it is assumed that researchers have the authority and power to make key decisions or steer the direction of the work without question and where research-ers demand curriculum be implemented in certain ways. In contrast, a hallmark of persuasive dialogue, either in classrooms or in co-design teams, is that diverse participants exercise agency based on their particular experiential background as well as their individual and collective goals. Because teachers and researchers have different expertise, experience, priorities, and power, persuasion allows diverse participants in design dialogue to navigate tensions and resolve disagreements. Maintaining persuasion rather than authority as the norm supports the buy-in of all group members for making substantive contributions to a collaborative process and generating curriculum products capitalizing on diverse expertise.

Context

The context of our co-design work is as follows. During the spring of 2015, the research team brainstormed four sketches of potential unit foci to include in a grant proposal. The research team brought to the project a certain set of commit-ments, including designing a course that would engage students in "deep learning, reflection, empathy, and fun." Our task in 2015–2016, developed in collaboration with our funder (Lucas Education Research), was to design a course around PBL principles. The course would include projects unified around a driving challenge with an essential question, collaborative work centered on production, and activi-ties that would feel authentic to the learner and audiences. Essential questions would connect to the overall theme of each unit, allowing for student-guided inquiry. The resulting educative materials would be published on an open-source platform. Funded in 2015, our full co-design team included 15 ninth-grade ELA teachers, 10 researchers, a district literacy coordinator, and a district educational technologist.[1]

Designing for Local Adaptation

We were committed to creating materials that could be adapted to local contexts (Kirshner & Polman, 2013). Within our co-design group, teachers taught in a variety of settings, representing six high schools within the two districts. The team prioritized developing materials that could be adapted to constraints and affordances of sites and course types. Ninth-grade ELA is not one specific course in these districts and elsewhere; rather, it is an umbrella term that encompasses many different course types, including honors, pre-International Baccalaureate, inclusion, English/social studies integrated, and regular English 9. Each course type and district had different constraints to which we had to conform. For instance, partnering districts (and schools) had different text requirements, with some teachers having more freedom to select texts than others. To support local adaptations, therefore, we planned our course to not require particular texts, but instead to offer themes that could be explored through different texts. Adaptations could be made to meet local curriculum demands, students' learning needs or interests, or a teacher's individual preferences.

Co-Design Team Formation

We began working as a full team in the summer of 2015, at our opening design institute. Teachers were enthusiastic about the potential of PBL to engage students meaningfully and to invigorate instruction. On the institute's first day, we sought to get to know one another and develop shared visions for PBL. We engaged in a short design sprint to begin developing a design culture. At day's end, the research team shared brief sketches of the four potential units that they had created for the grant proposal: Shattering Superman, The Singularity, It Happened Here, and Be the Change. The research team previewed ideas to garner excitement and to suggest a starting place for co-design. Team members stressed that the ideas were rough sketches intended to be further developed with teachers, emphasizing that teachers' expertise and knowledge of students and classrooms would be crucial to developing project-based units.

Later in the institute, we organized into four co-design teams, and each team's goal was to develop one PBL unit. Teachers selected teams based on their interest in the proposed topics. Each team ultimately had three or more teachers, a lead researcher, and one or more doctoral students with relevant interests and experience. Teams spent a few hours brainstorming and pitching ideas at the institute and then committed to working together during the fall semester to develop their units. Each teacher agreed to pilot the unit in their class during the spring semester of that same school year. Other than agreeing on timelines, approximate meeting frequency, and some initial responsibilities, each team set its own meeting schedule and agendas and divided the design work up as team members saw fit. Design teams agreed to use shared Google folders to organize their documents and Slack, an online messaging tool, for collaboration (see Garcia & Hunt, Chapter 11, this volume, for more information on how digital tools can be incorporated into partnerships). The research team met weekly to plan design workshops, develop and discuss research plans, and discuss implementation as it unfolded.

The full co-design team, including all researchers and teachers, met monthly during the fall semester to review and provide feedback on emerging unit plans and teachers' enactment of units.

In the case studies that follow, we describe the organization and outcomes of co-design processes for two of these four units in order to highlight how two different approaches to organizing the co-design process led to two different sets of outcomes.

Case 1: Be the Change

Personal Interests and Past Projects

I (Ashley) walk into the coffee shop and join my teammates: Amy, Jeannie, and Rachel, all teachers; Sela, a doctoral student; and Barbara, a professor.[2] We begin to talk about what the unit will look like; we have been trying to determine the big picture and essential questions. Inevitably, our discussion turns once again to defining what we mean by change, *a discussion that quickly becomes abstract and circular. Some of us see* change *as connected to personal experiences of change and growth, while others see* change *as connected to social change in the community and the world. In an effort to move the planning forward and get more concrete, we shift the conversation to designing, and teachers start to envision how some of these ideas might fit into their classrooms.*

Three distinct variations start to emerge as each teacher talks about a preexisting unit that they teach and how Be the Change could potentially fit into these units. Jeannie envisions integrating Be the Change into a unit she teaches around The Absolutely True Diary of a Part-Time Indian *by Sherman Alexie. Amy explains that the change unit needs to have a global focus in order to align with the integrated ELA/social studies world studies course she teaches. Rachel talks about her Problems and Solutions unit and thinks that this framing is already set up for students to "make a change."*

In the face of these different ideas and directions, it becomes apparent that we may not be able to identify one coherent approach, at least at first. Someone suggests designing three different variations of Be the Change to accommodate each teacher's unique contexts and situations, and then building on that to come back together to design a single coherent unit that could accommodate the local adaptations teachers had developed. We agree to follow this track, although it was not the original vision. In order to pursue three pathways, we decide to form three mini-teams, each with one teacher and the three researchers. After the meeting, I wonder what we will gain or lose from locating design as an individual rather than a collective activity.

Dividing and Conquering: Focusing on Individual Iterations

Two key tensions emerged during our group's design process, which impacted the way we structured the co-design work. First, a tension emerged early in our group's meetings that required us to strike a balance between conceptual planning and concretizing the unit into actionable learning activities. The group grappled with the core focus of the unit, questioning whether *change* should be conceptualized as personal change or broader advocacy for change. Reflecting this tension, the essential questions spanned both perspectives on change and included the following:

- What is change, and why does it matter?
- How have I changed? How have I been changed?
- How do people enact change?
- How am I going to be an agent of change? How are we going to be agents of change?

To address this tension and to accommodate the divergent interests and needs of the teachers, we collectively decided to suspend team planning to focus on each teacher's individual iteration of the unit. This changed the co-design configuration of our team; teachers co-designed with researchers rather than with one another. We chose to develop the unit inductively, starting with three individual adaptations and, from there, backing into a single coherent unit, based on the common themes that emerged across the units. Our original vision had involved developing a common unit and then creating local adaptations.

Structuring the co-design work in this way led to another tension: designing curriculum for a local context that could later be scaled involved tacking back and forth between planning for individual teacher enactment and designing for other classrooms. The teachers joined this particular design team because of the perceived connection to existing units they had taught previously. While the fit initially made sense to the team, it may have later become a barrier to our larger co-design goals for curriculum development because we established a pattern of focusing on each teacher's individual classrooms without establishing routines for zooming out to design for other classrooms. Additionally, it was difficult to identify commonalities among three distinct variations as each teacher emphasized different essential questions from our list and envisioned a different final project at the end of the unit. Working in mini-teams therefore resulted in design iterations that honored individual teacher preferences and contexts over broader ones. Thus, while a key design principle was to create materials that could be adapted to local contexts (Kirshner & Polman, 2013), we shifted to create materials for each teacher's context within our group, putting off the design of one coherent unit. By the end of the year, we had not identified or designed a coherent Be the Change unit.

Teacher Agency Directed Toward Individual Action

Teachers exercised agency when they worked in collaboration with researchers to design instruction for each of their classes (e.g., Polman & Miller, 2010). In each mini-team, teachers expressed interest in trying out new tools and strategies in their classrooms to align their units with key elements of PBL. For example, Jeannie and Amy implemented new teaching practices, such as multimodal composition and design sprints. However, they both returned to teaching their non-PBL units as they had done in the past, citing time and scheduling interruptions as barriers to the PBL implementation.

While all teachers on the team demonstrated agency, Rachel's participation reflected a deep commitment to co-design with a greater infusion of PBL. We discussed and planned many new ideas for Rachel's updated unit to align with PBL, and she incorporated nearly every new activity we developed together. We often co-created documents together, sending them back and forth for revisions. Sometimes Rachel started the document; sometimes the researchers started the document. When researchers visited Rachel's classroom, we often stayed for two periods, and Rachel frequently asked for feedback about the lesson or suggested a way to adjust it. She typically incorporated these changes into her next lesson. Sometimes Rachel emailed us to let us know how the day's lesson went or to share a student work sample. Rachel was the only teacher on the co-design team to enact an updated version of the unit that incorporated many PBL elements and to return to the research study for a second year. Rachel also opted to work during the summer so that we could continue to build on her work for the next iteration of Be the Change.

Collaborative Structures to Support Each Teacher in Their Context

Focusing on designing individual unit variations shifted the collaboration structures in co-design. Teachers on the Be the Change team had individualized support from researchers, and the researchers were heavily involved in the weekly classroom activities. Researchers often met with teachers or attended their class sessions multiple times a week. Teachers received support from researchers in creating lesson plans and instructional materials. While in the classroom, researchers performed a variety of tasks to support teachers, including co-teaching, providing feedback on lessons, or working with student groups.

While we planned to reunite periodically as a full design team to identify commonalities across the three strands, we only met again as a complete team twice. This was due in part to the volume and frequency of meetings we had with teachers individually, leaving little time or capacity for full design team meetings. When we did meet as a whole group, teachers shared what they were doing in their classrooms and described changes they would want to make to their preexisting units, but our team did not work on creating the coherent unit. In the end, we had a limited number of collaborative conversations that included multiple practicing teachers' voices.

At the end of the year, the Be the Change co-design team had not come to consensus on whether the common unit should focus on personal change or communal change through advocacy. In the following year, a newly configured co-design team formed to resolve these ambiguities and design a cohesive unit. That new unit incorporated many of the individual lessons and activities that had been designed for individual classrooms but required significant design and development work. The new team needed to determine the focus for change, revise essential questions to align with this unified focus, develop a common final product, and create daily lesson plans.

Case 2: It Happened Here

Whose Project Is It Anyway? Developing a Collective Vision

The excitement had been palpable in the car as Joe and I (Rebecca) took the hour-long drive through rolling farmland to Dover High. Though we were still getting to know each other, we already knew we had a shared commitment to working in a democratic fashion with our co-design team. We discussed plans to suggest rotating facilitators among the team members and tools to make sure to elicit everyone's voice.

In the classroom, we were joined by three teachers representing three schools: Amelia, Erica, and Jana. Together we were tasked with co-designing the It Happened Here unit. We opened the meeting with a discussion about continuing to share brainstorming and resources on Slack. As the facilitator, I opened the conversation: "Let's discuss our goals. What are broad ideas of resources we want to create together?"

Erica was quick to speak. "I don't feel like we can design anything without discussing the standards first." Her voiced frustration seemed to put up a roadblock, demanding to be addressed before we could continue on the path we'd started. "Will teachers in this group be forced to implement the unit? I mean, I can always modify it for my needs if I have to," Erica said. I felt my pulse quicken. This wasn't what Joe and I had hoped for—the implied division between researchers and teachers was in opposition to our hopes and intentions.

"The modifications you are picturing, what it would take to really do this in your classroom, are exactly what we as a design team want to know about and to include in how we create this project," Joe said. I added, "No one will be forced to teach anything, but we can build the unit with our real contexts in mind so that every teacher can adapt it for their context. Let's build something we want to teach."

Erica relaxed, and the feeling in the room shifted. We'd avoided thinking about our team as researchers versus teachers. We were in this together, and each of our voices, concerns, contexts, and ideas would count.

One Team Building One Unit to Support Individual Adaptation

In the beginning of that first team meeting, Erica articulated a tension she was experiencing that positioned our team as having two different sub-groups, one (researchers) with the power to force the other (teachers) to do something they might not want to do. Before we entered that meeting, Joe and Rebecca had discussed approaching this team with the assumption that everyone had expertise and that groups collaborated most successfully when each member was supported to leverage their expertise (Kirshner, 2010).

We recognized the need for our team to collaboratively identify goals and for our team members to feel individual responsibility to work toward those goals. When Erica raised her concern and revealed the tension she felt around power within the group, we drew on democratic principles to name the team as one entity with five members, all valued contributors who would work toward one goal. Still, within that one goal, we positioned teachers as having autonomy to decide what worked best for them and what adaptations to make for their classroom contexts.

The teachers on our design team exercised autonomy in their classroom implementations, and we encouraged them to bring challenges and affordances specific to their implementations to inform the group's design. The target was a single, adaptable unit, one that each team member would *want* to teach. This shaped the group's goals and practices. We focused on shared ownership of a large-scale product, the It Happened Here unit. This project invited students to investigate a newsworthy event and determine what had happened there, based on multiple perspectives, which they would gather through primary sources such as interviews.

The collaboratively created essential project questions were as follows:

- How does place matter? (If it had happened somewhere else, how might it be different?)
- How does time matter? (If it had happened at another time in history, how might it be different?)
- What is the power of sharing/telling stories? Whose (his)story is it?

The team honored the design principle of creating materials that could be adapted to local contexts by encouraging the development of a single set of materials for the unit (Kirshner & Polman, 2013).

Collaborative Structures to Support Building a Common Product

The It Happened Here team utilized several tools and structures to create the social settings and relationships needed to support democratic collaboration. For example, each meeting was facilitated by a different team member. While the researchers often created agendas for the meetings, the teachers agreed to review each agenda the day before the meeting and to add ideas and items. At each meeting's end, the team discussed who would facilitate the next meeting. This allowed for more horizontal collaboration, with a different person taking on the leadership role for each meeting.

On the shared Google Drive, we created several team charts that served as tools to support collaboration in building the shared unit. Throughout work together, we used these team charts in particular ways. During in-person meetings, we silently contributed to the same document; read through everyone's work, using the comment tool to note questions, concerns, or suggestions; and used the comments to guide a group discussion to make design decisions. The idea to create a team brainstorming chart emerged toward the end of our first meeting, to brainstorm different events that students could investigate and the products, texts, goals, and questions that would connect to the event.

The It Happened Here team started our second meeting with 10 minutes of silent collaboration, during which all contributed to the brainstorming chart simultaneously, putting everyone's ideas on the table before discussion. We used this strategy throughout the remainder of the school year. At one point, Jana suggested we work together in the charts outside of meeting time, setting several 30-minute time slots to "see each other in the document" and feel connected and supported even though we'd be working from four different towns. These virtual work sessions were highly productive, and we see the success of these sessions as an example of what can emerge through horizontal collaboration. The sessions could have fallen flat, had one of the researchers suggested them, or had the power dynamics between researchers and teachers been different. The various dialogic techniques of constructing shared documents helped to incorporate multiple voices in the emerging product.

When the time came to pilot our It Happened Here unit, Amelia suggested we keep a common team journal on Google Drive to share what we were trying and connect about what was working and what we needed to think through together. The teachers on the team contributed to the journal, and the researchers and teachers both used the comment tool to contribute ideas and encouragement throughout the journal entries. The collaborative structures used throughout our co-design team's process allowed us to feel joint ownership of the product.

Teacher Agency Directed Toward Collective Action

The teachers on the It Happened Here team expressed agency not just in the content of the unit but also in offering suggestions about collaborative processes. When Jana suggested scheduling times to work together in online documents, outside of face-to-face meetings, she was pitching a solution to alleviate the disconnection the team members felt between monthly meetings. Jana's expression of agency arose from a discussion in which the other teachers were expressing their desires to feel more connected to the project. This suggestion allowed us to take collective action between meeting times in order to create a stronger common product.

When Amelia suggested we use a shared journal during piloting, she shifted the team's collaborative focus. Until that point, we had been collaborating to create a common product. But as the teachers planned to pilot our team's product in their classrooms, their implementations became more independent and autonomous. Amelia expressed agency in suggesting that teachers stay connected with one another while implementing the unit in different contexts and with different texts and foci. Her suggestion allowed the team to collectively discuss ways to refine the common product as each team member worked out their individual implementation. While researchers observed classroom activities and actively commented in the teachers' collective journal, implementation of the unit was the responsibility of each teacher. The team negotiated these roles and responsibilities together, with Amelia's suggestion guiding the collaborative relationship. In these ways, the It Happened Here team operated as a community of learners, with all playing active roles.

At the end of the year, this team of teachers and researchers had designed a cohesive skeleton unit that teachers needed to personalize in order to implement it within their classrooms. The skeleton unit consisted of a coherent set of essential questions (see the list given earlier), a common final product, three interim products that moved students toward the final product, and a common final assessment aligned to standards and connected to the final product. Teachers then needed to determine the parameters for what students would investigate in their own classrooms. Amelia constrained topics of investigation by determining place; student groups chose topics to investigate that had happened in their small town. Erica constrained both the topic for investigation and the place by having students investigate the experiences of different sub-groups within their school. Jana shifted the focus of investigation to fit the requirements of her integrated English/history classroom by having students investigate individuals who had fought for human rights. All the teachers on the team engaged their students in practicing interviewing techniques, designing interview protocols, interpreting interviews through the lens of the essential questions, and storytelling about their investigation. All three teachers planned and enacted PBL units that were guided by the team's shared vision and design for the It Happened Here unit. In the following year, we were able to build on the solid skeleton that the co-design team created and use materials from all three of the teacher adaptations.

Reflections on Case Studies

Differences in these two cases shed light on the organization of co-design to support local adaptation. In one case, we worked from local adaptations to build a connected and coherent overarching unit. The Be the Change group started in mini design teams where teachers felt supported to develop lessons and new teaching practices that fit their own classrooms. While the team intended to inductively develop an integrated unit from these three variations, in the end, only one project-based version of Be the Change was fully developed; therefore, no coherent overarching unit was initially produced that blended ideas from the individual implementations. In It Happened Here, teachers and researchers began with a shared vision of the theme, which was further developed through extensive collaborative work, both in person and asynchronously. This team worked together to create a cohesive collective unit. In the implementation and local adaptation phase of this team's work, teachers looked to one another as resources as they planned for and began instruction in their individual classrooms.

In this concluding section, we note key trade-offs that emerged from our experience in terms of products created, work distribution, and participants' experience of agency.

How Do Co-Design Configurations Influence What Is Produced?

One of our teams (Be the Change) created materials for individualized local contexts, with the goal of later synthesizing them into one common unit, while the other team (It Happened Here) created common materials that were then adapted into local contexts. This led to differences in what was produced. The Be the Change team ended its year of co-design with one coherent locally adaptive unit and a collection of several additional activities that had never coalesced into units. These activities were used as a starting point for the next iteration of the team's unit design, and several were incorporated into other units. Yet, the individual unit designs left conceptual questions about the focus of the unit unanswered at the end of the year. When a new configuration of the Be the Change team formed the following year, team members had to return to the conceptual questions around *change*, determine a focus for the unit, and do a significant amount of designing and creating rather than refining materials for the next iteration.

In contrast, the It Happened Here team developed common materials that could be adapted to local contexts and created one cohesive skeleton that each teacher adapted for their individual classrooms. This team ended its year of co-design with a cohesive unit plan and three individual adaptations of that plan. When a new configuration of the It Happened Here group formed the following year to develop the second iteration of the unit, because the conceptual coherence had already been established, team members were able to move forward with the same base and develop more detailed materials that they determined were needed based on the data from the three pilot enactments. They were able to refine the unit and focus on building out pedagogical practices, such as incorporating a workshop model for storytelling, integrating texts into the unit, and including a reporter's notebook in which students would engage in daily practices of perspective taking.

The tradeoff between what the two groups produced has implications for future co-designers. We recommend working toward convergence as much as possible when co-designing with a team while framing individual adaptation as a necessary and crucial aspect of implementation. To do this, co-design teams must establish common goals early on and set norms for sticking to them. For example, committing to designing a common product and establishing norms around doing so might have supported the Be the Change co-design team to maintain its focus on project goals for co-design. Designing a single adaptable product can create a strong foundation for future iteration. From these experiences, we now envision co-design as a process that prioritizes collective goals and products ahead of individual aims.

How Is Work Distributed?

Working with teachers as co-designers positions all participants in active roles, which is a purposeful move away from the "sit and get" model of traditional professional development. Although both teams included active participation of teachers, there were benefits and challenges to the structures and methods of each. Teachers and researchers on the It Happened Here co-design team supported one another in ways that allowed for each teacher to exercise agency over the design process and what was designed. The Be the Change co-design team structured the work to privilege local contexts over the broader goals of the unit, which inadvertently diminished opportunities for teachers to support one another. Still, this structure kept teachers engaged in the design process. For the most part, teachers worked individually with researchers rather than collaboratively as a team of researchers and teachers.

Another indicator of roles was the greater breadth in forms of teacher agency observed within the It Happened Here team. For instance, when teachers planned their day-to-day classroom materials, they shared them with one another in the team journal. Though the entire team had access to this document, it was clearly made by and for teachers. When teachers created their daily lesson plans, they attended to their own context, interests, and commitments, but as they met throughout the piloting phase, they discussed ways to revise and refine the adaptable unit. This was useful for creating the product and made sense considering the team's shared vision.

The intense level of researcher support for each teacher on the Be the Change team was only possible for one semester, as it was time and labor intensive on the part of the researchers and the teachers. Although this level of support encouraged teachers to enact some new pedagogical practices, it was not enough to support all three teachers in enacting a new PBL unit. Such an intensive level of researcher involvement in teachers' classrooms is difficult to sustain. Further, it may not be desirable for all teachers or align with the vision of co-design as a process that seeks to engage teachers and researchers in persuasive dialogue (Wertsch, 1991). A danger in researchers providing significant support *to* teachers is that it can become one-way, in contrast to the ideal of co-design, where persuasive dialogue *with* teachers results in more diverse expertise being contributed.

Considering how work was distributed across these teams shows the types of agency that can be made available within co-design. We recommend working toward co-design teams that actively design the norms and processes they use in order to benefit from the expertise that each person brings to the collective. This may mean that group members step up or step back, depending on the phase of co-design work in order to maximize valued participation of each team member. Evidence from our work emphasizes the importance of engaging in co-design of both process and product that acknowledges teachers as professionals and invites them into an active community of learners (Rogoff, 1994), a key element of successful co-design.

Conclusion

Co-design can be an effective way to engage in RPPs. Although the two cases operated in distinct ways, the experiences in other co-design teams within our larger project presented many of the same trade-offs discussed above.

In this chapter, we have elaborated ways to surface and honor diverse expertise within co-design teams, through configurations and practices that encourage broad participation in persuasive dialogue. For instance, in our RPP, the practitioners brought intimate knowledge of their classroom contexts and students, whereas the researchers brought understanding of the core elements of PBL and theories of learning from current literature. Our work also emphasized key features for successful co-design teams, including creating a shared vision, working toward a shared product, and valuing collective goals over individual aims. As our partnership of teachers and university researchers continues on our journey together, we will seek to further explore and clarify the implications of our co-design configurations.

Acknowledgments

The project described in this chapter is based upon work supported by the George Lucas Educational Foundation. We would like to thank the editors of this volume for the excellent feedback and support.

Notes

* ★ Co-lead authors
1 We distinguish school-based practicing teachers from those working as part of the university team on all aspects of research and development of the course, referring to the latter as *the research team*.
2 All proper names are pseudonyms, with the exception of the authors.

References

Bakhtin, M. M. (1981). Discourse in the novel (C. Emerson & M. Holquist, Trans.). In M. Holquist (Ed.), *The dialogic imagination* (pp. 342–354). Austin: University of Texas Press.

Bransford, J. D., Brown, A. L., & Cocking, R. R. (2000). *How people learn: Brain, mind, experience, and school.* Washington, DC: National Academy Press.

Cohen, D. K., Moffitt, S. L., & Goldin, S. (2007). Policy and practice: The dilemma. *American Journal of Education, 113*(4), 515–548.

Cornelius, L. C., & Herrenkohl, L. R. (2004). Power in the classroom: How the classroom environment shapes students' relationships with each other and with concepts. *Cognition and Instruction, 22*(4), 467–498.

Desimone, L. M. (2009). Improving impact studies of teachers' professional development: Toward better conceptualizations and measures. *Educational Researcher, 38*(3), 181–199.

Fishman, B. J., Penuel, W. R., Allen, A. R., Cheng, B. H., & Sabelli, N. (2013). Design-based implementation research: An emerging model for transforming the relationship of research and practice. *National Society for the Study of Education, 112*(2), 136–156.

Herrenkohl, L. R., & Guerra, M. R. (1998). Participant structures, scientific discourse and student engagement in fourth grade. *Cognition and Instruction, 16*, 431–473.

Kirshner, B. (2010). Productive tensions in youth participatory action research. *Yearbook of the National Society for the Study of Education, 109*(1), 238–251.

Kirshner, B., & Polman, J. L. (2013). Adaptation by design: A context-sensitive, dialogic approach to interventions. *National Society for the Study of Education, 112*(2), 215–236.

Penuel, W., Fishman, B., Cheng, B., & Sabelli, N. (2011). Organizing research and development at the intersection of learning, implementation, and design. *Educational Researcher, 40*(7), 331–337.

Penuel, W. R., Roschelle, J., & Shechtman, N. (2007). Designing formative assessment software with teachers: An analysis of the co-design process. *Research and Practice in Technology Enhanced Learning, 2*(1), 51–74.

Philips, S. U. (1972). Participant structures and communicative competence: Warm Springs children in community and classroom. In A. Duranti (Ed.), *Linguistic anthropology: A reader* (pp. 370–394). New York: Teachers College Press.

Polman, J. L., & Miller, D. (2010). Changing stories: Trajectories of identification among African American youth in a science outreach apprenticeship. *American Educational Research Journal, 47*(4), 879–918.

Rogoff, B. (1994). Developing understanding of the idea of communities of learners. *Mind, Culture, and Activity, 1*(4), 209–229.

Vygotsky, L. S. (1978). *Mind in society: The development of higher mental process.* Cambridge, MA: Harvard University Press.

Wertsch, J. V. (1991). *Voices of the mind: A sociocultural approach to mediated action.* Cambridge, MA: Harvard University Press.

10

BUT WHAT DOES IT ACTUALLY LOOK LIKE?

Representations of Teaching Practice in the Work of Research–Practice Partnerships

Vera Michalchik and Jennifer Knudsen

Many studies have demonstrated that more equitable and mutual collaborations between practitioners and researchers can help create new types of educational opportunities for students—ones better grounded in instructional practices that account for the breadth of students' capacities, deepen their attunement to means for developing insights, and promote enhanced possibilities for their future learning (see Bevan & Penuel, Preface, this volume; Coburn, Penuel, & Geil, 2013). Such accomplishments require the development of common understandings among researchers and practitioners within a shared communicative space. This mutually accessible space, which can be thought of as a "trading zone" for researchers and practitioners, allows for the productive give-and-take of ideas, stories, data, guidelines, and other informational resources (Collins, Evans, & Gorman, 2007; Stein & Coburn, 2010). Interactions in trading zones benefit from the experiences and contributions of both researchers and practitioners, adding into the mix new forms of evidence for advancing educational practice. The pace of interchange in these new zones may be uneven, the processes messy, and details unanticipated, yet this collaborative approach can lead to creative new ways of addressing challenging issues of practice (Coburn & Penuel, 2016; Sawyer, 2011).

Although working together in a common space helps researchers and practitioners realize their shared commitment to educational improvement, common ground is not a given; rather, it needs to be created from the diverse and sometimes colliding perspectives of professionals coming from different communities and paradigms (Riel & Polin, 2004). Moreover, researchers and practitioners working together to achieve shared goals necessarily confront the task of creating a variety of resources that they both find useful, including developing a common language as well as practical tools for the improvement efforts at hand (Ikemoto & Honig, 2010). A representation of practice is a special kind of tool—overlapping in some ways with the functions of, say, templates for drafting lesson plans or assessments of student understanding. But rather than serving to directly support a task, representations of practice are a resource for imagining possibilities. Though not a window on reality, these representations stand in for reality, bearing direct similarities to what teachers (together with students) might do or aspire to, or even what they might avoid (Pulvermacher & Lefstein, 2016).

This chapter focuses on the role of *representations of teaching practice* as tools for achieving goals targeted mutually by researchers and practitioners. Because partnerships involve a kind of border crossing in which people must negotiate shared goals, they invite us to draw connections to other kinds of inter-professional collaborations, where "boundary objects" (Star & Griesemer, 1989) play a role in facilitating interaction in a trading zone. Within partnerships in education, these objects often take the form of a shared representation of practice. By shared representation, we mean a jointly accessible referent for negotiating meanings that makes it possible for collaborators to achieve agreed-upon mutual goals (Baxter, 2010; Howarth, 2006). But how do these representations come into being within the trading zone of a research–practice partnership (RPP)? What specific purposes do they serve? In this chapter, we seek to answer the question of what makes representations of teaching useful as a resource for shared work between researchers and practitioners.

Modeling Practice in RPPs

Consideration of useful representations of instructional practice needs to start with the recognition that teachers' work is complex (Koschmann, 2011), requiring, at a minimum, pedagogical techniques, subject matter expertise, learning theory, management skills, and insight into human relationships. In the moment, teachers must coordinate these various frames as they work to shape, understand, assess, scaffold, facilitate, direct, and inspire the efforts of individuals and groups, often large groups. Preparing to teach, for novices as well as for those further developing their repertoire, entails learning to enact valued norms and assumptions, that, however malleable, eventually coalesce into routines of practice (Hammerness, 2006). These routines serve as the building blocks for teachers' future efforts and the foundations on which they grow as professionals. In the process, teachers increasingly develop what has been called "professional vision"—the capacity to see and interpret patterns in what, to novices, might look uninteresting, inscrutable, or chaotic (Goodwin, 1994). Gaining experience renders the process of making sense of complexity more manageable.

A wide range of research programs on teacher professional development (PD) have recently centered on questions regarding useful representations. Much of this work considers the relationship of theory to practice and posits the importance of representations of practice as a means of embodying essential features of what teachers might learn or explore—for example, how to organize group work or identify evidence of student learning (e.g., Borko, Koellner, Jacobs, & Seago, 2011). Some research efforts have focused on teachers' contributions to the creation of narratives, scripts, and other representations they use in PD settings (Herbst, Chazan, Chen, Chieu, & Weiss, 2011; Zazkis, 2017). Because such teacher-developed representations sit at the nexus of teacher practice and research-based theory, these efforts can generate important insights for the process of developing equitable and mutualistic RPPs.

"But what does it actually look like?" is a common question teachers ask when learning about instructional innovations. Making practice visible in ways useful for improving it, however, is not necessarily easy. Even with the affordances of video and new technologies, for instance, it is difficult to capture the "right" aspects of teaching practice in representational form (Derry et al., 2010). The "right" representation would distill from the complexities of any given situation those features that need to be understood, unpacked, and appropriated in such way as to lead to better teaching.

RPPs may be a productive context for generating representations that can be used within and beyond the RPP itself. In the first instance, shared representations of practice would ideally serve common goals for members of an RPP. Ultimately, as they are refined, circulated, and successfully used, these types of representations would progressively become ways of seeing the world, frameworks to overlay on complexity that are effectively prescriptive in nature. They therefore could serve as highly portable shared cultural models or genres that simplify reality and, at the same time, instruct participants how to view and act on it. As a result, instead of the research community "being functionally inarticulate" regarding the practicalities of instruction, a collaborative approach could make clear "the importance of making competent instructional practice visible" (Koschmann, 2011, p. 5).

In one sense, then, an important part of the work of an RPP focused on increasing educational equity involves the development of easily recognizable patterns of practice designed to replace existing ones.[1] Judgments regarding the success of efforts to advance equity in education may rest on how well these efforts comport to norms embodied in the representations of new genres. Thus, as we consider new models for RPPs, we do well to examine the construction of codified representations *of* practice and their use *in* practice.

Analyzing Representations in RPPs

This chapter posits several fundamental dimensions for analyzing the co-constructive work of developing and using representations of teaching practice to help both practitioners and researchers better coordinate their efforts. Our list is not comprehensive or finely tuned, but it puts into play a set of considerations that may matter as researchers and practitioners together seek to create productive representations of practice within RPPs.

Dimension 1: Actors, Origins, and Drivers

This dimension accounts for the ways in which the collaborative work to build representations of practice is begun and sustained in relation to the central and often dynamically evolving goals of the partners. Who initiates the collaboration, drives the identification of the problems, and has oversight of the conditions for producing the representations—such as convening working sessions, owning video cameras or other apparatus, and organizing content—gives shape to the mechanisms through which meanings regarding reform emerge and become part of a partnership's activities (Ikemoto & Honig, 2010). Choices made within this process will largely determine the nature and substance of how representations of practice and other information are considered, created, and used (Howarth, 2006).

Many, if not most, partnerships celebrated as successful relationships between research and practice—such as Success for All, Institute for Learning, and QUA-SAR (Coburn & Stein, 2010)—have originated from researchers, whose work with practitioners evolved over time to embody the mutualism and long-standing character that define RPPs. In the QUASAR project, for example, teachers adapted tools originally created for research, such as data collection instruments, and repurposed them to use for improving practice, creating a dynamic process that iteratively improved the work of both the researchers and practitioners (Baxter, 2010). In other cases, RPPs have evolved from practitioners' initiative (Perry & Lewis, 2010).[2] A few other studies document the development of RPPs grown simultaneously by persons occupying research and practice roles (e.g., Bevan, Gutwill, Petrich, & Wilkinson, 2015), despite the inherent challenges and perhaps inconsequentiality of determining who, exactly, is a researcher and who is a practitioner (e.g., many full-time researchers are former teachers). The originator of the efforts may have implications for the ways in which the co-development process is intentionally structured to achieve full buy-in and participation of all parties.

Dimension 2: Features of the Representations

The reasons for the formation of an RPP will undoubtedly influence the nature of its representations—their media type, organization, level of detail or abstraction, and other concrete features. Are they textual descriptions, physical enactments such as role plays, or videos? Are they high-level models or replete with the details of focused interaction? Are they idealized exemplars or messy examples? Researchers have been actively investigating the impacts of varied forms of representations on teacher learning and considering a diverse array of features of the representations. For example, work on representational forms includes studies that highlight the differences in learning outcomes from narrative—both researcher-elicited (Schultz & Ravitch, 2013) and naturally occurring within research subjects' interactions (Horn, 2010). Others have compared the affordances of one medium with another, such as studying outcomes of teacher learning in PD using animations in contrast to live-action videos (Herbst & Kosko, 2014). Several researchers have taken up the topic of tools, more generally, as a jointly constructed resource serving to productively link research and practice (e.g., Baxter, 2010). This work is highly informative, but little, if any, of it addresses representations of practice within RPPs per se.

Efforts to address problems of instructional practice, including those undertaken through RPPs, necessarily will entail the creation of some type of agreed-upon referent for what instructional practice could or should look like. Analyses of RPPs optimally would include consideration of how shared representational resources embody temporal and spatial aspects of classroom interactions, balance the specificities of cases in relation to the generalities of models, and account for the affordances and constraints of the representational media in particular ways.

Dimension 3: Uses in Professional Development Activities

How are descriptions, role plays, videos, and other representations of teaching practice actually used when researchers and practitioners work together on improving instructional practices? Teaching requires the development of capabilities that build upon and extend existing forms of practice in ways that, in turn, become "more authentic, more efficient, more equitable" (Herbst et al., 2011, p. 92). Teacher preparation and professional learning, then, requires some degree of contemplation and interpretation of representations of instruction such that these existing forms can be re-created and applied by practitioners in new situations. Grossman and colleagues (2009) argue that this type of "pedagogy of practice" for professional education requires from the outset representations of practice as an integral part within a system of professional learning. Representations of practice can help novices (or newcomers to particular pedagogical approaches) decompose unfamiliar practices so that they can better see, name, and rehearse them as they progressively move to more authentic or realistic enactments. In this formulation, key questions to ask include the following:

> What facets of practice are visible through these various representations? Which facets remain hidden from view? How do these representations open up opportunities to investigate practice? How do novices use these various representations of practice and practitioners to construct their own professional identities? What do they learn from these representations that may go well beyond the instructor's purpose in using them?
>
> *(2009, p. 2068)*

If teaching requires a study of practice, improving teaching through RPPs requires representations of practice that are subject to both scrutiny and adaptation—with the benefit of insights from both research and practice—in the process of the partnership's work.

Dimensions 1 and 2—the genesis of the representations and their form—will interplay with the ways in which representations of practice are used—dimension 3—in shared efforts at instructional improvement. Specific to dimension 3 are the ways in which representations are malleable and revisable, particular to persons or situations, or part of the system of meanings and resources used in discussions among partners. All of these factors affect how existing, modified, or new representations of practice become part of efforts at creating new and more equitable opportunities for learning within variable local contexts.

Two Cases of Representing Practice

The following sections describe PD programs reliant on representations that embody insights about learning. The final section will analyze these cases to generate observations that might contribute to the work of future RPPs.

Case Study 1: Bridging Professional Development Through Disciplined Improvisation

The Bridging Professional Development project was designed to span the gap between workshops and classroom practice, specifically in the area of teaching mathematical argumentation within nondominant urban communities. Mathematical argumentation is foundational in the work of mathematicians and prescribed as a practice in the Common Core Standards for Mathematics (Common Core State Standards Initiative, 2010). For many teachers, helping students learn mathematical argumentation requires new pedagogical approaches, among them specific teaching moves that represent a shift in classroom discourse away from the one- or two-word "right answerism" typical in the initiation-response-evaluation pattern of traditional classrooms (Mehan, 1979).

In Bridging PD, teachers learn to provide conditions that present students with challenges and require them to draw on mathematical knowledge of others in the classroom community to interactively reason through these challenges. Under such conditions, mathematical argumentation and conceptual understanding co-develop (Knudsen & Shechtman, 2016). Socialized as normative practice through opportunities to observe and join in, engaging in mathematical argumentation additionally develops students' comfort and fluency with argumentation as a regular way of doing math. Furthermore, argumentation and other reasoning practices can become internalized as habits of mind even beyond the mathematics classroom (Resnick, Michaels, & O'Connor, 2010; Yackel & Cobb, 1996).

Beyond certain essential features, teachers' support for mathematical argumentation need not be formulaic and instead may follow contingent, creative, and variable solution paths (Shechtman, et al., in preparation). In this light, the

Bridging PD project derives its approach from research that conceptualizes teaching as disciplined improvisation (Burnard, 2011). The project uses actual improvisational acting techniques to provide teachers direct experience with the art form and explicitly connects this experience to teaching practice. These approaches are intended to help teachers prepare for the unforeseen, think on their toes, and adapt their teaching moves to their students' expression of their ideas—expressions that will differ between students, between classes, and between topics. The project helps teachers recognize the improvisational nature of teaching and, more importantly, how to actively apply improvisational approaches, particularly as they pertain to mathematical argumentation. These approaches are applicable both as they practice teaching with peers in the workshop environment and as they engage in these teaching practices with students in their classrooms (Knudsen & Shechtman, 2016).

Participants in Bridging PD learn to teach mathematical argumentation through "successive approximations of practice" (Grossman, et al., 2009; Knudsen, Stevens, Lara-Meloy, Kim, & Shechtman, 2017)—professional development activities that grow ever closer to actual classroom practice and enable teachers to develop and hone teaching moves for flexible classroom use. The goal of the workshop is to help teachers develop teaching moves aimed at specific purposes within a framework for mathematical argumentation, with phases of conjecturing, justifying, and concluding. Equipped with knowledge of the framework, teachers together with researchers follow specific steps for identifying, exploring, rehearsing, and building a repertoire of their own teaching moves to facilitate students' construction of mathematical arguments. To learn to teach in this way, teachers engage in a sequence of four types of activity that constitute successive approximations of practice (Kim, 2011):

1. *Scenario analysis.* Teachers begin by examining classroom scenarios presented in scripts derived from actual classroom dialogue but modified to highlight particular features of teaching argumentation in the classroom. In acting out the scenario together—for example, one in which teachers ask students to give a peer feedback on evidence supporting a conjecture—teachers identify moves and their purposes, considering alternatives and possible consequences.
2. *Teaching games.* After examining written representations of classroom practice, teachers engage in games that allow them to act out a variety of moves within the low-stakes workshop environment. They consider constraints, analyze their moves, and draw conclusions for use in their own teaching. The games are categorized by the argumentation framework, enabling teachers to focus on a particular set of moves for each of the phases in turn.
3. *Lesson planning.* Teachers take several rounds of script analysis and role-play into a lesson planning activity. Their plans account for different phases of classroom argumentation and include hypotheses regarding how discussion might unfold and the specific moves they might use. Planning goes beyond

notating the outline of a lesson and is based on a foundation of visualization—teachers' imaginings of what students may do and what they may do in response, playing out contingent paths.

4. *Rehearsals for the classroom.* Based on his or her lesson plan, each teacher leads an improvisational session focused on a particular element of classroom practice, such as clarifying conjectures, which is followed by a discussion. Fellow teachers are "endowed" with student characteristics to help them play out their roles. Unlike in the games, teachers can stop the action of the rehearsal and ask for help from PD facilitators or other teachers on what to do next. These rehearsals and replays are close approximations of practice, allowing teachers to actively test and refine moves specific to anticipated student needs (Horn, 2010).

In sum, the Bridging PD program provides teachers with a set of action moves for supporting argumentation, detailed lesson plans indicating likely places for specific moves, and practice with improvisationally using those moves in those lessons—all based on a disciplinary framework. The program aims to foreground types of teaching moves that support productive collaboration, intellectual risk taking, constructive feedback, and iterative improvement in students' mathematical practices. What begins as efforts to emulate authentic practice—playful pastiches re-presenting what they interpret from representations in scripts and scenarios—becomes a field-tested means for promoting student learning. Once teachers have taken the moves to their classrooms, the Bridging PD project offers them follow-on opportunities to regroup with their peers to reflect on how well the moves have worked with students.

Origin of Representations

Critical in the Bridging PD project has been the inclusion of a co-design year in each of its implementations (see Potvin, Kaplan, Boardman, & Polman, Chapter 9, this volume, for a discussion of co-design in RPPs). During the co-design year, the Bridging PD project team has worked to adapt the program to the circumstances of the schools and districts in which they have worked. Activities center on mutual examination of existing scenarios, joint participation in games, co-development of new scripts and teaching moves, and collaborative role plays and feedback. In the spirit of mutualism inherent in RPPs, Bridging PD was deliberately organized to have representations co-generated by both researchers and practitioners.

Forms of Representations

Although the project team provides participating teachers as much preparation as possible for adaptive implementation of supports for argumentation in actual practice, it does not use video to capture and demonstrate illustrative practice. This choice rests largely on the concern that video examples might be too salient or authoritative, too particular to the contexts or featured teachers' profiles, and too inflexible to be usefully combined with the program's improvisational approach (Herbst & Kosko, 2014; Hill, Beisiegel, & Jacob, 2013). Instead, the program focuses on representing practices that derive initially from simple scenarios provided by project staff but, over time, through several rounds of improvisation and role play, evolve into a flexible repertoire of well-articulated moves within frameworks built on the core features of mathematical argumentation (conjectures, justifications, and conclusions).

Uses of Representations

The Bridging PD program uses the structure of mathematical argumentation as the foundation for its trading zone—a space within which researchers and practitioners together improvise teaching moves. The scripts, moves, and other representations participants develop are categorized by this structure at every stage of their preparations and rehearsals, making representations an ongoing context for reflecting on practice throughout Bridging PD. Using the structure of mathematical argumentation provides the discipline in what Sawyer (2011) termed the "disciplined improvisation" of teaching. As in learning to perform improvisational theater, a simple framework enables greater improvisational freedom.

Case Study 2: Lesson Study for Teacher Collaborative Learning

Lesson study is a method of instructional improvement that originated in Japan in the late 1800s and is credited with the high quality of teaching in Japanese education (Morris & Hiebert, 2011). Increasingly adopted in the United States, the approach provides teachers practical techniques for learning from one another as they together set goals, plan lessons, and examine actual classroom implementation. Lesson study is most often used for mathematics, though it can be used for any topical or content area—such as English language learning in Hong Kong (Lee, 2008). Although it typically requires a great deal of time and skilled facilitation by an experienced coach for effective implementation, lesson study has been shown to improve instructional design and practice as well as student learning (Perry & Lewis, 2017). Representations in the lesson study approach are generated by teachers and take the form of documentation of a lesson's goals, implementation, and results.

The method is typically used by a small team of teachers working in a content area for several months and consists of four phases with the following features:

1. *Investigation.* The teaching team collectively decides on a particular student learning goal for a lesson. Teachers determine the goal based on student

characteristics considered within a long-term learning trajectory. Teachers conduct in-depth study of the content area, existing curricula, and research literature to generate possible instructional approaches.

2. *Planning.* Teachers use resources they have collected to design a detailed lesson plan, anticipating the problems students may experience during the implementation and charting possible moves to support students in overcoming challenges. Their write-up includes short- and long-term learning goals, activities, assessments, data collection points, and rationale for design.

3. *Implementation.* Teachers implement the lesson while peers observe the responses of students to various teacher moves, collecting data through notes and/or electronic means and comparing these data with anticipated outcomes.

4. *Reflection.* Teachers together discuss and document what did and did not succeed in that lesson vis-à-vis their original plans and any new or serendipitous results of the implementation that can lead to further refinement of the lesson for a subsequent iteration, with a focus on student learning of subject matter and consolidation of their own insights (Lewis, Perry, & Hurd, 2009).

Researchers have argued that this sequence of choreographed events helps teaching practice in part by making its underlying assumptions visible, that it builds teachers' professional community and identity, and that it produces resources that team members and others can use—which together lead to instructional improvement and consequent increases in student learning (Lewis et al., 2009; Morris & Hiebert, 2011). The research on lesson study overall emphasizes various processes through which these changes occur or lead to different outcomes. Some studies, for example, highlight the socio-emotional changes forged in collegial efforts that lead to motivation, accountability, and commitment to the work of improving instruction (Puchner & Taylor, 2006). Others emphasize agency in iterative testing of approaches (Fernandez, Cannon, & Chokshi, 2003) or the value of resource kits as an ongoing support for local teaching teams and broad sustainability (Lewis & Perry, 2014).

One noteworthy feature of lesson study is how much it resembles research: it functions as a system for building practitioner knowledge through examination of actual practice. As such, the lesson study approach relies upon generating meaningful and testable hypotheses, systematically exploring these hypotheses through gathering and analyzing appropriate evidence, and making efforts to generalize findings and abstract principles to other relevant settings (Fernandez et al., 2003).

Origin of Representations

Although lesson study is not necessarily a forum for collaboration between researchers and practitioners, lesson study groups typically include more experienced teachers or researchers as coaches. A key role of more experienced participants is to help hone what we described earlier in this chapter as teachers' professional vision.

Forms of Representations

Most of the work taking place in lesson study uses direct peer observations in classrooms, but video capture and other means of recording are also used for examining implemented lessons. Discussion of what is seen either directly or in recordings is always a mediating factor *and* an object of inquiry—another form of representation of practice. It is through observations, recordings, and, most universally, talk that teachers build shared representational frameworks for creating new, recognizable, and reproducible forms of practice.

Uses of Representations

The lesson study sequence of activities helps teachers see what is valuable to see in teaching practice and to represent these features of practice in ways that similarly serve as a reference for others. The research-oriented work of a lesson study team is instrumental in identifying which aspects of practice are made visible through representations, or, as Judith Warren Little suggested, how elements of practice are made "transparent" and with what "fullness and specificity" (2003, p. 918). Of teaching practice generally, she wrote:

> *What facets of classroom practice are made visible in out-of-classroom talk and with what degree of transparency?* By the facets or "face" of practice, I mean those categories and aspects of practice that are made available for consideration in the topics taken up in conversation and through any material artifacts that teachers bring with them, create in the moment, or otherwise have available. By transparency, I mean the degree of specificity, completeness, depth, and nuance of practice apparent in the talk and the associated artifacts.
>
> *(2003, p. 920, italics in original)*

Conclusion

The Bridging PD and lesson study examples illustrate the importance of representations of practice to ground and sustain the iterative co-development of instructional forms. Representations can be an integral element in the interchange of ideas about practice, possibilities for new approaches to teaching, and means for enacting advances in new settings. In Bridging PD, representations evolve as improvisational sequences approximating the scripts that are the shared starting point translating the practice of mathematicians into classroom activities. In lesson study, the determination of a goal, review of existing models, planning for enactment, and shared reflection on and revision of the actual lesson are owned by teachers collaborating with experienced others to shape how they come to interpret what they see and, in turn, re-present it for use.

A representation can thus serve as the empirical "substrate" on which evidence can be mounted and arguments built. Shaping a scenario, an illustrative video, a set of coherent moves, a narrative, a stepwise script, or even a static image that embodies critical elements of a pedagogical approach can serve multiple simultaneous purposes: supporting teacher professional learning, fostering relationships among improvement effort participants, and providing visibility into the effort for administrators and other stakeholders.

In this chapter, we have shown how representations of teaching practice, already a subject of study and design in other contexts, could enrich and further the work of RPPs. At the heart of all RPPs engaged in designing interventions is a shared commitment to addressing pressing problems of practice. This shared commitment is based on, and evolves from, mechanisms that build trust, leverage perspectives, and foster joint meaning-making. The use of representations, as shown in the two cases described in this chapter, create powerful contexts for (1) building relationships of trust (through discussions, reflections, etc.); (2) establishing common ground, mutual referents, and shared perspectives; (3) distilling and refining understanding to address persistent problems of practice; and (4) engaging in original analysis through communicating insights and possibilities. What origins, what forms, and what functions characterize representations all are idiosyncratically dependent on the problems of practice being addressed, the goals of the partnerships, and the ways in which possible solutions emerge, get tested, and evolve. This chapter points to the prospects for working on pressing educational challenges by bringing into closer alignment research on representations in teacher learning and the development of RPPs.

Notes

1 A pattern like the Initiation-Response-Evaluation (I-R-E) sequence identified by Mehan (1979) as dominant in inner-city elementary schools illustrates how widespread and pervasive a generic pattern can become.
2 Exemplified by the Bay Area Lesson Study project.

References

Baxter, J. (2010). The evolution of tools to support educational improvement. In C. E. Coburn & M. K. Stein (Eds.), *Research and practice in education: Building alliances, bridging the divide* (pp. 77–91). Lanham, MD: Rowman & Littlefield.

Bevan, B., Gutwill, J. P., Petrich, M., & Wilkinson, K. (2015). Learning through STEM-rich tinkering: Findings from a jointly negotiated research project taken up in practice. *Science Education*, *99*(1), 98–120.

Borko, H., Koellner, K., Jacobs, J., & Seago, N. (2011). Using video representations of teaching in practice-based professional development programs. *ZDM*, *43*(1), 175–187.

Burnard, P. (2011). Creativity, pedagogic partnerships, and the improvisatory space of teaching. In K. Sawyer (Ed.), *Structure and improvisation in creative teaching*. Cambridge: Cambridge University Press.

Coburn, C. E., & Penuel, W. R. (2016). Research–practice partnerships in education: Outcomes, dynamics, and open questions. *Educational Researcher, 45*(1), 48–54.

Coburn, C. E., Penuel, W. R., & Geil, K. E. (2013). *Practice partnerships: A strategy for leveraging research for educational improvement in school districts.* New York: William T. Grant Foundation.

Coburn, C. E., & Stein, M. K. (Eds.). (2010). *Research and practice in education: Building alliances, bridging the divide.* Lanham, MD: Rowman & Littlefield.

Collins, H., Evans, R., & Gorman, M. (2007). Trading zones and interactional expertise. *Studies in History and Philosophy of Science Part A, 38*, 657–666.

Common Core State Standards Initiative. (2010). *Mathematics standards.* Retrieved from www.corestandards.org/Math/

Derry, S., Pea, R., Barron, B., Engle, R., Erickson, F., Goldman, R., . . . Sherin, B. (2010). Conducting video research in the learning sciences: Guidance on selection, analysis, technology, and ethics. *The Journal of the Learning Sciences, 19*(1), 3–53.

Fernandez, C., Cannon, J., & Chokshi, S. (2003). A US–Japan lesson study collaboration reveals critical lenses for examining practice. *Teaching and Teacher Education, 19*(2), 171–185.

Goodwin, C. (1994). Professional vision. *American Anthropologist, 96*, 606–633.

Grossman, P., Compton, C., Igra, D., Ronfeldt, M., Shahan, E., & Williamson, P. (2009). Teaching practice: A cross-professional perspective. *Teachers College Record, 111*(9), 2055–2100.

Hammerness, K. (2006). *Seeing through teachers' eyes: Professional ideals and classroom practices.* New York: Teachers College Press.

Herbst, P., Chazan, D., Chen, C. L., Chieu, V. M., & Weiss, M. (2011). Using comics-based representations of teaching, and technology, to bring practice to teacher education courses. *ZDM, 43*(1), 91–103.

Herbst, P., & Kosko, K. W. (2014). Using representations of practice to elicit mathematics teachers' tacit knowledge of practice: A comparison of responses to animations and videos. *Journal of Mathematics Teacher Education, 17*(6), 515–537.

Hill, H. C., Beisiegel, M., & Jacob, R. (2013). Professional development research: Consensus, crossroads, and challenges. *Educational Researcher, 42*(9), 476–487.

Horn, I. S. (2010). Teaching replays, teaching rehearsals, and re-visions of practice: Learning from colleagues in a mathematics teacher community. *Teachers College Record, 112*(1), 225–259.

Howarth, C. (2006). A social representation is not a quiet thing: Exploring the critical potential of social representations theory. *British Journal of Social Psychology, 45*(1), 65–86.

Ikemoto, G. S., & Honig, M. I. (2010). Tools to deepen practitioners' engagement with research: The case of the Institute for Learning. In C. E. Coburn & M. I. Honig (Eds.), *Research and practice in education: Building alliances, bridging the divide* (pp. 93–108). Lanham, MD: Rowman & Littlefield.

Kim, H. J. (2011). *An exploratory study of teachers' use of mathematical knowledge for teaching to support mathematical argumentation in middle-grades classrooms.* Doctoral dissertation.

Knudsen, J., & Shechtman, N. (2016). Professional development that bridges the gap between workshop and classroom through disciplined improvisation. In S. Goldman & Z. Kabayadondo (Eds.), *Taking design thinking to school: How the technology of design can transform teachers, learners, and classrooms.* London: Taylor & Francis.

Knudsen, J., Stevens, H., Lara-Meloy, T., Kim, H-J., & Shechtman, N. (2017). *Mathematical argumentation in middle school—the what, why, and how.* Thousand Oaks, CA: Corwin Mathematics.

Koschmann, T. D. (2011). *Theories of learning and studies of instructional practice.* New York: Springer.

Lee, J. F. (2008). A Hong Kong case of lesson study—Benefits and concerns. *Teaching and Teacher Education, 24*(5), 1115–1124.

Lewis, C. C., & Perry, R. R. (2014). Lesson study with mathematical resources: A sustainable model for locally led teacher professional learning. *Mathematics Teacher Education and Development, 16*(1), n1.

Lewis, C. C., & Perry, R. R. (2017). Lesson study to scale up research-based knowledge: A randomized, controlled trial of fractions learning. *Journal for Research in Mathematics Education, 48*(3), 261–299.Little, J. W. (2003). Inside teacher community: Representations of classroom practice. *Teachers College Record, 105*(6), 913–945.

Lewis, C. C., Perry, R. R., & Hurd, J. (2009). Improving mathematics instruction through lesson study: A theoretical model and North American case. *Journal of Mathematics Teacher Education, 12*(4), 285–304.

Mehan, H. (1979). *Learning lessons: Social organization in the classroom.* Cambridge, MA: Harvard University Press.

Morris, A. K., & Hiebert, J. (2011). Creating shared instructional products: An alternative approach to improving teaching. *Educational Researcher, 40*(1), 5–14.

Perry, R. R., & Lewis, C. C. (2010). Building demand for research through lesson study. In C. E. Coburn & M. K. Stein (Eds.), *Research and practice in education: Building alliances, bridging the divide* (pp. 131–146). Lanham, MD: Rowman & Littlefield.

Puchner, L. D., & Taylor, A. R. (2006). Lesson study, collaboration and teacher efficacy: Stories from two school-based math lesson study groups. *Teaching and Teacher Education, 22*(7), 922–934.

Pulvermacher, Y., & Lefstein, A. (2016). Narrative representations of practice: What and how can student teachers learn from them? *Teaching and Teacher Education, 55*, 255–266.

Resnick, L. B., Michaels, S., & O'Connor, M. C. (2010). How (well-structured) talk builds the mind. In D. Preiss & R. J. Sternberg (Eds.), *Innovations in educational psychology: Perspectives on learning, teaching, and human development* (pp. 163–194). New York: Springer.

Riel, M., & Polin, L. (2004). Learning communities: Common ground and critical differences in designing technical support. In S. Barab, R. Kling, & J. Gray (Eds.). *Designing for virtual communities in the service of learning* (pp. 16–52). Cambridge, MA: Cambridge University Press.

Sawyer, R. K. (2011). What makes good teachers great: The artful balance of structure and improvisation. In R. K. Sawyer (Ed.), *Structure and improvisation in creative teaching* (pp. 1–24). New York: Cambridge University Press.

Schultz, K., & Ravitch, S. M. (2013). Narratives of learning to teach: Taking on professional identities. *Journal of Teacher Education, 64*(1), 35–46.

Shechtman, N., Knudsen, J., Michalchik, V., Stevens, H., & Kim, H. (in preparation). *Teacher professional development to support classroom mathematical argumentation.*

Star, S. L., & Griesemer, J. R. (1989). Institutional ecology, translations, and boundary objects: Amateurs and professionals in Berkeley's museum of vertebrate zoology, 1907–1939. *Social Studies of Science, 19*(3), 387–420.

Stein, M. K., & Coburn, C. E. (2010). Reframing the problem of research and practice. In C. E. Coburn & M. K. Stein (Eds.), *Research and practice in education: Building alliances, bridging the divide* (pp. 1–14). Lanham, MD: Rowman & Littlefield.

Yackel, E., & Cobb, P. (1996). Sociomathematical norms, argumentation, and autonomy in mathematics. *Journal for Research in Mathematics Education, 27*, 458–477.

Zazkis, R. (2017). Lesson Play tasks as a creative venture for teachers and teacher educators. *ZDM, 49*(1), 95–105.

11

OUR HOUSE COULD BE A VERY, VERY, VERY FINE HOUSE

The Tensions and Disenchantment of Collaborative Digital Tools Within Partnerships

Antero Garcia and Bud Hunt

> *Sitting around a weathered table, six of us schemed and planned and dreamed. An incubating vision of what would become an ongoing, fulfilling research-driven project was developed concurrent with a parallel set of schemes, plans, and dreams. While we developed our vision of enactment, we also began identifying the infrastructure for driving this vision home. Like newly minted contractors, we eyed the new intellectual plot of land that we'd invested in and began to determine the layout and infrastructure that would house our work. Our project's intellectual plot of land shaped how we communicated, organized, and shared with one another and with a broader public. Our moments of enchantment with a full complement of digital tools that worked seamlessly and productively to help us reach our goals were fleeting. Over time, we would wrestle with and be forced to fit our work to the constraints of the tools we had selected. Relying on specific tools for lasting tasks in partnership-driven work often meant recognizing initially invisible constraints and limitations that shaped how we work.*

We draw specifically on our experiences within an ongoing research–practice partnership (RPP) with classroom teachers, district administrators, students, and researchers across multiple school districts and universities in Colorado. The partnership began in 2015 and is still active today. RPPs, as noted throughout this volume, require trusting, mutualistic, and collaborative relationships. Timely and ongoing communication—across geographic distances, professional roles, and cultural practices—has been shown to be key to successful RPPs (Coburn, Penuel, & Geil, 2013). Our goal in building a technological communications infrastructure was to support equitable and timely decision-making across all levels and channels of the RPP. In this chapter, we describe challenges to such multi-channel communication and the ways in which the technological tools we adopted have and haven't served our partnership's needs for communication.

Our goals are to highlight decisions we made with these digital tools and how these choices affected our methods of practice and to offer guidelines for developing a communications infrastructure for projects within RPPs. As we reflect on how these tools shaped our work, we address the following questions:

- How do differing expectations of audience and purpose influence how an RPP communicates internally and externally?
- What power and structural dynamics impact who gets to speak in an RPP?
- How do different tools—and our understanding of their "purposes"—impact how communication happens?
- What is the potential for improved communication in an RPP through the use of social media tools?

Our answers to these questions grow from work principally focused on supporting teachers and students in ninth-grade English language arts contexts in Northern Colorado and linking them to researchers within our partnership. The partnership has included nearly 30 active team members, each of whom played different and evolving roles in building, planning, and teaching new curriculum materials as part of this project, and we chose tools that we believed could scale well to accommodate the needs and digital proficiencies of all of our members across multiple organizational contexts.

Getting Our House in Order

The tools detailed in this chapter were selected by an initial research team months before work with teachers, district administrators, and graduate students began. As a smaller collective envisioning the kinds of practices and methods of communication and dissemination we aspired toward, we identified three kinds of collaborative writing and production that we believed required an infrastructure to accommodate a rapidly expanding team of researchers and practitioners. We needed to be able to

- Clearly communicate with both the entire research team and with smaller groups within this team;
- Easily access files, edit files, and distribute files to the entire team; and
- Publicly share the progress, materials, and ideas that emerged from this work.

Though there are several popular options for the functionality we needed, we ultimately decided to utilize Slack, Google Drive, and WordPress as the main web-enabled tools for collaboration and communication within our RPP. To highlight how these tools have lived in this project, we imagine them as different parts of our partnership's home (Figure 11.1).

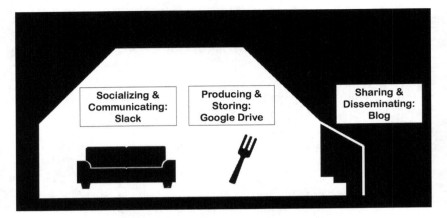

FIGURE 11.1 Envisioning How Our Digital Tools Function in Our RPP Home

- Slack is the *living room* for this partnership. This is where our project's family socializes and convenes.
- Google Drive is our *kitchen*. With a pantry chock-full of resources, this is where materials are prepared, reviewed, and stored.
- Our blog is the *porch*. This is the part of our house that extends into the broader world, inviting neighborly contact and growth.

Although this chapter details each of these tools, our assumptions about their uses, and the challenges they created for us as we tried to use them to communicate, create, and coordinate our activities, our account is not being written as an endorsement or review-based critique of specific tools. Rather, we highlight how our decisions about the kinds of work we needed to do led us to the tools we expected would support this work. Additionally, we surface the unanticipated consequences that resulted from how these tools functioned and were designed, which ultimately shaped how we did our work and our patterns of collaboration within the RPP.

We began our work with these new tools with much optimism about their potential. As our work progressed, members of our group occasionally voiced frustration over how some of these tools functioned; we recognized the familiar feeling of disenchantment that comes when hopes for the use of tools meet the real world. Not everyone wanted to write for our blog. Having a space where we could all draft resources together inside a Google Doc did not always mean that we did draft together. Social tools couldn't fix problematic social relationships and workflow challenges within our partnership.

Further, it is important to recognize the fact that different family members occupy different roles within the partnership's home. With teachers, researchers, graduate students, and community stakeholders each playing distinctive but complementary roles within the partnership, we realized that uses of Slack, Drive, and the blog did not need to be shared equally by everyone. Researchers needed a place to store material related to research (e.g., IRB documents and protocols), but teachers did not need access to these materials. Teachers and researchers on the same team, though, needed to know where and how to access materials they were co-developing and how to coordinate activity, which required the use of both Slack and Drive tools.

Communicating and Socializing: Slack as Our Living Room

In every project, there's a need to be in regular communication on many big and small ongoing details and issues. Where's the next meeting? Who's bringing snacks? Where are the presentation resources, and who's going to lead? As a new team with multiple procedural and practical items to discuss, we needed a way to be in conversation throughout the day. One big problem was that the "we" who needed to be in conversation changed regularly.

Managing a large team and making sure everyone is in the right communications loop is a difficult task. The size of our RPP fluctuated, over time, from an initial six to more than 40 individuals, with new participants joining roughly every academic year. As we began to work together, it seemed that communication tasks would eat up a considerable amount of personal and project capacity and bandwidth. We needed places and spaces where team members could engage each other, where new team members could ground themselves in our work, and where the team could come together and share ideas and be in conversation with each other. Some of that conversation was directly relevant to advancing our team's work. Other conversations were more about helping us grow together as a team. Our house needed a living room, where we could socialize and meet informally online when we couldn't be in the same physical spaces.

Group communication tools like Slack have been quickly adopted by many organizations and companies as simple ways to manage massive amounts of open discussion across a project or organization. At first, Slack might seem complex, but it is organized around a couple of basic concepts. There are two main types of content in Slack: public channels and private messages. Both types of content can handle text, images, links, and perhaps our favorite, emoji. Public channels are unthreaded, chronologically ordered message streams: the oldest message is at the top and the newest is at the bottom. The power of a public channel is that any member of our team can follow any of the project's public channels. Participants can self-organize to pay attention to any conversation on any topic and can ignore any conversation that isn't of interest. However, that does not necessarily mean that all participants feel comfortable enough with the tool to choose to do so. Public channels are searchable by any member of the team; even members who aren't following a particular conversation can locate relevant information in that conversation through a keyword search. Slack moves information out of individual email inboxes and into a team commons. With lots of people and activity to coordinate across our team, this was an appealing feature. Onboarding new team members was as simple as sending them an invitation and guiding them into the channels that made sense for their work.

When Bud (second author) first proposed Slack as a tool for communication within our team, several team members had heard of the messaging application but were still hazy about what Slack could do. We created several channels in which real-time conversations were archived. We coordinated meeting times in a #general channel, we highlighted project-based learning (PBL) resources in the #pbl-talk channel, and outlined the steps needed to complete a grant proposal in a private channel labeled leadership-team. However, with a team of only six at the time, our Slack felt empty and forced: Why were we writing in *another* application when we were already so used to email? It wasn't until the team began to grow in numbers that Slack began to make sense for us, and even then, it took a while to get used to the space.

While public channels made all conversations open to any team member who chose to read them, Slack's private messages function like other social media tools in that participants can create direct message streams between one or more persons and keep those conversations out of the eyes and ears of the larger team. In our partnership, centered around curriculum development, public channels are organized around the major areas of interest for our teams as well as the four major project ideas we wanted to develop. Private channels are set up for the leadership teams, our grad students, and for some of our development groups working on smaller pieces of our project.

We found that real-time messaging for our team worked best when our members could actually see and respond to messages in real time. Email is almost real-time, but several hours could elapse between responses. When a teacher or researcher needed just-in-time help, that might be too long to wait. Slack pops new messages onto your desktop or mobile phone, making them immediately evident; communication is both faster in Slack and more contextually rich. However, we also found that without installing the mobile version of Slack on our phones or the desktop version on our computers, several of our teammates did not see the flurry of near-constant activity on Slack until they logged in to the web version of the platform. As team members eventually embraced using the mobile version of Slack, the community grew in sharing, asking, and documenting important work in classrooms.

Slack has also been an important tool for archiving and bringing new team members up to speed. At the time we write this, there are 32 different public Slack channels available to our team. Ranging from detailed coordination for specific working groups to spaces for sharing personal details, our channels are diverse and encourage the cross-pollination of ideas, resources, and inquiry by all our members. At the same time, many of us have dozens of private channels and direct messages with other team members (Figure 11.2). Discussions about coordinating budgets, IRB protocols, and schedules for graduate students are often shared in spaces cordoned off from the public channels. In fact, most utterances in Slack have occurred in private channels, not public ones. Further study of the kinds of private messages that are produced (e.g., social talk, work-related inquiry) would help us better understand how power and openness manifest within our team.

Slack has truly become the living room of our project and has helped us cultivate a thriving social community; at the same time, we acknowledge that it has led to some social behaviors that have not always been so positive. Because any member of our team can privately message an individual or group within the system, Slack also can function as a backchannel for conversations during meetings. For better or worse, it isn't uncommon to see subtle smirks and attention focused on screens during meetings. In deciding to utilize Slack as a means for real-time discussion and socialization, we did not initially consider the consequences of encouraging private commenting and joking during meetings; passing notes in the back of class has been digitized via our team's use of Slack. Despite this, the social aspects and the ability for teachers to ask for resources and get

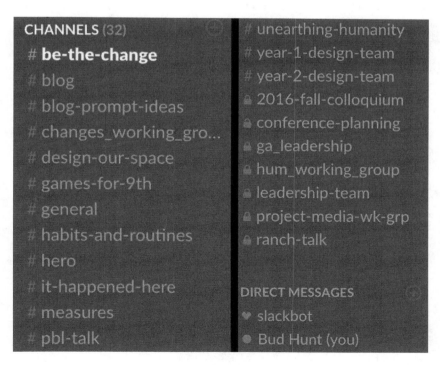

FIGURE 11.2 Some Public and Private Channels in Our Project's Slack

quick answers from the entire team has meant that Slack is a valuable and nearly constantly used tool for our partnership.

Slacking in Slack

As we noted, migrating our family from email as a main tool for communication to Slack was an initial challenge. It's one thing to build a space where teammates can freely share information and interact with one another. It's quite another to see the team immediately embrace the tool. Finding time for teachers to play with and explore Slack was an issue. Whenever you adopt a new platform, particularly one that's relatively new, you should give participants time to play with and take up the tools of the platform.

One challenge we faced was initial reluctance by some of our members to embrace this new tool. A sub-team in our project, tasked with developing and delivering one set of our curriculum project material, chose to not use Slack and to focus on email, a much more familiar and comfortable tool. While this meant that the sub-team could accomplish its task more quickly, it also meant that the rest of the team was unable to see team members' conversations, shared documents, and decisions made as the work was in progress. In a way, because their interactions did not occur in our family living room, we did not know they had occurred at all.

As our team learned the value of in-progress conversation, we realized that our sub-team unintentionally excluded others from its work practices. Specifically, we could not see or understand decisions made by the sub-team as it developed its work. These "missing decisions" became visible when project meetings took longer because the decisions conveyed through email had to be explained to the rest of the larger team. We had a hole in our collective understanding of what was worked on, what changed, and what was learned during the creation of that portion of our work. The decision to support communication outside of our living room was eventually reconsidered, and today, all teams' conversations occur, at least on some level, within Slack.

Preparing and Storing: Google Drive as Our Kitchen

As the team focused on building collaboratively developed curriculum, our project needed a consistent set of practices for writing, reviewing, and internally sharing materials that would be regularly consulted for several years.

If Slack is the project's living room, Google Drive as our file storage and collaboration solution is the project's kitchen. As a cloud-based storage platform, Google Drive synchronizes files that our team works on, regardless of where or on what devices files are accessed. As our kitchen, Google Drive is a singular place in which we produce materials for this project. With folders of content peppered with the resources we've completed or that remain half-baked as they undergo revision and feedback, the teacher lesson plans, research notes, and organizational nutrients that sustain our project are stored and developed in Drive. Coordination of who is working, where, and when is all done via Slack, but these messages ultimately point our members to files stored in Drive.

The decision to adopt Google Drive as our file storage tool for this project was made much easier by the fact that all the participating institutions—school districts, universities, and libraries—implement some form of Google Drive at the institution. The same habits for document management, then, are in play in some small way at each organization, and each participant had at least some familiarity with the tools and affordances of Google Drive prior to beginning work on our RPP project.

One of the most important tasks in setting up Google Drive for a large project spanning multiple roles and institutions is ensuring that file permissions and folders are set up correctly. Complicating this task is the fact that as teams shift throughout the life of a project, the exact nature of what *correctly* means can change. The appliances and pantry organization you decide on for baking might not be at all suitable for frying and candy making. What starts as a simple structure can quickly grow more complex.

We conceived of our project as a series of ever-smaller nested circles with each role—teacher, graduate assistant, researcher, and so on—living within the others, so the broadest level of permissions lived at the top, with subfolders beneath that restricted to smaller groups of collaborators. In some ways, this actually reinforced a hierarchy, one we did not intend, within the roles. Teachers had the fewest permissions, then graduate assistants, and so on. Similar to our Slack channels, the roles of the team members were also what we used as the foundation of our folder and permission structure. Also similar to our use of Slack was the need to teach the team how to use the folder structures we had set up. Finding time along the way of doing the actual curriculum design work to discuss the tools was a challenge. We spent significant time restoring documents deleted (presumably by accident!) by some of our members, had to figure out which institutional email addresses actually needed to be connected to which folders, and worked to establish practices for distributing materials so that teachers could nimbly tailor their instructional plans for their own needs. Reflecting on such challenges, we often had to do it wrong to learn how we actually needed things to be arranged.

Figure 11.3 highlights the top-level folders for our project. As "COW" is the acronym for our work, the common name made searching for the specific folders an intuitive process. Inside each group-named folder was a running record document for collaborative agendas and notes of each group. In running meeting documents, we added new material at the top of each document, with a table of contents utilizing date-based headers for each meeting. One could review the notes of a year's worth of meetings in reverse chronological order by opening one

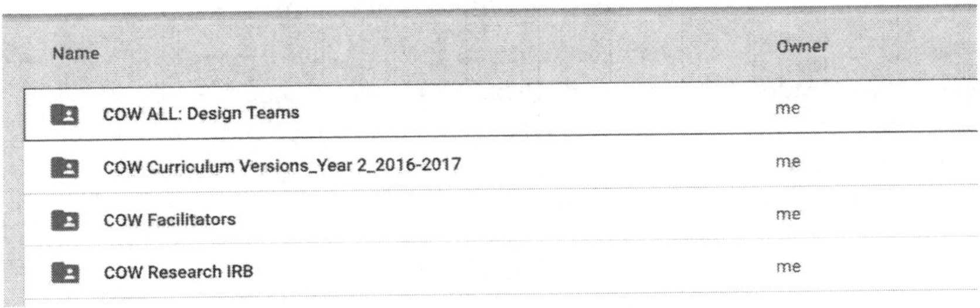

Name	Owner
📇 COW ALL: Design Teams	me
📇 COW Curriculum Versions_Year 2_2016-2017	me
📇 COW Facilitators	me
📇 COW Research IRB	me

FIGURE 11.3 Named Folders at Top Level

document and scrolling down. Because the notes were collaborative, anyone on the team could add to them. To support clear communication practices, we found it was essential to take time at the start of meetings to identify who was actually responsible for taking and curating notes in each meeting. When technology allowed us all to share in administrative roles, communication about who would take on each role became more important, not less.

No matter how friendly to co-editing and co-design our team might have been, we had to regularly attend to how we supported the practices of collaborative production and distribution. As with Slack, Google Drive didn't immediately make people engage in the practices we envisioned. Because changes happen in real time on any device currently viewing a document, some members of our partnership were initially hesitant to edit documents. Although everyone could edit, it frequently seemed that no one did.

An additional challenge for this curriculum development project has been version control—keeping track of what our projects looked like when they began and how they have progressed at each stage of their development. For smaller, document-level changes, this is easily achieved using Google's revision history feature, which will show you who made which changes across the document's history. But for larger revisions, an intentional numbering and renaming has been necessary.

Cooking to Everyone's Tastes

One tricky challenge of our research has been to create a document environment wherein we can allow for shared co-design of curricular resources and also track how individual teachers adapt these co-created resources for use within their own classrooms. While we're not sure we've managed to do this well, we have found one way to do so: create a space for the shared co-design work while replicating full "version releases" of our project resources to teachers throughout the year.

Figure 11.4 shows how we've created this space, ensuring that, while each participating teacher can only edit within their individual teacher folder, all can edit and revise within their team's shared folders. Version numbers and short change

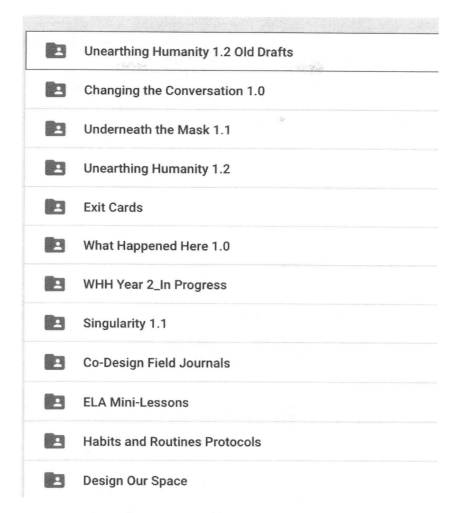

FIGURE 11.4   Curricular Resources Folder

memos at the time of release help keep everyone aware of major development changes to the resources. A change memo is a one-page document that briefly lists each major change or adjustment as well as some rationales for why changes were made. As curriculum materials for this project were continually revised, we numbered each version to best track and keep redundant copies of all versions of our work; teachers could compare, adjust, and revise their own copies of our project's current version of the curriculum relatively easily.

Technology has not been our friend when it comes to file naming conventions. Previously, when the number of characters allowed or available for naming a document was small and quickly exhausted, elaborate naming conventions were necessary for packing as much information into a file name as possible. With the advent of much larger limits for names, the purpose of a document's name has changed. Further, Drive encourages searching files using natural language. Now, the title of a document in Google Drive can, and should be, long and detailed; file names should be human readable rather than machine readable. A file name like "20170812_BH_SELFE_TC" is much less helpful for team discovery processes than "Bud Hunt's Self-Evaluation of Teaching Context, August 12, 2017" can be.

Ultimately, we realized that there were many options in Drive that—if unattended—could lead to challenges for the team. While it is easy to restore deleted text in a version of a document or locate a file that was deleted from the group's shared Drive, these are tasks that our project placed in the purview of just a few people on the team. Specifically, we designated a curator who prods, nudges, and administers the Drive for everyone to ensure that the project has specific individuals to reach out to for help.

Drive is by no means a perfect resource for supporting the production needs of our team. Though our kitchen-based work in Drive is not seamless, we want to recognize that our model of production is sustained by a tool that fosters real-time collaboration, persistent modes for annotation, and relatively accessible approaches to distributing customizable resources across our teaching team. In this regard, although our teammates have had to orient toward the specific systemic features of Google Drive, the tool has guided what collaborative production looks like for our team.

Sharing and Communicating: WordPress as Our Porch

> Committed to documenting the lessons our large team was learning along the way, our project needed an easily accessible space to interact with a broader public and scholarly community. Through sharing written reflections, multimodal pastiche, and images of work samples from our project, we continue to aspire to a "working open" approach to project dissemination using our public WordPress blog.

While blogs are the "oldest" tools discussed here, their use as public dissemination spaces of work in progress is still foreign to many academics and educators. On our own team, we have mixed experience with online publishing as a tool for dissemination of our project's key resources to the public.

We envisioned our project's blog run with WordPress software functioning as an open, semi-public space for the project to describe our ongoing activities to others. With the blog as our front porch, we imagined that conversations that happened on the blog would be overheard by others, and that others might join in from time to time. One of the goals of our project is to create open educational resources (OERs) that can be freely shared, reused, and adapted by others. We thought the blog might be a place where we could tell stories of the project as well as release some of the resources we created in order to fulfill our goal of creating OERs. It is also possible, or so we believe, that the struggle itself, and our narratives about it, might well serve as an OER of its own.

In our prior work, our respective professional blogs have served well for that type of sharing, and they have also served as places where we can think out loud and write our way through problems and opportunities of practice. As teachers, both of us wrote to improve our practice. Along the way, we made personal and professional connections with others who were engaged in similar work. To our thinking, a project blog could serve many of the same purposes, while also serving to help tell many of the little stories of the project in an informal way.

That's not really how the space has worked out in this project so far. Although our blog has led to the drafting and sharing of some interesting or "aha!" moments from our work together, it certainly isn't the hub of activity we envisioned. If we're being honest with ourselves, our porch is feeling a little dusty and under-used. We have struggled as a team to use the space regularly and to do the types of sharing we thought we would be doing. There are a few reasons for this gap between vision and reality.

For one, it takes significant additional *time* to draft, revise, and share the stories of our project that we believe could be of interest, even at an early stage. There are many online spaces clamoring for our time and attention, and we struggle with maintaining our own personal blogs, so this isn't a criticism of others on our team but a recognition of a genuine challenge. All members of our team want the stories of our work to be shared, but generating those stories is still a task that we are working to build into our daily routines. If there is not a member of your team assigned to "project story curation" detail, that might be a good role to intention-ally support and develop. Like taking meeting notes, it's a job that everyone thinks everyone else will do.

For much of our project's team, the format of a blog is new and the audi-ence is often unclear: knowing who our community is and what they want to know from us takes time. The time spent drafting a post that might be read by a *potential* audience seems less important than the use of that same time to draft a conference proposal or a paper draft that may well be seen and read by a known or guaranteed audience. In addition, blog posts are not necessarily valued as part of the tenure and promotion processes to which many of us are held account-able. The expectations and prior experience with the blog format has led to some confusion and some disinterest in using project time for blog posts. Fur-ther, our team differs in experience and comfort with the idea of sharing work in progress in a space where it might be seen. In considering the intentional efforts required for sustaining a culture of sharing, we recognize that our own project's challenges with sharing are tied to comfort and familiarity, as well as to larger structural issues of power, both localized within our project and tied to sociohistorical roots. What is "good enough" for some of our team is not yet "good" for others.

Related to audience, the *format* of the blog itself is new and unfamiliar to many. While a blog is just a container for words and media, there are some genre conventions that exist outside of traditional academic presentation and publication environments. As a team of academic researchers and classroom educators, the kinds of writing genres, lengths, and conventions varied widely for our members. Our blog has featured posts of several thousand words in length with myriad APA-style citations, 200-word posts with multiple hyperlinks, and multimodal posts filled with images, videos, and GIFs. Deciding what and how to write can feel intimidating. Considering the combined complexities of the purpose and audience and the worries over format, quite often, it's easier to stay inside the house rather than venturing out onto the porch.

Of all the tools we've employed in this project, the blog is the one that continues to confound us the most. While we continue to believe that blogging as a team habit has great potential, we have struggled to develop the blogging habit, considering the challenges we've identified. A larger question remains: Are stories of work in progress of value to our project and to the larger educational community outside the context of formal academic publishing and conferences? Despite the powerful norming practices that have helped shape strong in-group practices for our project, our diverse identities within this RPP highlight the different orientations, familiarity, and sense of safety in speaking across and with members beyond our team in public spaces.

From Building a House to Sustaining a Home

Perhaps you have found yourself in a situation similar to ours. You build a new home, outfit it and design it as best as you can, and then begin to settle in. You and your housemates start to inhabit the spaces, developing habits and routines that inform how and when you use the kitchen, the living room, and the porch. Some of these are positive and useful, even productive. But other habits and routines are not as helpful. That cabinet you thought made sense by the back door just gets in the way. The front porch catches the light just at the moment you thought would be the best time to use it. Someone else is always using the toaster. Conflict happens, and in some moments, you want to call a contractor and begin a renovation. No matter what tools you adopt as a team, they will not create the perfect home for your project. Projects are staffed by people, and people are less predictable than the plans we make for them.

We began this chapter by questioning how communication practices change internally and externally when focusing on the needs of a context-specific RPP. We asked ourselves how power structures and group dynamics shape and affect the online practices we ended up adopting alongside tools like Slack, Google Drive, and WordPress. By describing our RPP as a home, we wanted to offer a unique tour of the contexts of communication for our RPP. Though we highlight the constraints and limitations of each of the tools of communication, we want to specifically note that we have sought to integrate them with practices that aim for transparency as much as a possible; such transparency did not guarantee the equitable distribution of power in our RPP but did provide mindful conditions for addressing this need.

Likewise, while we also opened this chapter by reflecting on the power dynamics of who gets to speak within our RPP, we want to underscore that trust and relationships centered how we saw our home operating amicably. As such, it is imperative not to overlook the relational aspects of how we used the tools described in this chapter to support partnership work. The structures embedded in our communication tools imply specific power dynamics that we attempted to surface with the members of this project. For example, there are areas of our Drive that are not accessible to teachers; we have private Slack channels that discuss larger, budgetary aspects of the project; and posting to the blog is not fully open but rather requires administrative approval. These layers of privacy are there for important reasons, but they also imply often unspoken levels of power within projects like this one. We designed the structures of Slack and Drive to meet the individual needs of teachers and researchers, and we did this with a specific viewpoint of research and the roles of various stakeholders in this project. These levels of power within the project are not a secret—we have discussed how and why certain tools cordon off access for some of our members. While we have tried to make issues of power clear, we still look for ways to make these constraints more explicit to all team members. Discussing these decisions and being clear about how our work drives toward larger goals helps address the power and structural dynamics within our RPP.

Challenges to Communication in Our Partnership Evident From the Use of Tools

Reflecting on another of our opening questions—how the purposes of different tools shape how communication happens—we made a list of some of the challenges that arose as we worked with these different tools. Often, when thinking about posting, publishing, or sharing information within our project, some of the initial hesitancy stemmed from individuals' comfort with where their work and ideas fall across the following spectra:

- *Public versus private*: When are we sharing or speaking with each other, and when are we engaging a larger audience? When do both things (potentially) happen?
- *Done versus done enough:* How do we know a project is finished? When is a resource complete?
- *Neat versus messy:* At what point are we comfortable sharing materials across our project? At what point can we share work with the general public?

- *Fast versus slow:* How long is too long to work through a sticky issue? When is sharing an insight useful, and when is it premature? When is taking time an asset? a liability?

These areas of hesitation and concern can seem very different, but in many ways they overlap. Classrooms and learning systems move quicker than the traditionally slow pace of research. "Open" and "fast" practices—lauded in descriptions of today's technology-driven start-ups—are a lived reality within our own RPP. Neither side of these dualities is more correct than the other, but differences in beliefs, comfort, and experiences can lead to internalizing ways of working and approaching work that tend to favor one side or the other. Our learning within our own RPP leads us to consider how other partnerships might weather similar struggles. Deliberately surfacing *why* certain kinds of practices are taken up (such as our discussion with our team that certain research protocols and materials were not shared with the entire team) and exploring what boundaries of digital use are malleable (such as what may be lost when not all of our members are utilizing Slack) are important for addressing possible challenges head on. We wonder, too, how other RPPs work to address issues of power and who gets to speak or write when; members of an RPP will have different understandings of the definitions of the spectra we offered here, and agreeing on how an RPP operates is a choreographed dialogue that, we believe, should happen intentionally.

As we continue to consider how social media tools could improve communication within our RPP, the divides we have highlighted point to how individuals' comfort, familiarity, and sense of agentic communication fall across multiple dimensions of consideration. In *improving* one context—making work faster—an RPP must also consider how communication speed shapes the other dimensions on which its work falls. The rooms in our home have been shaped and weathered over several years of use at this point; they may not be perfect, but they are the tools we are accustomed to.

A feeling of uncertainty sometimes manifests in our project through questions such as, "Do I post this idea to the Slack? To the blog? Or is it just an email?" While our tool sets allow for lots of choices as far as the publicness of work, our team did not explicitly discuss these issues as fully as we might have. We assumed that the blog would be a welcome place for first-draft thinking, but our colleagues' discomfort with this raised concerns and inhibited our use of the tool. We believe that working openly can reposition everyone involved in our project. When we discover in the open, we present our ideas to the team and to the world in ways that suggest that we are all learning, all learners, and that there is more to learn from each other. Modeling this openness can encourage others to take risks and changes the traditional power dynamics of researchers, teachers, and students.

Issues of power, audience, and comfort all play into how comfortable the members of your team will ultimately feel in the house that you build together. In particular, we recognize that much of this chapter questions what *kind* of social practices are found in the digital tools utilized by our partnership today and the constraints they create. While many of us quickly acculturated to the communication practices encouraged by a tool like Slack or felt comfortable navigating the Borges-esque structures of locating files in Google Drive, others—researchers, students, and teachers alike—found these spaces unwelcoming. Some folks won't mind putting their feet up on the coffee table from the start. Others will avoid wearing shoes on the carpet. One team member might eat all of your yogurt in the fridge. The correct answer for your project might not be to decide everyone's level of comfort but to ask questions about who and when and how your team is composing and creating for its audiences, as well as what those audiences might be. Being open and direct about expectations, intentions, and hopes for the use of your tools can help create the home environment that matches your project's needs.

Reference

Coburn, C. E., Penuel, W. R., & Geil, K. (2013). *Research–practice partnerships at the district level: A new strategy for leveraging research for educational improvement.* Berkeley, CA and Boulder, CO: University of California and University of Colorado.

INDEX

active learning 121
Advancing Academic Language for All!
   (AALA) 40
Advancing Coherence and Equity in State
   Science Education (ACESSE)
   project 26
Afterschool Alliance 24–25
American Institutes for Research 122
Auburn School Department 51; *see also*
   EDC-Auburn partnership
authorship agreements 70

Be the Change (case study) 139–142, 146
blogs/blogging 102, 108, 166–167,
   174–178
Boston Plan for Excellence (BPE) 39
Boston Public Schools (BPS) 33, 46
boundary objects 151
Bridging Professional Development
   project 155–158, 160
Bronfenbrenner, U. 18
Buck Institute of Education 124
Building Capacity for State Science
   Education (BCSSE) 25, 26

cafecitos 93–94
Catalyzing Comprehension Through
   Discussion and Debate project 44
Center for Research on the Educational
   Achievement and Teaching of English
   learners (CREATE) 40
Center for the Advancement of STEM
   Education 24

civic values 10
cloud-based storage platforms 170
co-design model: approach to 136–137;
   Be the Change case study 139–142,
   146; Bridging Professional Development
   project 155–158; configurations
   influencing product 146–147; context
   of 137; as design-based implementation
   research element 136; designing for
   local adaptation 137–138; developing
   project-based learning curriculum by
   135; engaging in persuasive dialogue
   137; It Happened Here case study
   142–145, 146; work distribution
   147–148
co-design teams 136, 138–139
coherence 127–128
collaborative work 8, 143
collective decision-making 105
collective orientation 108–109
Common Core Standards for
   Mathematics 155
communications: blogs/blogging 102,
   108, 166–167, 174–178; challenges to
   177–179; done vs. done enough 177;
   fast vs. slow 178; Google Drive 144, 166,
   170–174; as key to successful RPPs 164;
   neat vs. messy 177; privacy layers 177;
   in-progress conversation 170; public vs.
   private 177; Slack 138, 166–168, *169*,
   170; speed shaping 178; web-enabled
   tools for collaboration 165–166;
   WordPress 174–176

community-based participatory research (CBPR) 87, 93–94; *see also* CU Engage
community engagement 72–73, 75, 77, 81, 86–89
community of learners 136
community organizing 87–88
consultants 12
Council of State Science Supervisors (CSSS) 24–26
CU Dialogues 91–93, 95
CU Engage: CU Dialogues 91–93, 95; description of 88; fostering participation across institutions 96; participatory action research 89–91; power dynamics 91–92; redefining community 90–91; spotlighting 90, 91–92; working within complex systems 96–97
curricular resources 42, 128, 130, 172–173, *173*

decision-making: collective 105; counsel-based approaches to 105; data-driven 68–69, 79; democratic practices in 95; evidence-informed 4, 131; partnership arrangements and 34; technological communications infrastructure in 164
deeper learning 121, 122, 124
democratic evidence in education: aligning with democratic principles 3–4; building relationships 7–8; communication of 4–5; example of 7; new infrastructure focused on learning 12–13; preexisting beliefs influencing 4–5; professional roles and identities in 10–12; shared values 8–10; as tool for productive dialogue 6; as weapon vs. dialogue 5–7
democratic principles 143
Denver Collaborative on Racial Disparities in School Discipline 75, 79–80
Denver Public Schools (DPS) 66–67; *see also* DU-DPS partnership
Denver School-Based Restorative Practices Partnership 77
design-based implementation research (DBIR) 34, 54
design-based research–practice partnerships 35, 127, 136
design charrettes 112
design research 112
Developing Assessments of the Next Generation Science Standards 27

dialogue 10
digital tools: blogs/blogging 102, 108, 166–167, 174–176, 177–178; Google Drive 144, 166, 170–174; Slack 138, 166–168, *169*, 170; social practices in 178–179; WordPress 174–176
disciplined improvisation of teaching 158
distributed inter-organizational networks 102–105, 115–116
distributed RPP network 20
Division of Student Equity and Opportunity at DPS *see* DU-DPS partnership
document management 171
done vs. done enough, in communications 177
DU-DPS partnership: addressing beliefs and assumptions 69–73; assessing intervention impact 73–75; collaborators characteristics 79–80; conducting validity checks 70–71; creating formal authorship agreement 70; design 67–68; expanding community engagement 75; funding for 80–81; hypotheses of 69–70; purpose of 67; racial discipline gaps 71–72; reciprocal benefits of 78; stakeholder groups 68; strengthening promising practices 75–77; supporting community engagement 72–73; sustainability of 77–78

EDC-Auburn partnership: altered views of school leaders 61; building relationships 55–56; building trust 53; co-investigative approach to 54; developing group hypothesis 59–60; developing shared language 56–57; emphasizing alignment 53; evolving partnership 63–64; forming of 52; funding for 54–55; goal of 51; initial exploration phase 59; mathematical learning shifts 62–63; professional learning community meetings 58; promoting educational change 60–61; supporting shifting needs 58–59; teacher shifts in confidence 61–62
education decision-making, skepticism in 9–10; *see also* decision-making
Education Development Center (EDC) 51
Education Testing Service (ETS) 36
educators: engaging with researchers 20–22; influencing Word Generation topics 36; mutualistic collaborations to

facilitate change 61; ongoing learning 129; professional development for 45, 124; project-based learning and 129–130; roles, identities and skills 11
effectiveness studies 17, 40
email vs. real-time messaging 168
enduring partnerships 34
equity in education 26–27
Every Student Succeeds Act (ESSA) 21
evidence democracy *see* democratic evidence in education
evidence in education *see* democratic evidence in education
evidence-informed decision-making 4
experiential learning vs. traditional learning 123
Explain Everything screencasting tool 57, 60

fast vs. slow, in communications 178
field site partnerships 34
file naming conventions 173–174
file storage tools 171
flexible situational thinking 96
Fosnot, C. T. 58
Framework for K–12 Science Education 25–26

generalizability 18, 19
Google Drive 144, 166, 170–174
Graduate School of Social Work (GSSW) 67; *see also* DU-DPS partnership
group communication tools 167; *see also* Slack (online messaging tool)

Hive NYC Learning Network: community white paper *114*; description of 100; as distributed inter-organizational network 102–105; engaging in collaborative design 111–112; engaging in network-wide field scan 104; founding of 101; functions of 101; funding for 101; funding opportunities 102; participatory knowledge building 113–115
Hive Research Lab 100
Housing Facilities Services (HFS) 91
Humble Inquiry (Schein) 12
humility 9

improvement infrastructure 27–28
improvisational acting techniques 156–158
innovators 130–131
in-progress conversation 170

Institute for the Study of Knowledge Management in Education 130
Institute of Education Sciences 13, 41, 44, 45, 47
instructional innovations 19, 152
internal coherence project 38
interpersonal values 8–9
It Happened Here (case study) 142–145, 146

joint work: building collective orientation in 108–111; in distributed networks 105–107

knowledge-building process 113–115
knowledge commons 106
knowledge production 18–19, 22

labor-management collaborations (LMCs) 13; *see also* research–practice partnerships (RPPs)
laggards 130
language minority (LM) learners 37
learning brokers 113
lesson study for teacher collaborative learning 158–160
long-term partnership arrangements 34
Lucas Education Research 130

Math and Science Partnership Network (MSPnet) 24
Math Congress 58
mathematical argumentation 155–156
mathematics curriculum 56
membership campaigns 88
memorandums of understanding 54
Middle School Quality Initiative 45
Mozilla Foundation 101–102; *see also* Hive NYC Learning Network
Mozilla Hive NYC Learning Network *see* Hive NYC Learning Network
multi-channel communications *see* communications
multi-organizational networks, research–practice partnerships and 100
mutual respect 8

National Association for Research in Science Teaching (NARST) 24
National Center for Education Research 13
National Center for Research–Practice Partnerships 24

National Council of Teachers of
Mathematics (NCTM) 24
National Education Policy Center 21
National Network of Education
Research–Practice Partnerships 8, 13
National Research Council 9, 33, 46, 122
National Science Foundation (NSF) 13, 52
National Science Teachers Association
(NSTA) 24
neat vs. messy, in communications 177
negotiation 10
networked improvement community
(NIC) 26
networked research–practice partnerships
113–115; see also Hive NYC Learning
Network; research–practice partnerships
(RPPs)
network participation structures 108
networks for learning 101
networks that learn 101
New York City Department of
Education 45
Next Generation Science Standards
(NGSS) 20

one-to-one digital devices 51, 57–58; see
also EDC-Auburn partnership
open educational resources (OERs)
174–175
opportunity commons 106
optimism 10

Padres & Jóvenes Unidos 66, 72–73
parent engagement project 93–94, 96
participatory democracy 88, 95
partnerships: characteristics of 33–34;
engaging with professional associations
24–25; infrastructures for 27–28; lack
of sufficient funding for 27; with Latino
parents 93; learning from each other 19;
problem-solving 35; responsiveness and
its relationship to impact 25–27; see also
research–practice partnerships (RPPs)
pedagogy of practice 154
post-program slump 107, 108
power dynamics 91–92, 143
preexisting beliefs, influencing information
processing 4–5
problem of practice 35–37, 46, 55, 58,
69–72, 89
problem-solving partnerships 35
professional development: customizing
128–129; improving student's learning
competencies 124; improvisational

acting techniques 156–158; lesson
study for teacher collaborative learning
158–160; pedagogy of practice 154;
teacher-developed representations
151–152; see also representations of
instructional practice
Professional Learning Committee 25
professional learning community (PLC)
meetings 58
professional vision 151
project-based learning: building a learning
community 129–130; coherent learning
trajectories 127–128; as curricular
approach to student proficiency
122–123; deploying at-scale professional
development 128–129; developing
curriculum by co-design model 135;
developing deeper learning outcomes
122–123; developing supportive
infrastructures 130; equity-related
challenges in 123–125; intrapersonal
and interpersonal competencies 123;
at macro, systems-level 123–124;
in mathematics 122–123; multiple
literacies in 127; primary implementers
of 130–131; randomized controlled trial
of 122–123; rigorous learning goals
126–127; students learning through
126–127; tensions between macro- and
micro-factors in **125**; where/when
teachers learn about 128–129
public channels, Slack 167–168
public vs. private communication 177

QUASAR project 153

racial discipline gaps 66, 71–72
randomized controlled trials (RCTs) 17,
40, 122–123
reading comprehension 36
Reading for Understanding initiative 41,
43, 44, 47
reading interventions 38
Reading Inventory and Scholastic
Evaluation (RISE) 36
real-time messaging 168
reform fatigue 135
Regional Educational Laboratory
program 13
replication 18
representations of instructional practice:
analyzing 152–155; case studies
155–160; co-constructive work
of developing and using 152–155;

complex work of teachers 151–152; definition of 150–151; features of 153–154; forms of 157–158, 160; lesson planning 156–157; in lesson study approach 158–160; origins of 157, 159; rehearsals for the classroom 157; scenario analysis 156; teacher-developed 151–152; teaching games 156; uses in professional development activities 154–155; uses of 158, 160, 161; *see also* professional development

research adoption 88

research alliances 34–35

Research + Practice Collaboratory 19, 20, 22, 52

research–practice partnerships (RPPs): authorship agreements 70; brokering future learning opportunities *110–111*; building new structures 13; communication of 164; core operating principles 11; democratic potential of 85; design-based 35, 127; emergent principles 95–96; as emerging field 8; engaging educators and researchers 20–22; equitable project-based learning experiences and 125–126; memorandums of understanding in 54; multi-organizational networks and 100; Practice Brief *110–111*; supporting youth learning in networks 106–107; working in the open as approach to 115–116; *see also* DU-DPS partnership; EDC-Auburn partnership; partnerships; Strategic Education Research Partnership (SERP); university–community partnerships

restorative interventions (RIs): expanding resources for 77; increasing trustworthiness to stakeholders 75–76; shifts in policy and practice 74; strengthening schoolwide delivery 76; students participating in 72

RISE assessment 38–39, 40–41

scientific values 9–10

screencasting 60, 62–63

shared learning agenda 122

Slack (online messaging tool) 138, 166–168, *169*, 170

Smart School Discipline Law 67

spheres of activity 18

spotlighting 90

STARI curriculum 44–45

STEM learning 18, 21

STEM Practice Briefs 22–23

STEM Research Briefs 22

STEM Teaching Tools 21, 23–24, 25

Strategic Adolescent Reading Intervention (STARI) 39

Strategic Education Research Partnership (SERP): adapting to changing environment 40–41, 42–43; background of 33–35; as design-based implementation research partnership 34–35; focusing on Boston Public Schools' problem of practice 35–37; funding for 47; goal of 39–40, 45–46; partners 43–44; partnership characteristics 33–34; supporting professional development 45; *see also* research–practice partnerships (RPPs)

student participatory action research project 96

teacher agency 143–145

teacher-developed representations 151–152

teachers *see* educators

Teaching in Context (Allensworth) 6

top-down reform 136

trading zones 150, 151

traditional learning vs. experiential learning 123

transfer, process of 122

tuning, process of 109

university–community binary 86

university–community partnerships 86–88, 91–92, 96; *see also* CU Engage

University of Chicago Consortium on School Research 12

weblog *see* blogs/blogging

Word Generation (vocabulary program): enhancing for second language learners 45; expansion of 42; influenced by teachers 36–37; initial design principles 36; materials for 44–45; program results 37–38; randomized controlled trial of 40; successfulness of 44; testing of 37

WordPress 174–176

working in the open 107, 115–116

Young Mathematicians at Work 57

Printed and bound by PG in the USA